Spiritual Approaches in the Treatment of Women With Eating Disorders

Spiritual Approaches in the Treatment of Women With Eating Disorders

P. Scott Richards, Randy K. Hardman,
and Michael E. Berrett

American Psychological Association • Washington, DC

Published by
American Psychological Association
750 First Street, NE
Washington, DC 20002
www.apa.org

To order
APA Order Department
P.O. Box 92984
Washington, DC 20090-2984
Tel: (800) 374-2721
Direct: (202) 336-5510
Fax: (202) 336-5502
TDD/TTY: (202) 336-6123
Online: www.apa.org/books/
E-mail: order@apa.org

In the U.K., Europe, Africa, and the Middle East, copies may be ordered from
American Psychological Association
3 Henrietta Street
Covent Garden, London
WC2E 8LU England

Typeset in Goudy by World Composition Services, Inc., Sterling, VA

Printer: Vail-Ballou Press, Binghamton, NY
Cover Designer: Naylor Design, Washington, DC
Technical/Production Editor: Genevieve Gill

The opinions and statements published are the responsibility of the authors, and such opinions and statements do not necessarily represent the policies of the American Psychological Association.

Library of Congress Cataloging-in-Publication Data

Richards, P. Scott.
Spiritual approaches in the treatment of women with eating disorders / by P. Scott Richards, Randy K. Hardman, and Michael E. Berrett.
p. cm.
Includes bibliographical references and index.
ISBN-13: 978-1-59147-393-0
ISBN-10: 1-59147-393-4
1. Eating disorders in women—Religious aspects. 2. Eating disorders in women—Treatment. I. Hardman, Randy K. II. Berrett, Michael E. III. Title.

RC552.E18R52 2006
616.85'2606—dc22 2006001146

British Library Cataloguing-in-Publication Data
A CIP record is available from the British Library.

Printed in the United States of America
First Edition

We dedicate this book to every woman who is suffering with an eating disorder, who is searching for light, hope, peace, and power beyond herself, to assist her in the journey of healing and recovery.

CONTENTS

PREFACE

During our careers, we have noticed that those with spiritual beliefs, and especially those who live congruently with their spiritual beliefs, seem to make more dramatic gains in the recovery process and in maintenance of treatment gains. We have repeatedly heard from patients that their own focus on religious or spiritual issues in treatment, whether within the therapeutic relationship or "on their own," including their faith in their own spiritual tenets and consequent life activities and choices, were some of the most powerful catalysts for positive change.

Over the years, in many thousands of hours of face-to-face interactions with individuals, couples, and families, we have become more aware of how relationships with self, God, and others are interconnected and need to be addressed and integrated in successful therapeutic change. We believe that these relationship experiences, whether perceptual, emotional, or spiritual, have great long-term impact on healing, change, and recovery. We listen closely to clients to understand where they are willing to go in exploring spiritual–religious experiences. We have become more and more willing over the years to discuss spiritual concerns and needs openly and directly because clients are so eager to explore them.

As a result of this personal learning over time, which we consider a blessing from our clients, we began conceptualizing those spiritual themes that were both recurrent and powerful in the lives of our patients with eating disorders. This has led to designing a spirituality workbook, a spirituality group in treatment, spiritual interventions in treatment, research on the efficacy of spiritual interventions in treatment outcomes, and a number of professional publications about spirituality and eating disorders. Ultimately, this focus has led us to integrate spiritual perspectives and interventions more comprehensively into our eating disorder treatment program.

During the past 10 years we have provided treatment in inpatient, residential, and outpatient treatment settings to many women with eating disorders. Approximately 75% of our patients come from Utah, California, Idaho, and Colorado, but the rest come from throughout the United States. Most of our patients are between 15 and 24 years old, but some have been as young as 12 and as old as 54. Most of our patients are Caucasian; approximately 10% have another racial heritage (African American, Asian, or Hispanic). About 55% of our patients are Latter-Day Saints, 25% to 30% are Protestant or Roman Catholic, and 4% to 5% are Jewish or Muslim. Approximately 10% to 15% are not affiliated with a religious denomination but view themselves as having their own spiritual beliefs.

We invite patients to explore spiritual issues related to their recovery, if they desire, during their treatment. Our spiritual emphasis is nondenominational and culturally sensitive to patients from a wide variety of theistic religious backgrounds. Our perspective is also consistent with the recommendations of numerous professionals that spiritual interventions should not be used alone but integrated with standard psychological and medical interventions (Richards & Bergin, 1997). Our patients participate in a variety of needed therapies to ensure comprehensive treatment and progress toward recovery, including medical evaluations and treatment; nutrition monitoring and counseling; and individual, group, and family therapies.

We have noticed that for women who believe in God, deep spiritual struggles are often a major impediment in their ability to recover from an eating disorder (Collins, 2000; Lewis, 2001; Richards et al., 1997). Many have earlier in their lives felt a connection to God and a degree of personal spirituality. Many have participated in religious observations, but almost all of them have lost these connections through the course of their eating disorder. Consider the following comment from a patient in our treatment program illustrating the potentially devastating effects of an eating disorder on faith and spirituality.

> The eating disorder consumed every aspect of my life. My life was centered entirely on food and weight. I felt unworthy and undeserving of having a relationship with God. I hated myself and did not think it was possible for anybody, including God, to love me. I did not feel that I was good enough to merit a relationship with God.

Many of our former patients believe that faith in God and their personal spirituality have been essential in their healing and recovery. We have witnessed many times the hope and strength that come to patients as they renew their faith in God, as the following statement from a former patient confirms:

> I don't think I would have made it through treatment if it weren't for my faith and spirituality. There were so many times when I felt like I

> couldn't go on a minute longer, and it was in those moments that I trusted that God would take care of me. Even when recovery no longer felt possible, I was able to hold on to my faith that anything is possible if we only trust God and trust ourselves.

When women begin to turn away from the eating disorder and return to their faith, a new hope for recovery is kindled. Spiritual discussions and interventions can greatly help women with eating disorders reconnect with themselves, with others, and with their God in healing and life-changing ways.

Although we believe that the spiritual is not the only worthwhile modality of treatment and indeed that the best treatment is multimodal and multidisciplinary, we find that the spiritual is often an extremely important aspect of healing and recovery. Two research studies we have conducted at our center have provided evidence that spiritual growth and healing during treatment is positively associated with positive patient outcomes (Richards, Berrett, Hardman, & Eggett, in press; Smith, Richards, Fischer, & Hardman, 2003).

Identifying and finding healing solutions to the religious and spiritual aspects of eating disorders require time, patience, kindness, repetition, and emotional work over an extended period of time. Despite the challenges, mental health professionals who are willing to open themselves up to the healing potential of their clients' faith and spirituality can be an important support in the recovery process. In the pages that follow, we present theory, research, and in-depth clinical cases that help document and illustrate the importance of spirituality in the etiology and treatment of eating disorders. We hope that the book will prove helpful to you as you consider the role of spirituality in your own practice or research.

ACKNOWLEDGMENTS

We are grateful to Susan Reynolds, our acquisitions editor at the American Psychological Association (APA), for her encouragement and support from the beginning of this project. We appreciate the valuable feedback we received from Susan Herman at APA, other members of the APA development team, and two external reviewers. Their feedback was crucial and helped us improve the book in many ways. We also appreciate the helpful editorial assistance of Susan Black at Brigham Young University and Genevieve Gill at APA. Their expertise with the English language helped make the book much more readable than it would otherwise have been.

We are grateful to Kari A. O'Grady, a doctoral student at Brigham Young University, who assisted us in writing portions of the manuscript. Her talent and dedication improved the book and helped us move it forward to completion at a time when burnout was threatening to stall the project. We also thank Bobbi L. Carter, a former colleague, who shared her expertise for this book by writing the initial draft of the chapter on 12-step groups.

We acknowledge all of the wonderful and amazing women who have been patients at Center for Change. We thank them for opening their hearts and minds to change and recovery from an eating disorder. Their courage and determination have changed us as well in that healing process. We also thank the very talented and loving staff at Center for Change. Their dedication blesses the lives of the women who have been and who are in treatment at the Center.

We thank our wives, Marcia Richards, Aline Hardman, and Karen Berrett. Their love and support over the years has brought us joy and given us strength. Finally, we give thanks to God whose loving kindness and inspiration has sustained us throughout our own journeys of healing, growth, and service.

I

INTRODUCTION, THEORY, AND RESEARCH

1

FAITH, SPIRITUALITY, AND EATING DISORDERS

Medical and psychological professionals are increasingly aware that religious and spiritual influences may often be beneficial in human health and healing (Benson, 1996; Emmons, 1999; Koenig, McCullough, & Larson, 2001; Richards & Bergin, 1997, 2000; Shafranske, 1996; Worthington, Kurusu, McCullough, & Sanders, 1996). This awareness has led to the integration of spiritual perspectives and interventions into mainstream medical and psychological training and practice (Miller, 1999; Richards & Bergin, 1997, 2000, 2004; Shafranske, 1996).

As recently as 10 years ago, only a few medical schools offered courses in spirituality and healing. Now more than half of U.S. medical schools have such courses (Puchalski, Larson, & Lu, 2000). Many medical practitioners now regard faith and spirituality as important resources in physical health and healing and are willing to discuss spiritual issues with patients (Puchalski & Larson, 1998; Puchalski et al., 2000). Within the mental health professions, religion is now openly recognized as one type of diversity professionals are ethically obligated to understand and respect (e.g., American Counseling Association, 1995; American Psychological Association [APA], 2002). More and more courses and continuing education workshops are being offered concerning spiritual issues in psychological treatment. Many psychotherapists now use spiritually oriented approaches and interventions in their practices (Miller, 1999; Richards & Bergin, 1997, 2000, 2005; Sperry & Shafranske, 2005).

Spiritual treatment approaches encourage psychotherapists to address clients' spiritual concerns when relevant and to use language and interventions that demonstrate honor and respect for the healing potential of their clients' faith. They also use a wide variety of specific spiritual techniques or interventions, including for example, praying privately for clients, teaching religious and spiritual concepts, encouraging forgiveness, taking a history of clients' religious and spiritual backgrounds, making reference to scriptures, respecting spiritual meditation, encouraging religious relaxation and imagery, conducting in-depth religious–spiritual assessments, and praying with clients (Richards & Bergin, 1997, 2005).

Buddhist, Hindu, Christian, Jewish, Muslim, and ecumenical theistic psychotherapy approaches have been described (e.g., Epstein, 1995; Hedayat-Diba, 2000; McMinn, 1996; Rabinowitz, 1999, 2000; Richards & Bergin, 1997, 2005; Rubin, 1996). Other spiritual approaches have been based on Jungian, transpersonal, psychodynamic, cognitive, interpersonal, humanistic, and multicultural psychologies (e.g., Elkins, 1995; Faiver, Ingersoll, O'Brien, & McNally, 2001; Griffith & Griffith, 2002; Helminiak, 1996; Kelly, 1995; Lovinger, 1984; West, 2000).

The use of spiritual interventions in psychological treatment has increased dramatically during the past decade. As summarized in Table 1.1, spiritual perspectives and interventions have now been integrated with virtually all mainstream therapeutic traditions and treatment modalities and with a great variety of clinical issues and client populations, including addictions, anxiety disorders, eating disorders, dissociative disorders, trauma victims, antisocial and psychopathic personality disorders, postpartum depression, and so on (Richards & Bergin, 2005). It is beyond the scope of this book to describe the variety of ways that such treatments have been used, but we refer interested readers to recent publications that do so (e.g., Richards & Bergin, 2005; Sperry & Shafranske, 2005).

Despite the proliferation of spiritual approaches in clinical practice, outcome research concerning their effectiveness with various clinical issues and populations lags far behind, although it has increased during the past 2 decades. There are now several published articles that review these studies, including a meta-analysis of eight outcomes studies dealing with religiously accommodative cognitive therapy approaches (McCullough, 1999) and several narrative reviews (e.g., Oman & Thoresen, 2001; Worthington et al., 1996; Worthington & Sandage, 2001). Although much research work remains to be done, there is some empirical evidence that spiritual approaches are as effective, sometimes more effective, than secular ones, particularly with religiously devout clients (McCullough, 1999; Richards & Bartz, 2006). In particular, several studies have provided evidence that spiritually

TABLE 1.1
Applications of Spiritual Approaches Described in the Professional Literature

Theoretical orientations	Therapeutic modalities	Clinical issues	Special populations
Psychodynamic	Individual therapy	Addictions	African Americans
Adlerian	Group therapy	Anxiety disorders	Latinos
Behavioral	Family therapy	Eating disorders	Asian Americans
Cognitive	Child therapy	Stress	Native Americans
Rational–emotive behavior therapy	Inpatient	Attention-deficit disorder	The elderly
Person centered		Compulsive gambling	Jews
Existential		Dependency	Buddhists
Gestalt		Depression	Lesbians, gay men, and bisexuals
Constructivism		Dissociation	Women
Transactional analysis		Trauma	Gifted individuals
		Antisocial personality disorder	
		Self-injurers	
		Transplant surviors	
		Postpartum depression	
		Sadomasochism	
		Cancer	

oriented (Christian) cognitive therapy approaches are as effective for the treatment of depression as standard (secular) cognitive approaches (Hawkins, Tan, & Turk, 1999; Johnson, DeVries, Ridley, Pettorini, & Peterson, 1994; Johnson & Ridley, 1992; McCullough, 1999; Pecheur & Edwards, 1984; Propst, 1980; Propst, Ostrom, Watkins, Dean, & Mashburn, 1992). There is also some evidence that 12-step treatment approaches that affirm the importance of faith in God or a higher power are effective for treating addictions (Miller, 1999; Ringwald, 2002).

LACK OF RESEARCH ON SPIRITUALITY IN THE EATING DISORDERS FIELD

Despite the widespread professional interest in spirituality that now exists, research concerning the relationship between spirituality and eating disorders is still relatively sparse. The small numbers of studies that have examined these issues during the past decade have nonetheless provided some evidence that spirituality may be important in both etiology and recovery. For example, several researchers have observed relationships between eating disorder prevalence or severity and religious affiliation or devoutness (e.g., Garfinkel & Garner, 1982; Rowland, 1970; Sykes, Gross, & Subishin, 1986; Sykes, Leuser, Melia, & Gross, 1988; Ziegler & Sours, 1968). Other researchers have found that when recovered patients are asked what helped them recover from their eating disorder, many women report that their faith and spirituality were important (e.g., Hall & Cohn, 1992; Hsu, Crisp, & Callender, 1992; Mitchell, Erlander, Pyle, & Fletcher, 1990; Rorty, Yager, & Rossotto, 1993). Others have found that spiritual exploration and growth during treatment is positively associated with better treatment outcomes (e.g., Garrett, 1996; Richards et al., in press; Smith et al., 2003). We review these and other studies in more depth in chapter 2.

Despite such indications that religion and spirituality may be important in the etiology and treatment of eating disorders, these topics have rarely been addressed in scholarly journals or books focused on eating disorders. For example, a systematic review of the *International Journal of Eating Disorders*, a prestigious journal that specializes in publishing empirical studies about eating disorders, found that only 0.8% ($n = 8$) of more than 1,033 empirical studies published in this journal from 1993 to 2004 included a measure of religion or spirituality as a variable (Richards & Bartz, 2006). The neglect of spirituality extends to other professional journals: for example, only 2.2% ($n = 4$) of 186 empirical studies published from 1999 to 2004 in *Eating Disorders: Journal of Treatment and Prevention* included religion or spirituality as a variable. Finally, the *Practice Guideline for the Treatment of Patients With Eating Disorders*, published by the American Psychiatric Association Work Group on Eating Disorders (2000b), does not use the words *religion* or *spirituality*, nor does this publication discuss the possible role of spiritual issues in etiology or treatment other than to briefly acknowledge that 12-step groups may be helpful in treatment.

IMPORTANCE OF RELIGION AND SPIRITUALITY IN THE TREATMENT OF EATING DISORDERS

During the past decade we have provided treatment to hundreds of women with eating disorders in our inpatient, residential, and outpatient eating disorder treatment programs. These experiences have convinced us that religious and spiritual issues are often significant in both the etiology of and the recovery from eating disorders. We have observed a variety of important religious and spiritual issues with which patients often struggle, including deficits in their sense of spiritual identity, negative images of God, feelings of spiritual unworthiness and shame, fear of abandonment by God, guilt over and a lack of acceptance of sexuality, dishonesty, difficulty having faith, and reduced capacity to love and serve. Consider the following two case vignettes, which illustrate the importance of spiritual issues in etiology and treatment.

LeAnn

LeAnn came from a small farming community in the western United States where she lived with her husband and two children. She lived in a small trailer on a farm and had a part-time job at a bank. LeAnn's eating disorder became so severe that she was no longer able to care for her children properly. This was her primary motivation for seeking treatment: She loved her children and wanted to be a good mother.

During treatment, LeAnn disclosed many of her religious beliefs. One of her beliefs was that there was a loving God watching out for her. LeAnn also disclosed that she prayed for people every day, many times a day, but was unable to pray for herself. She was unwilling to ask God for anything for herself, even though she encouraged her children and other people to pray for themselves.

LeAnn's feelings of spiritual unworthiness and shame were preventing her from fully exercising her faith in God. Because she felt alienated and undeserving of God's help, LeAnn had made her eating disorder her object of worship. She had come to believe that her eating disorder would give her a sense of control and security rather than turning to God to help her with her problems. Thus, LeAnn's spiritual shame and alienation had contributed to the development and maintenance of her eating disorder.

When LeAnn realized that she was not willing to do for herself what she asked other people to do, she decided she needed to change this incongruence. LeAnn started praying for herself. She prayed for specific kinds of help: for help to overcome her negative body image, her self-hatred, and her low self-esteem. As she prayed for herself, LeAnn found that over time she did not need the eating disorder to give her a sense of control and security. Instead, she learned to have more faith in God and to gain security from her belief that God would be there for her, love her, and answer her prayers.

As LeAnn recognized and challenged her belief that she was unworthy and undeserving of God's assistance, she began to turn again to God through prayer as her source of guidance, security, and courage; she also began to give up the false belief that her eating behavior was the solution to her problems. She recognized that the eating disorder provided a false sense of control and security, that in reality it made her less in control of her life and her well-being. LeAnn's recovery accelerated as she learned to place her faith in the healing power of God and in the love and support of her husband and family.

Donna

Donna was an 18-year-old woman of Persian descent, a U.S. citizen whose family was Muslim. The family had lived in the United States for 20 years. The parents had been married more than 25 years. She had an older brother and an older sister. Donna's parents were hesitant to "let her grow up."

Donna, however, felt a desire to grow up and have freedom, but she also felt guilty any time she said or did anything that went against the wishes of her father. Donna found it confusing to distinguish the traditions of her Persian ancestry, the principles of the Islamic religion, and the personal preferences and wishes of her parents.

During family therapy, Donna's therapist helped her and her parents explore issues of control and freedom. Donna wanted to have normal young adult privileges similar to those of her peers. One intervention the therapist used was to ask the parents to watch the movie *Fiddler on the Roof* (Jewison, 1971). Although the movie features a Jewish family, the therapist felt that because the pain the characters experience in the movie is rooted in their attachment to religious tradition, the particular religion in the movie was of less importance than the pain itself. Watching the film helped them get in touch with the struggles and issues that need to be resolved when children begin to go against the traditions of their fathers and "win their own way." It also gave them a chance to think about unhealthy and healthy ways to allow Donna to grow up and find her own way.

Although Donna was not religiously orthodox, she did believe in God and she expressed a strong desire to "do what is right." Being somewhat familiar with the Islamic religious tradition, Donna's therapist discussed with her the story of Abraham's sons, one of whom "sold his birthright for a mess of pottage" by giving away that which was of most value to him for something that was short-lived. Donna came to recognize that her eating disorder was a "mess of pottage," so to speak, that helped her feel secure in the short term but would not allow her to have those things that were important to her, including health, happiness, and rewarding relationships. This spiritual metaphor helped motivate Donna to persist in treatment even during times of discouragement.

Donna was increasingly able to have a voice and speak up for herself without feeling guilt. She was able to tell her parents that her eating disorder was a way for her to have some sense of control and power in her life in reaction to her parents' fear of letting her grow up. Through discussions with her therapist and her parents, Donna was able to learn that she could love her parents and yet still have a different opinion with them about what might be best for her as a young adult woman. She came to realize that she could express her love to her parents in ways other than making sure she had their approval at all times and in every decision. She was able to gain her parents' support to take drivers' education and get a driver's license. She was also able to convince her parents to allow her to start college. With their blessing, she moved out of her parents' home to live in student dorms, and after 1 year, she moved into her own apartment.

As illustrated in these case vignettes, as well as in several full-length case reports in chapter 10, we have found that attending to eating disorder patients' spiritual issues during the treatment process is often crucial for successful treatment and recovery. With this understanding, we inform patients at the beginning of treatment that their faith and spirituality can be included as part of treatment. We conduct a religious and spiritual history and assessment of our patients as part of a multidimensional assessment strategy (Richards & Bergin, 2005). We invite patients to set spiritual goals to assist them in their recovery. We incorporate spiritual interventions into individual, group, and family therapy when doing so seems appropriate for our patients. We have found that spiritual interventions such as spiritual discussions, spiritual bibliotherapy, prayer, spiritual imagery and meditation, repentance, forgiveness, and service often help our patients in their spiritual exploration and growth. We also invite our patients to participate in structured spirituality and 12-step groups. We provide additional opportunities for spiritual exploration and growth depending on our patients' preferences and needs. We say more about these spiritual issues and intervention strategies throughout the book.

PURPOSES OF THE BOOK

The first purpose of *Spiritual Approaches in the Treatment of Women With Eating Disorders* is to describe why we think faith and spirituality are important in the etiology and treatment of women with eating disorders. The second purpose of the book is to describe a theistic spiritual framework for conceptualizing and treating eating disorders. The third purpose is to describe clinical guidelines and interventions that may assist mental health professionals in their efforts to include spirituality in treatment with women who have eating disorders.

The book is intended for practitioners and researchers in clinical and counseling psychology, as well as psychiatry, clinical social work, and marriage and family therapy, particularly those who treat or conduct research about women with anorexia nervosa, bulimia nervosa, and eating disorders not otherwise specified. We hope this book will draw attention to the neglected topic of faith and spirituality in the field of treating eating disorders. We hope that it will encourage and give direction to both practitioners who wish to understand more fully how faith and spirituality might assist patients on their journeys of recovery and scholars who wish to do research in this domain.

As we mentioned in the Preface, our approach to treating eating disorders is multidimensional, including contemporary state-of-the-art approaches, such as pharmacological, nutritional, cognitive–behavioral, family, interpersonal, group, and recreational therapeutic interventions. Our spiritual approach does not replace these proven treatment methods but enhances them. In this book, we seek to build on what professionals already know by describing how a theistic spiritual approach can augment what mental health professionals are already doing in their practices. Although the book will provide readers with new information and skills for incorporating spirituality into treatment, it will not require them to go back to school or to acquire additional certification to do so.

In the Western Hemisphere and Europe, more than 80% of the population professes adherence to one of the major theistic world religions—Judaism, Christianity, and Islam (Barrett & Johnson, 2002)—and thus we think a theistic perspective of eating disorders and their treatment may provide a more culturally sensitive approach, particularly for those who are devout (Bergin, 1980; Richards & Bergin, 2000). In addition, we think that the spiritual resources found in the theistic religious traditions, if more fully accessed by professionals, could help enhance the efficacy of eating disorder treatment.

Our theistic spiritual approach should not be confused with pastoral or religious counseling, both of which are done by religious clergy or other individuals who have some type of ecclesiastical role or position within a religious organization (Richards & Bergin, 2005). Our approach is for licensed mental health professionals. It is solidly grounded in mainstream medical and mental health treatment methods. It builds on these contemporary approaches by helping professionals understand how they can include the spiritual dimension in their work.

Our theistic approach is most suitable for patients and therapists who believe in God or a higher power, but we find that many aspects can also be applied in culturally sensitive ways with patients who believe in Eastern or other nontheistic forms of spirituality, as well as with patients who do not believe in God. We encourage therapists to respect and work within their patients' belief systems, and our approach offers considerable insight into how they can successfully do so. Therapists who are not personally theistic will undoubtedly find some aspects of our framework incompatible with their beliefs, but we hope they will not conclude that there is nothing of value for them in this book. They may still find considerable benefit in the overall guidelines we offer for incorporating spirituality into eating disorder treatment. At the least, the book should help them enhance their ability to work sensitively with their patients with eating disorders who believe in God.

In this book, we share insights from our clinical experience and findings from research studies we have conducted, along with findings and clinical insights from other scholars and practitioners. We discuss how religious and spiritual issues may influence the development and maintenance of eating disorders, as well as how patients' faith and spirituality can be used as resources in treatment. We also describe in detail a number of clinical case examples to help mental health professionals understand the role of faith and spirituality in the recovery process.

Because most of our clinical experience with eating disorders has been with women and because approximately 90% of those who struggle with anorexia nervosa and bulimia nervosa are women (American Psychiatric Association, 2000a; Romano, 2005a, 2005b), this book focuses on the treatment of women. Although there are some differences between women and men regarding concerns about body shape and weight (e.g., most women want to be thinner whereas some men want to be heavier and some want to be thinner) and how eating-disordered behaviors are manifest (e.g., men are more likely to use exercise and steroids as a body change strategy whereas women are more likely to restrict or purge), both female and male individuals with eating disorders appear to struggle with underlying issues concerning their sense of identity and self-esteem (McCabe & Ricciardelli, 2004). Because our spiritual approach focuses on helping affirm and strengthen patients' sense of identity and worth, we believe that much of the information in this book may be helpful in the treatment of men and boys with eating disorders. We hope that clinicians and researchers will clinically and empirically test the usefulness of the spiritual approaches we describe for male patients with eating disorders.

DEFINITIONS OF *RELIGIOUS* AND *SPIRITUAL*

Given the confusion that often surrounds the terms *religious* and *spiritual*, we wish to clarify what they mean to us, how we use them when we work with patients with eating disorders, and how we use them in this book. Pargament (1999) defined *religious* as "the search for significance in ways related to the sacred" (p. 12). We like his definition; when we use the terms *religious* and *religiousness*, we are referring to sacred beliefs, practices, feelings about God, and other ultimate concerns (Emmons, 1999) that are often, but not always, expressed institutionally and denominationally (e.g., church attendance, participation in public religious rituals).

Pargament (1999) defined *spirituality* as "a search for the sacred" (p. 12). We like his definition, but we would expand it from our perspective to include a search for and "attunement with God or the Divine Intelligence that governs or harmonizes the universe" (Richards & Bergin, 2005, p. 22). When we use the term *spiritual* we are referring to invisible phenomena associated with thoughts and feelings of enlightenment; vision, harmony with truth; transcendence; and oneness with God, nature, or the universe (cf. James, 1902/1936). We also consider spirituality to include human experiences such as love, gratitude, honesty, and compassion.

Although we agree with those who have argued that polarizing *religious* as an institutional activity and *spirituality* as a private or individual expression is an oversimplification (Pargament, 1999), studies have shown that these are the main criteria that people use to distinguish between these terms. Furthermore, when people refer to themselves "as spiritual but not religious," they often mean they are not affiliated with an organized religion, but they do feel connected with God or other sacred things (Zinnbauer, Pargament, & Scott, 1999). Given this usage, we think there is some value in distinguishing between the terms *religious* and *spiritual* in this manner, remembering that "virtually every major religious institution is quite concerned with spiritual matters" and that "every form of religious or spiritual expression occurs in a social context" (Pargament, 1999, p. 9).

In a clinical context, we have found it important and helpful to use a broad definition for spirituality to give patients plenty of room to figure out what spirituality means to them. We view religious activities and practices such as attending church, reading scriptures, praying, and so on as potentially good and helpful, but we think spirituality is much more than these practices. Spirituality also includes experiences such as feeling compassion for someone, loving someone, being loved, being able to feel hope, receiving inspiration, feeling enlightened, being honest and congruent, and feeling a sense of life meaning and purpose. We say more about helping clients understand and recognize the many ways that spirituality can be understood and experienced in chapter 5.

BACKGROUND INFORMATION ABOUT EATING DISORDERS

To help readers understand how our spiritual approach complements other contemporary eating disorder treatment methods and to assist readers who may appreciate some general background information about eating disorders, we now briefly describe (a) diagnostic criteria and general informa-

EXHIBIT 1.1
Diagnostic Criteria for Anorexia Nervosa

A. Refusal to maintain body weight at or above a minimally normal weight for age and height (e.g., weight loss leading to maintenance of body weight less than 85% of the expected; or failure to make expected weight gain during period of growth, leading to body weight less than 85% of that expected).
B. Intense fear of gaining weight or becoming fat, even though underweight.
C. Disturbance in the way in which one's body weight or shape is experienced, undue influence of body weight or shape on self-evaluation, or denial of the seriousness of the current low body weight.
D. In postmenarcheal females, amenorrhea, i.e., the absence of at least three consecutive menstrual cycles (a woman is considered to have amenorrhea if her periods occur only following hormone, e.g., estrogen, administration).

Specify type:

Restricting Type: During the current episode of anorexia nervosa, the person has not regularly engaged in binge eating or purging behavior (i.e., self-induced vomiting or the misuse of laxatives, diuretics, or enemas).

Binge-Eating–Purging Type: During the current episode of anorexia nervosa, the person has regularly engaged in binge eating or purging behavior (i.e., self-induced vomiting or the misuse of laxatives, diuretics, or enemas).

Note. From *Diagnostic and Statistical Manual of Mental Disorders* (4th ed., text rev., p. 589), by the American Psychiatric Association, 2000a, Washington, DC: Author. Copyright 2000 by the American Psychiatric Association. Reprinted with permission.

tion concerning eating disorders; (b) prevalence statistics for eating disorders, including information about age of onset and the course and outcome of the disorders; and (c) physiological and psychological consequences of eating disorders. We conclude by providing a brief overview of the rest of the book.

Description and Prevalence of Eating Disorders

According to the *Diagnostic and Statistical Manual of Mental Disorders* (4th ed., text rev.; *DSM–IV–TR;* American Psychiatric Association, 2000a), eating disorders in general are characterized by severe disturbances in eating practices and in perceptions of body weight and shape. Specifically, individuals with *anorexia nervosa* have significant distortions in body perception, intense fear of gaining weight, and refusal to maintain appropriate body weight (less than 85% of the normal weight for their age and height; see Exhibit 1.1). Individuals with anorexia nervosa exhibit an obsessive preoccupation with food, dieting, and body weight and shape (Romano, 2005b; Wilson & Pike, 2001).

The typical age of onset for anorexia nervosa is late adolescence to early 20s (Hoek & van Hoeken, 2003). Although some older individuals may develop the disorder, few individuals do so after age 40 (Romano, 2005b). The onset of illness is often associated with a stressful life event, such as leaving home for college, termination or disruption of an intimate relationship, family problems, or physical or sexual abuse. The course and outcome of anorexia nervosa are highly variable. Some individuals recover fully after a single episode, some exhibit a fluctuating pattern of weight gain followed by relapse, and others experience a deteriorating course of the illness over many years. Hospitalization may be required to restore weight and to address fluid and electrolyte imbalances.

The prevalence of anorexia nervosa among females is approximately 0.5% to 3.7%, and the prevalence for males is approximately one tenth of that (American Psychiatric Association, 2000a; Hoek & van Hoeken, 2003; Romano, 2005b). Studies conducted over the last few decades indicate an increasing prevalence of anorexia nervosa (Hoek & van Hoeken, 2003; Romano, 2005b). It appears to be most prevalent in industrialized societies in which there is abundance of food and in which, especially for females, being considered attractive is linked to being thin. The disorder is probably most common in the United States, Canada, Europe, Australia, Japan, New Zealand, and South Africa, but little systematic work has examined prevalence in other cultures. Individuals who immigrate from cultures in which the disorder is rare to cultures in which it is more prevalent may develop anorexia nervosa as thin body ideals are assimilated. There is evidence that anorexia nervosa is increasing among minority populations, including Latinos and African Americans.

Individuals with *bulimia nervosa* participate in binge eating (eating significantly larger amounts of food in a limited period of time than most individuals would eat in a similar context) and then go through inappropriate compensatory practices to prevent weight gain (e.g., induction of vomiting, use of laxatives and diuretics). Bingeing is typically accompanied by a feeling of being out of control (American Psychiatric Association, 2000b; see Exhibit 1.2). Individuals with this disorder typically have an excessive fear of gaining weight, and they determine their self-esteem mainly by their body weight and shape (Romano, 2005a).

The typical age of onset for bulimia nervosa is late adolescence, with a large number of individuals presenting with the disorder in their 20s and 30s after having lived with it for a significant period of time (Romano, 2005a). The binge eating frequently begins during or after an episode of dieting. Disturbed eating behavior persists for at least several years in a high percentage of clinical samples. Hospitalization may be required to restore weight and to address fluid and electrolyte imbalances. The course of the illness may be chronic or intermittent, with periods of remission alternating with recurrences of binge eating.

The prevalence of bulimia nervosa among females is approximately 1% to 3.7%, and the prevalence for males is approximately one tenth of that (American Psychiatric Association, 2000a; Hoek & van Hoeken, 2003;

EXHIBIT 1.2
Diagnostic Criteria for Bulimia Nervosa

A. Recurrent episodes of binge eating. An episode of binge eating is characterized by both of the following:
   (1) eating, in a discrete period of time (e.g., within any 2-hour period), an amount of food that is definitely larger than most people would eat during a similar period of time and under similar circumstances.
   (2) a sense of lack of control over eating during the episode (e.g., a feeling that one cannot stop eating or control what or how much one is eating).
B. Recurrent inappropriate compensatory behavior in order to prevent weight gain, such as self-induced vomiting; misuse of laxatives, diuretics, enemas, or other medications; fasting; or excessive exercise.
C. The binge eating and inappropriate compensatory behaviors both occur, on average, at least twice a week for 3 months.
D. Self-evaluation is unduly influenced by body shape and weight.
E. The disturbance does not occur exclusively during episodes of anorexia nervosa.

Specify Type:

Purging Type: During the current episode of bulimia nervosa, the person has regularly engaged in self-induced vomiting or the misuse of laxatives, diuretics, or enemas.

Nonpurging Type: During the current episode of bulimia nervosa, the person has used other inappropriate compensatory behaviors, such as fasting or excessive exercise, but has not regularly engaged in self-induced vomiting or the misuse of laxatives, diuretics, or enemas.

Note. From *Diagnostic and Statistical Manual of Mental Disorders* (4th ed., text rev., p. 594), by the American Psychiatric Association, 2000a, Washington, DC: Author. Copyright 2000 by the American Psychiatric Association. Reprinted with permission.

Wilson & Pike, 2001). This disorder appears to be increasing (Hoek & van Hoeken, 2003) with roughly similar frequency in most industrialized countries, including the United States, Canada, Europe, Australia, Japan, New Zealand, and South Africa. Few studies have examined the prevalence of bulimia nervosa in other cultures. In clinical studies in the United States, individuals presenting with this disorder are primarily Caucasian, but the disorder has also been reported among other ethnic groups including Latinos and African Americans.

Approximately 50% of individuals presenting at tertiary treatment programs for eating disorders are diagnosed with *eating disorder not otherwise specified* (NOS). This diagnostic label is assigned to individuals who present with a disorder of eating but who do not meet all of the criteria required to be diagnosed with anorexia nervosa or bulimia nervosa. This diagnosis seems to be particularly prevalent among adolescents (American Psychiatric Association, 2000a, 2000b). Exhibit 1.3 provides additional information about eating disorder NOS.

EXHIBIT 1.3
Diagnostic Criteria for Eating Disorder Not Otherwise Specified

The eating disordered not otherwise specified (NOS) category is for disorders of eating that do not meet the criteria for any specific eating disorder. Examples include the following:

1. For females, all of the criteria for anorexia nervosa are met except that the individual has regular menses.
2. All of the criteria for anorexia nervosa are met except that, despite significant weight loss, the individual's current weight is in the normal range.
3. All of the criteria for bulimia nervosa are met except that the binge eating and inappropriate compensatory mechanisms occur at a frequency of less than twice a week or for a duration of less than 3 months.
4. The regular use of inappropriate compensatory behavior by an individual of normal body weight after eating small amounts of food (e.g., self-induced vomiting after the consumption of two cookies).
5. Repeatedly chewing and spitting out, but not swallowing, large amounts of food.
6. Binge-eating disorder: Recurrent episodes of binge eating in the absence of the regular use of inappropriate compensatory behaviors characteristic of bulimia nervosa.

Note. From *Diagnostic and Statistical Manual of Mental Disorders* (4th ed., text rev., pp. 594–595), by the American Psychiatric Association, 2000a, Washington, DC: Author.

Physiological and Psychological Consequences of Eating Disorders

Individuals with eating disorders have the highest rate of treatment seeking, inpatient hospitalization, and attempted suicide of common psychiatric disorders (Stice, 2001). According to the National Institute of Mental Health (Spearing, 2001), "The mortality rate among people with anorexia has been estimated at 0.56 percent per year, or approximately 5.6 percent per decade, which is about 12 times higher than the annual death rate due to all causes of death among females ages 15–24 in the general population" (p. 5). Mortality rates for bulimia nervosa are much lower, but some women do die from this disorder, and the health consequences can be severe.

Anorexic and bulimic patients put their bodies at risk for severe medical consequences, ranging from gastrointestinal distress to death. Although most individuals with eating disorders endeavor to present a facade of good health, the severity and variety of their physical ailments tell an alarmingly different story. Those with bulimia who engage in extreme purging by laxatives or vomiting may show obvious electrolyte imbalance in lab work. Those with anorexia may yield somewhat normal blood lab values but later have sudden failure of the heart or another organ (American Psychiatric Association, 2000b). A wide variety of other serious physical consequences may result from eating disorders, including cardiac and skeletal myopathies, irregular menstruation or amenorrhea, esophageal tears, gastric ruptures, cardiac arrhythmias, peripheral edema, bradycardia, hypothermia, hypotension, bleeding diathesis, yellowing of the skin associated with hypercaratenemi, hypertrophy of the salivary glands, normochromic mormocytic anemia, impaired renal function, osteoporosis, muscle loss and weakness, kidney failure, dry hair and skin, permanent loss of dental enamel from vomiting, calluses or scars on the hand from repeated contact with the teeth, irregular bowel movements, peptic ulcers, pancreatitis, electrolyte imbalance, and cardiac arrest, as well as other medical complications not listed here (American Psychiatric Association, 2000b).

Eating disorders can also be extremely disruptive psychosocially for individuals with the disorder and their families. Individuals with eating disorders often become preoccupied with thoughts of food, demonstrate inflexible thinking, withdraw socially, experience feelings of ineffectiveness, and have restrained initiative and emotional affect (American Psychiatric Association, 2000a, 2000b). Family routines, decision-making capacities, and developmental needs are often interrupted or neglected by the extreme amount of attention that is given to the eating disorder (Eisler, le Grange, & Asen, 2003).

Individuals with eating disorders have restricted emotions and are frequently unable to identify their feelings. What they are aware of is extremely negative thoughts related to their body—an effective diversion from their emotional turmoil and pain. Their thoughts are obsessively locked on the irrelevant, and their feelings are avoided and hidden, even from themselves. In addition, eating disorders frequently co-occur with other psychiatric disorders including obsessive–compulsive symptoms; depressive symptomology; major depressive disorder; posttraumatic stress syndrome; and bipolar, anxiety, personality, and substance use disorders, which further impair the individual's functioning (American Psychiatric Association, 2000a, 2000b; Myers & Mitchell, 2005; Romano, 2005a, 2005b).

It is widely agreed that there is no single cause for eating disorders. Although concerns about weight and body shape underlie all eating disorders, these disorders appear to result from a convergence of many factors, including cultural and family pressures and emotional and personality disorders. Genetics and biologic factors may also play a role (Kaye et al., 2004). Chapter 3 discusses more about contemporary theories of etiology.

In regard to treatment, it is widely agreed that nutritional and medical stabilization, pharmacological treatments, and psychological interventions are often all needed. Psychological treatments often include several treatment modalities, including individual, group, and family therapy. Cognitive–behavioral, psychodynamic, and interpersonal therapies are most often used. A multidisciplinary team approach with consistent support and counseling is essential for long-term recovery from all severe eating disorders. Depending on the severity and type of disorder, team members may include physicians specializing in relevant medical complications, dietitians, psychologists and other mental health professionals, and nurses. All should be skilled in treating eating disorders. We say more about contemporary theories and approaches to treating eating disorders in chapters 4 and 5.

PLAN OF THE BOOK

In chapter 2, we review theory and research about religion and spirituality in eating disorder etiology, treatment, and recovery. Although this domain of theory and research has not yet received sufficient attention, we discuss several books and a relatively small number of studies that contribute to understanding the relationship of religion and spirituality with eating disorders.

In chapter 3, we describe the theistic view of personality and therapeutic change that influences our understanding and treatment of eating disorders. We discuss how this perspective adds to other contemporary etiological theories of eating disorders, including biological, psychodynamic, cognitive–behavioral, family systems, and interpersonal approaches. We explain how eating disorders can be a spiritual problem. We discuss how the false pursuits of an eating disorder can undermine patients' sense of spiritual identity and worth as well as their relationships with God, family, and friends. We describe common spiritual issues that many patients with eating disorders manifest during treatment, including negative images or perceptions of God, feelings of spiritual unworthiness and shame, fear of abandonment by God, guilt or lack of acceptance of sexuality, reduced capacity to love and serve, difficulty surrendering and having faith, and dishonesty and deception.

In chapter 4 we describe our view of the role of spirituality in healing and recovery from eating disorders. We briefly summarize the theistic view of therapeutic change on which we ground our understanding of this recovery from eating disorders. We discuss the theistic perspective in the context of its contribution to other contemporary understandings about therapeutic change in eating disorders. We describe how we seek to help women with eating disorders learn to listen to their hearts and reaffirm their eternal spiritual identity and worth, a concept that is described in depth in the chapter. We offer suggestions for helping patients learn to again place their faith in God, in significant others, and in their own divinely given capabilities instead of in the dangerous pursuit of their eating disorder.

In chapter 5, we describe the theistic view of psychotherapy on which we base some of our treatment approach to eating disorders. We describe its theological and theoretical foundations, as well as its perspective on the treatment process and clinical issues that need to be addressed with these patients. We discuss how the theistic perspective of treatment adds to other contemporary theories of eating disorder treatment. We provide an overview of our inpatient, residential, and outpatient treatment programs. We discuss a variety of ways that we integrate theistic perspectives and interventions into our treatment center, and we offer some general process guidelines for such integration.

In chapter 6, we describe a theistic view of the assessment of eating disorders and explain why we think a religious and spiritual assessment should be a part of a multidimensional assessment approach. We describe a multilevel, multidimensional assessment approach. We describe dimensions of religiousness and spirituality that we think are clinically important. We provide examples of religious and spiritual assessment questions that can be asked on written intake questionnaires or in clinical interviews. We also describe several examples of standardized religious and spiritual assessment measures that could be useful in clinical practice.

In chapter 7, we describe a variety of interventions that we use when conducting individual, group, and family therapy with patients who have eating disorders. We first describe some interventions we use that are explicitly religious or spiritual in nature. We then describe a variety of therapeutic interventions we use in group, family, and individual therapy that are not explicitly religious or spiritual but that are valuable for helping patients explore spiritual, emotional, and relationship issues associated with their eating disorders.

In chapter 8, we describe a spirituality group and workbook that we have been using for several years in our treatment center's inpatient and residential eating disorder treatment program. We describe the findings of an empirical outcome study that evaluated the effectiveness of adding this group to our inpatient treatment program. We provide information about how practitioners who are interested in using the spiritual growth group and workbook in outpatient or inpatient settings can obtain support material from our treatment center.

In chapter 9, we describe how 12-step groups (similar to the 12-step groups of Alcoholics Anonymous) can be tailored for use with eating disorder patients. We discuss how to implement such groups in inpatient, residential, and outpatient settings and provide information about how practitioners can obtain support for implementing such groups.

In chapter 10, we propose a research agenda about theistic treatment, spirituality, and eating disorders. We describe research designs and outcomes measures that we think may be useful for conducting research on spirituality

and eating disorders. We offer some recommendations about how scholars and practitioners can contribute in this domain of theory, research and practice.

In chapter 11, we describe in detail several case reports that illustrate the use of spiritual interventions with patients in treatment for eating disorders. The case reports help illustrate why and how spirituality can serve as a resource in treatment and recovery.

In chapter 12, we share the findings from a recent follow-up survey of former patients in which we asked them to share their views about what role faith and spirituality played in their treatment and recovery from eating disorders. This chapter contains personal recovery stories, patient views about which spiritual interventions were most helpful to them, and messages they wished to share with other women who struggle with eating disorders.

2

SCHOLARSHIP ON RELIGION, SPIRITUALITY, AND EATING DISORDERS

This chapter reviews existing scholarship regarding the possible roles of religion and spirituality in the etiology, treatment, and recovery from eating disorders. We wish to emphasize that little empirical research has been done on these topics, and those studies that have been done often have methodological shortcomings that limit their usefulness (e.g., small sample sizes, limited generalizability). As we mentioned in chapter 1, from 1993 to 2004, only eight empirical studies that included religion or spirituality as a variable were published in the *International Journal of Eating Disorders*, the premier scholarly outlet for studies about eating disorders. Because of the dearth of empirical studies about spirituality and eating disorders, we devote considerable space in this chapter to the discussion of theoretical literature that has explored the possible relations between religion and spirituality and eating disorders.

Beginning with scholarship concerning etiology, we briefly review theoretical literature that has examined the relationship between anorexia nervosa, asceticism, and religion. We then discuss preliminary empirical evidence that bulimia nervosa may be associated with less devout religious attributes. Shifting focus to treatment issues, we review growing evidence from survey and interview studies that many patients with eating disorders view faith and spirituality as important resources in their recovery. We also discuss the current lack of scholarly literature concerning ways to integrate spiritual perspectives and interventions into eating disorder treatment. We encourage researchers in the eating disorders field to include religion and spirituality more frequently as variables in their studies.

ANOREXIA NERVOSA, ASCETICISM, AND RELIGION

Psychological, biomedical, and sociocultural models for the etiology of eating disorders have all been proposed (Brownell & Fairburn, 1995; Lelwica, 1999). Scholars who favor the sociocultural model have given considerable attention to possible connections among anorexia nervosa, asceticism, and religious tradition. Although these writers differ on a variety of issues, many agree that ancient self-starvation or asceticism and modern anorexia nervosa are both fueled by women's need for more control, autonomy, and individuation in a male-dominated society.

In the book *Holy Anorexia,* Bell (1985) examined the historical evidence and concluded that women who engaged in self-starvation, whom Bell referred to as "holy anorexics," moved from being considered "holy" by the male hierarchy of the Catholic Church, to being considered evil (possessed by demons), and finally to being considered "ill." As the Catholic Church redefined "saintliness" and female saints began to be recognized for their good works, "holy anorexia" waned. It is historically unclear whether the holy anorexics self-starved to search for God or to search for a way to become undesirable marriage partners. There is some agreement, however, that holy anorexia was due to gender conflict and thus to attempts by some females to be more in control of their lives.

In the epilogue to *Holy Anorexia,* William N. Davis pointed out that the holy women Bell described differed from modern people with anorexia in that no mention was made of a "dread of fatness, and a self-conscious, unremitting pursuit of thinness . . . the hallmark of anorexia nervosa" (Davis, 1985, p. 181). Davis acknowledged, however, that holy anorexia and anorexia nervosa are similar in that

> both states are characterized by an unwillingness to eat, but one is driven by the desire to be holy and the other by the desire to be thin. . . . And, whether in the service of holiness or thinness, they [the women] determinedly relish the effects of starvation. (p. 181)

Davis also suggested that "there is good reason to equate medieval holiness with contemporary thinness [because they] both represent ideal states of being in the cultural milieus under consideration" (pp. 181–182). He pointed out that in medieval Italy, the highest ideal was holiness, whereas today female adolescents learn from the media and other messengers of contemporary Western culture that thinness is the feminine ideal.

From Fasting Saints to Anorexic Girls (Vandereycken & Van Deth, 1994) also examines the history of self-starvation in an attempt to understand the etiology of anorexia nervosa. The authors assumed that mental disorders, including anorexia nervosa, are culture-bound syndromes and argued that self-starvation began in a religious context. Throughout history, some Christians have engaged in excessive fasting and other ascetic practices. Eventually the Roman Catholic Church established some rules regarding how stringent a religious fast needed to be. In the 15th and 16th centuries, fasting lost much appeal and became somewhat divorced from religion. In the 15th century, extraordinary fasting was deemed to be the work of witchcraft. In the 16th century, fasting girls were a spectacle of entertainment. Women would fast for months and years at a time, confounding doctors and laypeople. When skeptics started to test these spectacles empirically, it was confirmed that many could go months without food.

Beginning in the 16th century, medical explanations began to supplant demonological ones. From the 17th century on, demonological explanations of illness were increasingly disputed. In the 18th century, skepticism increased; however, demonological explanations of fasting were not completely erased. In the 19th century, the phenomenon of hunger strikes began. These were different from hysteria, however, in that they were conscious, deliberate struggles for power. In the late 19th century, as the naturalistic medical view became more influential, fasters came to be viewed as cases of hysteria. They were viewed not as dishonest or evil but as delusional (i.e., they believed that they were fasting for long times but really were not).

Vandereycken and Van Deth (1994) argued that even though various forms of self-starvation have taken place throughout history, similarities do not imply that they all had the same etiology. These researchers suggested that the fasting saints of the past were not concerned with getting fat because their culture did not value thinness. Despite the commonalities between the fasting saints of the past and the anorexics of today, Vandereycken and Van Deth argued that there are significant differences between them. The fasting saints of the past were motivated by a need for power in a male-dominated religious culture, but they had no fear of fatness. Fasting saints manipulated a religious rite to gain power. Vandereycken and Van Deth acknowledged that modern-day anorexia nervosa is also an attempt to get power but that it includes a fear of fatness born of cultural influences.

Another book examining the relationship between fasting and eating disorders is *Starving for Salvation* (Lelwica, 1999). Lelwica discussed Rudoph Bell's *Holy Anorexia* (1985) and Caroline Walker Bynum's *Holy Feast and*

Holy Fast (1987), as well as other sources discussing historical perspectives on female fasting practices. Lelwica suggested that before a slender body shape was the hallmark of ideal female beauty, fasting was a means for women to define themselves and manipulate their environment. Catherine of Siena gained notoriety by fasting, which enabled her to intervene in the political and religious crises of her time—until she died of starvation.

Lelwica (1999) suggested that in *Holy Anorexia,* Bell viewed anorexia as a timeless struggle for female autonomy in the face of patriarchal control. In *Holy Feast and Holy Fast,* however, Bynum (1987) considered ancient eating problems to be tied to the context of medieval Christianity. Lelwica (1999) argued that to Bynum, fasting wasn't intended to gain autonomy but instead represented "women's creative efforts to use the resources and roles available to them—food, feeding and their bodies—to shape their worlds and to achieve sanctity" (p. 28). Bynum (1987) viewed the eating problems of medieval women as religious and those of today as more superficial (related to appearance). Lelwica argued against this, saying that the eating problems of today are also spiritual and explaining that many of her students identify with Catherine of Siena's strategy for cultivating purity, virtue, and public admiration through fasting.

Lelwica (1999) accepted the idea that people have an inherent need for a source of ultimate meaning in their lives. She pointed out that ancient women looked to religion to provide that sense of meaning. She argued that religion has failed to meet women's needs and has actually exacerbated their problems through its male chauvinism and Cartesian dualism. As a result, women now turn to the pursuit of thinness in an attempt to meet their spiritual needs for meaning and salvation from pain and uncertainty.

> Today . . . for many girls and women, including those who believe and participate in organized religion, a media-saturated, consumer-oriented culture provides the primary images, beliefs, and practices through which the truths of their lives are sought and defined. . . . For many of them, a network of symbols, beliefs, and rituals centering on bodily appetites and appearances constitutes an ultimate frame of reference—a "secular" salvation myth . . .
>
> The pictures in women's magazines are not simply images of women. They are also bodily symbols. More specifically, they are icons of womanhood, pointing to a seemingly transcendent truth—a feminine ideal—that many girls and women recognize as Ultimate. . . . For many of their viewers, these images serve what has historically been a religious function: that of mediating the search for meaning in a world of uncertainty, injustice, longing and pain. (Lelwica, 1999, pp. 5, 41)

Lelwica (1999) argued that eating disorders point to spiritual hunger and a need for a sense of meaning and wholeness. She suggested that a spiritual transformation is needed to overcome an eating disorder and that traditional religions could assist women with eating problems if they were more egalitarian.

In addition to these books, a number of journal articles have explored the relationship among anorexia, asceticism, and religion. For example, Mogul (1980) argued that when a woman reaches puberty or gets pregnant, she feels a need to establish herself as a relatively independent being with an autonomous sense of self and identity. To do this, young women call on a variety of inner resources. To counter the upsurge of libidinal energy, the woman's ego and superego must be strong enough to protect her against the danger of being overwhelmed and adaptive enough to allow her to explore and master her new potentialities. In this effort, the ego makes use of defenses established or consolidated in latency—namely, intellectualization and asceticism. Mogul pointed out that asceticism can be a valuable protective mechanism; however, it can also become perverted and spread into the suppression of real needs, such as food. Mogul suggested that people with anorexia have an exaggerated wish for aesthetic and moral superiority (Mogul, 1980).

Huline-Dickens (2000) wrote an article pointing out that there are many connections between the Judeo-Christian religious attitude and the individual with anorexia and that there are many psychopathological features common to both. She cited the work of historians who have tried to understand historical self-starvation. She argued that the Judeo-Christian culture socializes women and inculcates them with a high level of powerlessness and guilt. Negative views of the self are inevitable when women are considered to be the cause of sin and evil. Because greed has caused sin, abstinence from food can thus be seen as penitential—the means to redeem the sinner and reconnect her to the estranging Father.

Huline-Dickens (2000) posited that cognitive therapy approaches focusing on guilt, shame, and self-denial would be useful in treatment. For adolescents, she suggested that treatment should consider the religious and cultural meanings and explanations of the illness that the patients and their families give. She also recommended that the therapist be aware that some religious systems of belief are not helpful to recovery and that such beliefs should be examined rationally.

Banks (1992) argued that even though eating disorders are probably caused by some unconscious conflicts, many people with anorexia and bulimia understand their self-starvation in terms of religious meaning and symbolism. She suggested that studies be done to determine whether women in non-Western cultures also orient their eating-disordered behavior within religious meanings. Banks took an anthropological approach to examining how culture is involved in anorexia nervosa. In particular, she tried to highlight the importance of considering the patient's own subjective interpretations of food refusal and thinness in working toward an understanding of this disorder.

Banks (1992) pointed out that some people with anorexia may understand their symptoms through sets of cultural symbols different from those held by diagnosticians, medical practitioners, and psychologists. She argued that the failure of some medical practitioners to treat cases of chronic anorexia successfully may be due to their failure to take the patient's own subjective meanings into account.

Banks (1992) concluded that her own research on anorexia patients in Minnesota showed that they express their desire to restrict intake of food through religious conceptions about food, the body, and sexuality provided by their religious traditions. Contrary to popular belief, they are not motivated by cultural ideas of thinness. Banks described two case studies that point to the importance of considering religious conceptions about the body and about food in attempting to understand anorexia in the contemporary United States.

Banks (1992) also discussed some clinical evidence for a relationship between religion and contemporary anorexia nervosa. She also pointed out that in the 1980s, several people recovering from anorexia have published their autobiographies, and some touch on the ethical, moral, and religious themes of their patterns of food refusal. Banks encouraged researchers to investigate more systematically and directly the religious beliefs and practices of people with anorexia. She also suggested that cross-cultural research might investigate the extent to which these cases of self-starvation are religiously motivated and expressed.

In another article, Banks (1997) examined the use of religious symbols and idioms in the subjective experiences of two contemporary women with anorexia nervosa. This article showed how both women used notions of asceticism central to their religion to express personal concerns with growth, separation, and loss. Their religious beliefs helped them construct a personal meaning system in which they did not see themselves as sick but as moral and religious.

One of these women, Jane, viewed her self-starvation as fasting. Her fasts coincided with the church calendar. The Lutheran Church does not require fasting as a precondition for taking Holy Communion, but Jane would fast anyway and used the notion that fasting is holy to construct personal meaning for her starvation. Jane would also appeal to God and Jesus to help her to control her desire to eat food and to lose weight.

The other woman, Margaret, reported that a man from her church who visited her family couched his dedication to self-starvation in religious terms. Thus, he gave Margaret a religious context within which to understand self-starvation. She called the story of her life a "Christian miracle." She almost died, and she interpreted her survival as an act of God due to her faith. Margaret believed that "there is not fat in Heaven."

Banks (1997) argued that these two cases challenge models of anorexia nervosa that understand the condition exclusively in terms of cultural foci and on dieting and secular ideals of beauty and bodily thinness for women. Banks suggested that these cases show the continuing persistence into the 20th century of an association between religiosity and self-starvation noted by historians during the early Christian medieval and late Victorian periods.

Shafter (1989) argued that anorexia nervosa and hysteria result from social pressures that stifle women's freedom and leave them without any outlet of personal expression or control. She asserted that the determination of what constitutes madness has been handed over to the combination of religion, medicine, and law.

> I would like to try to set "women's madness" within the historical context of the social and largely the patriarchal institutions which have shaped it both from within and without. . . . sociocultural and economic factors operate on a macroscopic level to influence the way pathology is experienced and expressed by the patient, defined and treated by the healing professions, and responded to by society at large. (Shafter, 1989, p. 77)

Shafter (1989) concluded that people with anorexia have been unable to assert themselves and make their own choices and compromises in a society where the guidelines consist of either hidden messages or impossible ideals. Under such conditions, the pursuit of thinness provides a circumscribed, tangible, and easily managed goal.

McCourt and Waller (1996) wrote a paper in which they disputed the theory that the high prevalence of eating disorders among Asians living in Britain is due to acculturation to Western standards (thinness). They argued that a better explanation is that eating disorders are due to a culture clash between the restrictive Asian–Muslim culture and the more liberal Western culture.

McCourt and Waller (1996) discussed three aspects of Islam that may contribute to the development of eating disorders: (a) the decadence of Western culture is seen as threatening; (b) many Muslims are very protective of their daughters, discouraging them from associating with boys and limiting their educational opportunities; and (c) parents fear that women will be promiscuous if they are allowed freedom outside the home.

McCourt and Waller (1996) suggested that when Asian–Muslim families move to the United Kingdom, the parents become concerned about the encroachment of Western culture on their daughters, and hence they pull in, becoming overly protective and restrict their daughters' freedom even more than they would in their home country. The loss of control in the daughters' lives can lead to eating disorders.

In addition to historical and sociocultural works that have discussed the relationship of anorexia nervosa, asceticism, and religion, a small number of empirical studies have examined it. For example, Joughin, Crisp, Halek, and Humphrey (1992) sent out 2,300 surveys asking registered members of the Eating Disorders Association in the United Kingdom (the majority of whom had been or were currently afflicted with anorexia nervosa) about their religious beliefs and their eating disorder symptoms. Participants included 851 respondents who met the researchers' inclusion criteria. The researchers found that the more important religion was to the participants, the lower their body mass index was; this was especially true for Anglicans, among whom asceticism is perhaps more prevalent than in the other groups studied. The authors concluded that this finding supports the notion that asceticism is used by individuals to justify or supplement the anorexic defense of weight loss. They also found that respondents who experienced some kind of religious conversion seemed to experience less severe weight loss than those who had not converted. The authors concluded from these findings that religious beliefs are an important consideration when treating eating disorders. They suggested that it may be helpful to challenge patients' defense mechanisms, including their portrayal of anorexia as asceticism.

Wilbur and Colligan (1981) empirically examined the cognitive, behavioral, and personality traits of a sample of 34 adolescent and female young adults with anorexia, comparing them with two control groups of nonpsychotic female psychiatric patients. The patients with anorexia were admitted to a treatment unit over a period of 5 years, although the length of treatment received by the patients was not specified in the article. The patients were matched with the control groups on the basis of similar demographics. The Minnesota Multiphasic Personality Inventory, the Devereus Adolescent Behavior Rating Scale, and the Wechsler Intelligence Scale were used as assessment measures. The findings indicated that there was less psychotic disturbance among the patients with anorexia than in the matched control sample. Patients with anorexia nervosa had significantly higher scores on items concerning poor health and religious fundamentalism but lower scores on family problems.

M. H. Smith, Richards, and Maglio (2004) examined the relationship between eating disorder symptoms and religious orientation as measured by the Eating Attitudes Test and the Body Shape Questionnaire and by the participants' religious orientations in a sample of 129 female undergraduate students and 316 female patients in an inpatient eating disorder treatment program. They found that there was not a significant relationship between intrinsic religiousness and severity of eating disorder symptoms among women with anorexia nervosa.

BULIMIA NERVOSA AND RELIGIOUS ORIENTATION

Little has been explored empirically about the relationship between bulimia nervosa and religion, although the two studies we found on this topic both provided suggestive evidence that bulimia nervosa may be associated with lower levels of religious devoutness than is anorexia. In the Joughin et al. (1992) study discussed in the preceding section, the researchers also reported findings relevant to bulimia nervosa. They found that correlations between the Eating Disorder Inventory Bulimia subscale and the religious belief questionnaire revealed a

> significant correlation between increasing pathology on this scale and decreasing current importance of religion. Further, increasing pathology on the subscale was correlated with a perceived weakening of the subjects' religious beliefs and decreasing importance of their religious belief relative to either parent. (Joughin et al., 1992, p. 402)

Thus, more bulimic symptoms were associated with weaker religious beliefs among the respondents. The authors theorized that

> it seems most likely that profound religious belief . . . cannot be sustained when the individual repeatedly gives in to the "sin" of gluttony. The individual may feel too guilty to continue to profess an important religious belief, or may feel deserted by . . . her faith. (Joughin et al., 1992, p. 404)

The study by M. H. Smith et al. (2004) described in the previous section provided some additional empirical support for the idea that women with bulimia may be less religiously devout. Smith et al. (2004) found a positive relationship between eating disorder symptoms as measured by the Eating Attitudes Test and Body Shape Questionnaire and extrinsic religiousness among women with bulimia nervosa or subclinical bulimic symptoms. They concluded that women who are involved in religion for extrinsic reasons (e.g., for personal and social gains and for acceptance) have more bulimic symptoms than do women who are more devout and committed to their religion.

FAITH AND SPIRITUALITY AS RESOURCES IN RECOVERY

Several studies provide evidence that women who have recovered from eating disorders believe that their faith and spirituality were important in their healing and recovery. Mitchell, Erlander, Pyle, and Fletcher (1990) reported from a follow-up study they had conducted with patients who had bulimia nervosa that

> the single most common write-in answer as to what factors have been helpful in their recovery had to do with religion in the form of faith, pastoral counseling, or prayer. Since we had not inquired about this systematically, we were somewhat surprised by the number of these responses and decided this should be explored further. (p. 589)

In an effort to further explore these issues, Mitchell et al. (1990) surveyed 50 women with bulimia nervosa. They found that 88% of the women with bulimia believed in God, and approximately 60% prayed or worshiped privately at least several times a month. Only 18% of the women had sought help for their eating disorder from a representative of their place of worship, but those who had felt after doing so that they had received support, encouragement, advice, sympathy, and renewed faith. Mitchell et al. (1990) concluded that

> [m]ental health professionals are frequently uneasy in dealing with religious issues, yet clearly religious issues are important for many patients with bulimia nervosa. Therapists should consider discussing each patient's religious needs as part of their intervention and be willing to refer to a member of the clergy when appropriate. (pp. 592–593)

Hall and Cohn (1992) also conducted follow-up surveys of former patients, asking 366 women and 6 men which activities had been helpful in their recovery from bulimia and other forms of problem eating. Of the respondents, 59% said that "spiritual pursuits" had been helpful, and 35% said that a spiritually oriented 12-step program, Overeaters Anonymous, was helpful to them.

Hsu, Crisp, and Callender (1992) did follow-up interviews of six patients who had recovered from anorexia nervosa to find out what the patients believed had helped them recover. One patient indicated that her religious beliefs, including prayer, church attendance, and faith in God had helped in her recovery. Hsu et al. (1992) acknowledged that the influence of religion on recovery was "an area that we did not inquire about at all in our interview[s]" and that it was thus "unclear whether it played a part in the recovery of others" (p. 348). They acknowledged that this "oversight is perhaps indicative of our indifference to the ethical and transcendental aspects of the patients' illness" (p. 348).

Rorty, Yager, and Rossotto (1993) interviewed 40 women who considered themselves to have recovered from bulimia nervosa to find out what had helped them recover. Many of the women (25%–40%) had participated in a 12-step program such as Overeaters Anonymous, Alcoholics Anonymous, or AlAnon and had found the "spiritual aspects" of these programs helpful. Others had sought out other forms of spiritual guidance. Rorty et al. (1993) concluded that "nonprofessional contacts, such as support groups of various kinds and including a spiritual focus in some cases, are important components of the healing process for many women" (pp. 259–260).

Garrett (1996) interviewed 32 participants with anorexia about their self-starvation and their recovery from it. She found that participants referred to anorexia as a spiritual quest, and for many of them, recovery involved rediscovery of the self. Garrett (1996) theorized that the development of anorexia is the negative part of a ritual that initiates a girl into maturity and that the recovery is a positive part of the same ritual, initiating the girl into a fuller way of living. Garrett suggested that the whole process serves as a tool to help the girl master her fear of death. She concluded that the women in her study understood their self-starvation and recovery in spiritual ways and that they "regarded anorexia nervosa as a distorted form of spirituality and a misguided way of life, even when they were engaged in it" (p. 1493). She further explained,

> "Spirituality" was the word most participants used to explain both anorexia and recovery as sequential parts of an ongoing expansion of consciousness; from a phase involving inner search and social isolation to a new stage they described as greater awareness of connection with the material and social world and of powers which lay both inside and outside themselves. . . . The word spirituality was most often introduced by participants themselves in the course of their narrative. . . . All participants claimed that recovery requires an experience of something (a material reality and/or an energy) beyond the self. They named it "spirituality" or referred to it as "love," as God or as Nature. (Garrett, 1996, pp. 1490, 1493)

In addition to the surveys of former patients, there have been several other studies, case reports, and testimonials that point to the conclusion that attending to religious and spiritual issues may be important in treatment and recovery. For example, in a correlational study, Smith, Richards, Fischer, and Hardman (2003) examined the association between growth in spiritual well-being and other positive treatment outcomes in a sample of 251 women who received inpatient treatment for their eating disorders. The researchers found that improvements in spiritual well-being were significantly associated with positive gains in attitudes about eating and body shape, as well as healthy psychological functioning. Smith et al. (2003) concluded that regardless of patients' religious orientation and affiliation at the beginning of treatment, if they experienced spiritual growth during treatment, they were more likely to experience reductions in eating disorder symptoms and psychological distress.

Dancyger et al. (2002) empirically compared 8 Orthodox Jewish girls with 72 non-Orthodox Jewish patients in a day treatment program. The subjects were compared on demographic data, treatment data, the Beck Depression Inventory, the Eating Disorder Inventory, and the Family Adaptability and Cohesion Evaluation Scale. Of the eight Orthodox patients, four were ultra-Orthodox (the strictest form of Judaism) and four were modern Orthodox (not as strict).

At the time of admission, all of the Orthodox adolescents were on psychotropic medications, compared with 45% of the non-Orthodox patients. The Orthodox group had a significantly longer stay in contrast to the others. In addition, members of the Orthodox group were more likely to perceive their families as more cohesive and to have a less rigid structure. At discharge there were no significant differences between the Orthodox and non-Orthodox groups in terms of outcome. The ultra-Orthodox patients were 3 years younger at the onset of illness and stayed at the facility 8 weeks longer than the modern Orthodox patients. All of the ultra-Orthodox patients developed their eating disorder during summer camp; only one modern Orthodox developed hers in this setting.

The authors concluded that the course of the eating disorders in Orthodox Jewish patients does not differ significantly from the presentation and course in the non-Orthodox patients. Nonetheless, Dancyger et al. (2002) suggested that their work shows that Orthodox young women face some issues and experience some dynamics that lead to the development and perpetuation of their eating disorder, especially the ultra-Orthodox patients. For example, several of the young women in the program felt threatened by the possibility of an early marriage, and this became a factor in their refusal to reach their goal weight. The authors also suggested that the eating disorders became the only forms of rebellion available to the ultra-Orthodox patients, who might be rigid, perfectionistic, and obedient in most other ways. The authors concluded that these cultural and religious differences did require that the treatment staff be sensitive and attentive to several details, including (a) making sure these girls had kosher foods, (b) following specific guidance on how to handle religious fasting, and (c) eliciting the input and support of clergy.

Manley and Leichner (2003) described five recurrent themes of anguish and despair that they have seen in adolescents with eating disorders: (a) feeling undeserving of help, (b) feeling helpless and hopeless in coping with the eating disorder itself, (c) having marked difficulty with recognizing and expressing feelings, (d) experiencing ambivalence about treatment, and (e) mistrust of health care providers. Manley and Leichner suggested that these themes need to be recognized, attended to, and validated in the individual patient. They suggested a treatment that is narrative, feminist, cognitive, and spiritual.

Manley and Leichner (2003) explained that narrative therapy helps clients to articulate their story. Feminist therapy helps clients recognize that despair arises in a context beyond their own intrapsychic difficulties—the context of the mass media and that they can reclaim their voices and validate their feelings and needs. Cognitive therapy can help patients learn that *feeling* hopeless does not mean that things *are* hopeless.

Manley and Leichner (2003) suggested that a focus on spirituality may be life affirming for the adolescent and enable her to recognize that suicide has no place in her own personal ethical framework. A spirituality group may empower adolescents to discover and implement in their lives the values that are of great personal significance to them. Motivational work that sensitively encourages patients to discover that there is a dissonance between their own values and the requirements of an eating-disordered lifestyle may also be helpful. Lastly, they suggest that family therapy, or at least parental counseling, is an essential component of treating adolescents with eating disorders.

By presenting four cases of women with eating disorders, Morgan, Marsden, and Lacey (2000) shared their views that religion was both beneficial and deleterious to their patients' prognosis. The first case was of a woman who believed that her hearing impediment was God's punishment. In middle age, she displayed punitive religious devotions that eventually turned into anorexia nervosa. She responded to behavioral therapy, and her religious beliefs became more sustaining than punitive.

In the second case, a woman used religious arguments to justify low weight. The clinical team was not sure how to show respect for her faith as they challenged her dysfunctional beliefs. Eventually a pastoral counselor who enjoyed religious credibility with the patient helped her to recognize which of her religious beliefs were faulty and were serving as anorectic defenses.

The third woman saw psychodynamic therapies as a challenge to her faith, and as a result she did not make full use of the treatment. The fourth woman was a nun who was overwhelmed by guilt and starved herself in expiation (atonement for sin), which led to the development of anorexia. Through psychotherapy, she was able to make sense of her experiences and restore her weight, albeit at the loss of her religious faith.

Morgan et al. (2000) concluded that these cases demonstrate complex interactions between religion and mental disorders in which neither component can be ignored. For some, religion was containing or reparative; and for others it exacerbated the eating disorder. The authors also expressed their view that pastoral counseling by a hospital chaplain may be beneficial given that such persons may be better prepared than mental health professionals to understand and place patients' religious experience in context.

IMPLEMENTING SPIRITUALITY IN TREATMENT

Despite claims by increasing numbers of eating disorder treatment programs and professionals that they include spirituality in treatment, scholarly literature that describes how professionals integrate spiritual perspectives and interventions into treatment is currently scarce. Several professionals have described how they use 12-step groups in the treatment of eating disorders (e.g., C. L. Johnson & Sansone, 1993; McGee & Mountcastle, 1990; Wasson & Jackson, 2004; Wormer & Davis, 2003; Yeary, 1987). Newmark (2001) described how she incorporates spiritual direction and counseling into her work as a registered dietician working with patients who have eating disorders. We have published and presented several manuscripts describing how we integrate spirituality into our work with eating disorders (e.g., Hardman, Berrett, & Richards, 2003; Richards et al., 1997). Although a number of other professionals have expressed their belief that attending to religious and spiritual concerns may be important in treatment, they have provided scant specific guidance about how to do so (e.g., Jacoby, 1993; Jersild, 2001; Manley & Leichner, 2003; Mitchell et al., 1990; Morgan et al., 2000; Rorty et al., 1993). Clearly, more professional literature that helps clinicians understand how to ethically and effectively incorporate spirituality into the treatment of eating disorder patients is needed.

CONCLUSION

Although relatively little scholarly literature has explored eating disorders and religion and spirituality, a few general conclusions are possible. First, a number of theorists believe that both ancient self-starvation and modern anorexia nervosa are driven by women's need for more control, autonomy, and individuation. Historically, women struggled with a patriarchal religious hierarchy, and currently women must assert themselves in a male-dominated consumer society. Second, many women interpret their eating disorder in religious ways. Third, religion may be important in eating disorder etiology, although the relationship is not yet well understood. Increasing numbers of mental health professionals believe that religion should be taken into consideration during assessment and treatment, although few guidelines have been offered for doing this. Fourth, many former patients believe that their faith and spirituality played an important, even a central, role in their recovery. Little is currently known, however, about how professionals can help patients with eating disorders tap into the resources of their faith and spirituality during treatment. We encourage researchers in the eating disorders field to investigate more systematically and frequently the relationships between religion and spirituality and eating disorder etiology, treatment, and recovery. The lack of empirical research about religion and spirituality is a glaring deficiency in the eating disorders field.

II

A THEISTIC SPIRITUAL FRAMEWORK FOR TREATING EATING DISORDERS

3

A THEISTIC VIEW OF EATING DISORDERS

In this chapter, we briefly summarize contemporary theories of eating disorder etiology. We point out how a theistic view adds to the understanding of eating disorders and describe why we regard eating disorders as a spiritual problem. We describe 10 false, dysfunctional beliefs commonly held by women with eating disorders and explain how pursuing these beliefs undermines their spirituality and their relationships. We also discuss the most common and significant religious and spiritual issues that we have observed in working with patients who have eating disorders, including (a) negative images or perceptions of God, (b) feelings of spiritual unworthiness and shame, (c) fear of abandonment by God, (d) guilt or lack of acceptance of sexuality, (e) reduced capacity to love and serve, (f) difficulty surrendering and having faith, and (g) dishonesty and deception.

THEORIES OF EATING DISORDER ETIOLOGY

Exhibit 3.1 briefly summarizes some of the most prominent theories of eating disorder etiology, along with our theistic view. It is beyond the scope of this book to discuss all of the existing etiology theories in detail. Instead, we briefly summarize a number of the general theoretical perspectives.

EXHIBIT 3.1
Theories of Etiology for Eating Disorders

Cognitive–behavioral	Family systems	Interpersonal	Psychodynamic	Biological	Feminist	Theistic
Eating disorders are caused and maintained by maladaptive beliefs about food, weight, and body shape, as well as positive reinforcement of these beliefs. Patients believe that their personal worth is based on their weight and body shape. They seek to regulate their emotions and stress with food.	Historically, eating disorders were theorized to be caused by rigid, enmeshed, conflict avoidant family systems, but this view of etiology has not received consistent empirical support. Patients' symptoms are still understood in the context of family processes. Current literature focuses on the impact of the eating disorder on the family system.	Eating disorders are caused by one of four areas of interpersonal distress: grief (loss of person or relationship), interpersonal role disputes (conflict from differing expectations), interpersonal deficits (socially isolated or unfulfilled), role transitions (change in life status). The eating disorder provides a sick person role that helps relieve the woman of the stress associated with the caretaker role.	Eating disorders may represent an attempt to defend against or cope with a variety of issues, including rebellion against the family, effort to seek help for parents and self, and attempt to gain self-esteem, hold back suicidal impulses, reverse pressures of sexuality, delay growing up, and somatize anxiety or anger.	Disturbances in brain physiology (e.g., serotonin activity) may create a physiological vulnerability for eating disorders. Eating-disordered behaviors cause malnutrition and other physical and psychological disturbances, which can interfere with neurological cues for satiety and food intake, as well as impair thinking.	Eating disorders are caused by the internalization of objectification, sexual harassment, sexual abuse, dating abuse, or unreasonable gender role expectations. Eating disorders are coping strategies used to combat adverse social contexts. Women try to gain control over a chaotic life through food. Media communicate that thinness is power.	Deficits in spiritual identity and feelings of spiritual unworthiness contribute to feelings of alienation from God and significant others. Eating disorders represent an attempt to gain a sense of identity and worth and to feel a sense of control and security in life. Patients place their faith in the eating disorder instead of in God and the love of significant others.

Cognitive–behavioral perspectives suggest that eating disorders are caused and maintained by a cycle of maladaptive beliefs regarding food, eating, weight, and body shape (Pike, Devlin, & Loeb, 2004). In addition, positive reinforcements for the attitudes involved in the eating disorder help maintain the behavior (Birmingham & Beumont, 2004; Waller & Kennerley, 2003). Patients typically feel that their personal worth and self-esteem are based on their body weight and shape (Birmingham & Beumont, 2004; Pike et al., 2004). They struggle to regulate their emotions and strive to gain control over their emotions and stress level through food (Waller & Kennerley, 2003).

Family systems theories intimate that eating disorders are best understood within the context of the family (Eisler, le Grange, & Asen, 2003; Shwartz, Barrett, & Saba, 1985). Historically, family systems theories attributed eating disorders to dysfunctional family patterns (e.g., rigid, enmeshed, conflict avoidant), but empirical evidence has not supported a family etiological model (Dare & Eisler, 1995, 1997). Current literature focuses more on the impacts of the eating disorder on the family system rather than the impacts of the family on the etiology of the eating disorder (Dare & Eisler, 1995, 1997; Levine, 1996).

Interpersonal theories state that eating disorders are caused by distress in one of four interpersonal areas: (a) grief—loss of an important person or relationship in the patient's life, (b) interpersonal role disputes—conflicts that arise from discrepancies in expectations for the relationship or for the other in the relationship, (c) interpersonal deficits—feelings of social isolation or a lack of satisfaction and fulfillment in the patient's personal life, or (d) role transition—change in the patient's status in life (Tantleff-Dunn, Gokee-LaRose, & Peterson, 2004; Wilfey, Stein, & Welch, 2003). Interpersonal theories also suggest that individuals who develop eating disorders typically assume the caretaker role in their interpersonal relationships. The eating disorder is developed as a way to relieve the individual from the stress of the caretaker role (Tantleff-Dunn et al., 2004).

The psychodynamic perspective has generated a variety of theories of etiology, including those of self psychology, object relations theory, ego psychology, and Jungian theory (Herzog, 1995; C. Johnson, 1995). From a psychodynamic perspective an eating disorder may also represent (a) simultaneous efforts to be loyal to but rebel against the family, (b) a way of seeking help for the parents or oneself, (c) a way of holding back suicidal impulses, (d) an effort to reverse the pressures of sexuality, (e) a means to remove oneself from relationships, (f) a means to delay growing up, (g) a way to elevate self-esteem, and (h) a way of somatizing anxiety or anger (Herzog, 1995). One prominent psychodynamic theory of etiology concerns fears of sexual maturity. Fears of sexual maturity, it is theorized, develop in "families in which the father is kind but passive and the mother is aggressive and castrating" (Keel, 2005, p. 72). Girls in such families develop an unconscious hatred of femininity because of their preoedipal mother conflict (Keel, 2005). This hatred may lead to a fear of being controlled by their mothers or to a fear of becoming women like their mothers. The eating disorder, then, appears to be a means of gaining control over such fears (C. Johnson, 1995).

Biological theories suggest that disturbances in brain physiology (e.g., serotonin activity) may create a physiological vulnerability for eating disorders (Kaye, 2002; Kaye et al., 2004). There is also evidence that genetic variants may contribute to the development of eating disorders (Kaye et al., 2004). Furthermore, eating-disordered behaviors can cause malnutrition and other physical and psychological disturbances which can interfere with neurological cues for satiety and food intake, as well as impair thinking (Treasure & Szmukler, 1995; Walsh, 1995, 2002).

According to some feminist theories, eating disorders develop when individuals internalize messages that objectify females (Gilbert, Keery, & Thompson, 2005; Smolak & Murnen, 2004). The feminist perspective also suggests that some individuals develop eating disorders in response to sexual harassment, sexual abuse, and other forms of abuse experienced in dating relationships (Smolak & Murnen, 2004). Eating disorders may also function as a coping mechanism for unfulfilling and unreasonable role expectations that are placed on women, or as a response to the media's message that thinness is an effective means to power (Gilbert, Keery, & Thompson, 2005). In sum, eating disorders are viewed as an attempt to gain control over a chaotic life created by socially oppressive and adverse conditions (Piran, Jasper, & Pinhas, 2004).

A THEISTIC VIEW OF HUMAN NATURE AND PSYCHOPATHOLOGY

Our view of eating disorders is grounded theoretically in the theistic worldview and in the theistic understanding of personality and psychopathology described by Richards and Bergin (1997, 2005) and summarized in Exhibit 3.2. The core axioms of this orientation are that God exists, humans are the creations of God, and unseen spiritual processes exist through which God communicates with human beings (Bergin, 1980; Richards & Bergin, 1997).

According to this perspective, human development and personality are influenced by a variety of systems and processes (e.g., biological, cognitive, social, psychological), but the core of identity and personality is spiritual (Richards & Bergin, 2005). Human beings are composed of both a mortal body and an eternal spirit or soul that continues to exist beyond the death

EXHIBIT 3.2
Theistic View of Human Nature and Psychopathology

View of human nature	View of psychopathology
People have agency, although both environmental and biological factors can restrict their choices. Human beings are multisystemic organisms (i.e., biological, social, cognitive, psychological, and spiritual). Human beings have a spirit or soul that is eternal in nature. Spiritual processes exist that allow human beings to communicate with a supreme being. Human beings have great potential for growth and can realize their potential by seeking for spiritual awareness and growth. Human beings can also follow a path of deterioration by neglecting their spiritual growth and choosing evil.	Psychological disturbance and symptoms can be caused by a variety of influences, including physiological (e.g., neurotransmitter depletions), familial (e.g., abuse, marital conflict) social (e.g., prolonged work-related stress), cognitive (e.g., irrational thinking), and spiritual (e.g., moral transgressions) problems. People who neglect their spiritual growth and well-being are more likely to suffer poor mental health and disturbed, unfulfilling interpersonal relationships.

Note. From *A Spiritual Strategy for Counseling and Psychotherapy* (2nd ed., p. 113), by P. S. Richards and A. E. Bergin, 2005, Washington, DC: American Psychological Association. Copyright 2005 by the American Psychological Association.

of the mortal body. This eternal spirit is of divine creation and worth, and it constitutes the lasting or eternal identity of the individual. The spirit interacts with other aspects of the person to produce identity and personality.

The potential development of a person's spiritual identity can go awry because of abusive parenting, social chaos, biological deficiencies, self-destructive choices, and so on, so that a mortal overlay develops and obscures the person's eternal identity. Bergin (2002) described the mortal overlay as "the unique, complex set of characteristics that covers or 'overlays' our spiritual selves during earthly life. It is the combined physical body and mortal mind with all their positive and negative features acquired through biology, genetics, and life experience" (p. 29).

The eternal spiritual identity or self may become obscured by genetic defects and other disorders of the physical body, abusive and other hurtful life experiences, distorted perceptions and debilitating emotional symptoms, and dysfunctional coping mechanisms. But when people get in touch with their eternal spiritual core, with all of its dignity and power for enhancement, the negative aspects of the mortal overlay begins to dissolve, and they begin to overcome their pathologies and grow in healthy ways (Ellsworth, 1995). We say more about the process of healing and therapeutic change in the following chapter.

According to the theistic view, people who believe in their eternal spiritual identity, follow the influence of God's spirit, and live in harmony with universal moral principles are more likely to develop in a healthy manner socially and psychologically (Richards & Bergin, 1997). Spiritually mature people have the capacity to enjoy loving, affirming relationships with others, have a clear sense of identity and values, and behave in harmony with their value system (Bergin, 1980). They also feel closeness and harmony with God and experience a sense of strength, meaning, and fulfillment from their spiritual beliefs. People who neglect their spiritual growth and well-being may be more likely to suffer emotional disturbance and conflicted, unfulfilling interpersonal relationships.

Eating Disorders as a Spiritual Problem

We believe that at their core eating disorders are a spiritual problem. Almost all women with eating disorders have distorted and lost touch with their sense of identity and worth. This identity loss is pervasive to the extent that they lose touch with virtually every healthy aspect of their identity until their identity *is* their eating disorder. They no longer are capable of seeing themselves as women, daughters, mothers, artists, creations of God, and so on but see themselves exclusively *as* an eating disorder, or as the expression of an eating disorder. Their whole sense of identity revolves around their body and their eating disorder. A 19-year-old former patient who participated in a survey we conducted about the role of faith and spirituality in recovery wrote,

> An eating disorder doesn't want just a part of your life, it wants it *all*—it demands it all. This was the case for me. Before I knew it, I was consumed by my eating disorder and spent 110% of my time thinking about food, weight, etc.

A 22-year-old former patient wrote,

> Having an eating disorder hurt my spirituality and relationship with God just as it hurt everything else. There *was* nothing else—only an eating disorder to occupy my time and energy.

For many patients, the loss of their spiritual sense of identity is an extremely painful part of their experience. Many patients feel that they have lost God or that God has left them. They no longer feel worthy or deserving of God's love. A 25-year-old former patient wrote,

> My eating disorder destroyed my relationship with God. It blocked me from God and I lost all faith and trust in God. I became very angry with God because I felt like God had abandoned me. Eventually, I just stopped thinking about God. My eating disorder became my God and my body became the Devil.

A 22-year-old former patient wrote,

> My eating disorder robbed me of my relationship with God. I was in a personal anguish that shred my soul and threatened my spiritual and mortal life. I felt no love and saw no mercy. Anger consumed me. I felt abandoned and worthless. My heart turned bitter and hard. I cut God out of my life completely. My eating disorder robbed me of my self-worth. I felt like nothing. I could not feel love, for I was unlovable. I could not give love, for I was incapable. I lost my self-respect and went against all I believed to be true. It was a downward spiral that almost led to my death.

These statements help illustrate the damage an eating disorder can do to a woman's sense of spiritual identity and worth and to her relationship with God. One of the sad consequences for women who suffer with eating disorders is that through the course and development of the eating disorder, they often lose touch with what is most powerful within themselves. They become numb or lose contact with the feelings of their heart or spiritual identity and worth.

The Impact of a Broken Heart: A Loss of Spiritual Identity

We have noticed often in our observation of artwork created in the early weeks of a patient's treatment that the majority of patients' artistic self-expressions show a broken heart. Some of these hearts have holes in them; others are bound in chains, imprisoned behind bars, torn apart, covered in black, darkened, pierced, broken off or damaged; and some are very small or nearly invisible. These artistic expressions communicate that within the painful experiences and consequences of anorexia and bulimia the women have lost the ability to connect in a positive way with that aspect of their identity most easily described by the metaphor of the heart. They have lost touch with their sense of spiritual identity, with all of its worth, dignity, and capability.

As an eating disorder worsens, the ability even to recognize the impressions and intuitions of the heart is lost in internal conflict and turmoil. The consequence of this inner confusion is that the women do not trust themselves to have valid impressions, desires, or intuitions that would help them correct the negative choices and decisions they are making. As they hide from their emotions, the drive for control over their environment becomes a substitute for the need to listen to the heart. The heart feels too far away, and the impressions are too vague to trust.

As we listen to patients who are in the depths of despair, consumed by the inner conflict associated with anorexia or bulimia, we notice that they associate anything to do with their hearts as emotionally painful. Thus, their sense of themselves is painful. They can lose the ability to recognize the influence of the heart in their lives because they are either trying to control and monitor everything through their minds, or they have numbed or detached themselves from anything emotional. Any emotional pain can be interpreted to mean that the very core of who they are—their hearts—are bad, damaged, or unacceptable. This symbolic connection between emotional pain and the heart of the individual is one reason they have portrayed their hearts as damaged or broken.

We have also observed that many women with eating disorders develop a very rigid "either–or" conceptualization of who they are. On one side they interpret pain, inner conflict, or difficult emotional experiences to mean they have failed—that there is something wrong with them. The other side of the "either–or" equation is the belief that if they could just find the right answer or the magic solution, all of the pain, addiction, or conflict would go away. They are constantly bombarded by this false equation that says,

> [i]f I am struggling, if there are problems, and if the eating disorder is running my life, there is something wrong with me and I am a failure; or I am failing for having not discovered or figured out the right or magic answer to stop it. Once I have the magical answer, then all of the inner conflict will go away.

Because the conflict and pain do not go away, this bind becomes a downward spiral taking them further from recognizing or trusting their hearts.

One of the most significant consequences for those who have forgotten or who have lost their ability to listen to their hearts is that they lose their ability to feel love and to recognize spiritual feelings. For many, to lose that connection to love is a loss of spiritual relationship with God. They feel distant and far removed from God's influence and love. They also lose their ability to feel connected to family and friends. They can feel lonely and empty, even in the presence of those who genuinely love and care for them.

Many women with eating disorders also lose their ability to discern right from wrong. They lose their ability to know what is most important in life. They lose their ability to be congruent and honest. They place all of their faith and value in looks, performance, and body image, rather than in God, love, relationships, and honesty. These are some of the ways that eating disorders undermine a woman's spirituality.

DYSFUNCTIONAL ATTEMPTS TO FILL SPIRITUAL NEEDS: 10 FALSE BELIEFS OF EATING DISORDERS

In our clinical work, we have observed that women with eating disorders often pursue one or more of the 10 false or dysfunctional beliefs (listed

EXHIBIT 3.3
Ten False Beliefs and Pursuits of Women With Eating Disorders

1. My eating disorder will give me control of my life and emotions.
2. My eating disorder will effectively communicate my pain and suffering.
3. My eating disorder will make me exceptional.
4. My eating disorder will prove that I am bad and unworthy.
5. My eating disorder will make me perfect.
6. My eating disorder will give me comfort and safety from pain.
7. My eating disorder will give me a sense of identity.
8. My eating disorder will compensate or atone for my past.
9. My eating disorder will allow me to avoid personal responsibility for life.
10. My eating disorder will give me approval from others.

in Exhibit 3.3) at the expense of their relationship with God, with themselves, and with other individuals. Instead of reaching out to God and to others for help to cope with and heal from painful life events, they pursue one or more of these false beliefs. In a spiritual and religious sense, therefore, these pursuits become false idols that undermine their spiritual identity and prevent them from genuinely worshipping and connecting with God. Rather than worshipping God and having faith in God's healing power, they believe that the eating disorder will provide the solution to their emotional and spiritual problems. These unhealthy beliefs become the objects of their faith and attention, contributing to their feelings of alienation from God's healing influence and from the supportive influence of other people.

False Belief 1: My Eating Disorder Will Give Me Control of My Life and Emotions

Many women who suffer from eating disorders experience an overwhelming fear of "not being in control" or of losing the sense of control that they have. The pursuit of control at all costs eventually becomes the narrow crusade of their eating disorder. They try to be in full control of their environment, avoiding any feelings associated with being out of control. Many of these women have suffered painful experiences in childhood that they could not control or stop. They are terrified of trusting anyone because trust has become associated with disappointment or pain. They have an illusion that by avoiding food or getting rid of their food they are in control of their circumstances and can avoid the things that they are so afraid of, such as pain, disapproval, criticism, and abandonment. The eating disorder gives them a false sense of being in control.

One way this false belief affects women's spiritual lives is that they will not relinquish their illusion of control long enough to believe that someone outside of themselves can care for them, accept them, or love them. They do not believe that other people or God will see more in them than they see in themselves. As a result, they keep people and God at a distance, refuse to allow themselves to become vulnerable, and subsequently avoid emotional intimacy or closeness in all relationships. They substitute a false sense of control for meaningful and loving relationships with God and others.

False Belief 2: My Eating Disorder Will Effectively Communicate My Pain and Suffering

Women with eating disorders may believe that their eating disorder is the only way to express their pain and suffering, along with their feelings of unacceptability. They hide their pain behind the illness in hopes that others will respond to their sickness with love, kindness, or understanding. Actually this form of communication is an ineffective means of soliciting help from others, and it is usually not met with supportive or helpful responses. Women with eating disorders are often told that they are selfish and seeking attention—that they just need to eat and everything will be fine.

This false communication impacts the spiritual life of women with eating disorders in that they are often not willing to be direct and honest with themselves or with God. Instead of expressing their pain in their prayers with God, they talk about how fat they feel. Instead of sharing how lonely, inadequate, or empty they feel, they tell God and others that they are "bad," that they do not deserve love and acceptance. They are frightened to ask specifically for what they want or need from God or from other people.

False Belief 3: My Eating Disorder Will Make Me Exceptional

Many women with eating disorders believe that their eating disorder makes them exceptional—both "better than" and "worse than" others. Many with eating disorders say, "This is the one thing I can do better than anyone else. This is the one thing that I can do well." As a consequence, doing the eating disorder well becomes a false form of self-acceptance, replacing true acceptance from themselves and desire for acceptance from God and others. The belief that they have more will power, strength, or discipline than women who give in to their hunger and need for food and nourishment sets them apart in their own minds, but this belief also keeps them separate, unhappy, isolated, and disconnected from the healing that comes from relationships with other people and with God.

Women who have this belief do become exceptional—exceptional in their refusal to allow any kind of genuine acceptance, kindness, or support to benefit them emotionally or spiritually. Paradoxically, this pursuit of exceptionality—of being special through their eating disorder—distorts their view of the ways that they *are* unique and leaves them feeling *uniquely bad.* Ironically, most of these women will do anything they can to help another woman recover from her eating disorder, believing the ability to overcome it exists, but only in others.

The pursuit of being exceptional can be a significant barrier to recovery from an eating disorder because the individual often feels that she is an "outcast," thus exempt from love, kindness, forgiveness, or support. The sufferer believes that somehow empathy, compassion, mercy, and grace apply to other people, but not to her. She feels like there is something inherently wrong with her, and her shame-based thinking says, "Other people deserve kindness and love, but I don't. I deserve contempt, hatred, and rejection."

This false sense of being the exception can be a major barrier to maintaining a spiritual life or a relationship with God. Many women with eating disorders have stopped praying because they feel like they are unforgivable, unacceptable, or undeserving of a relationship with God. The extreme notion that the rules are different for them keeps them from actively pursuing relationships with God, religious leaders, or with other significant people—relationships that would help them in their recovery. Their own false pursuit of exceptionality reinforces their sense of being empty and alone.

False Belief 4: My Eating Disorder Will Prove That I Am Bad and Unworthy

Women with eating disorders can use the disorder as evidence that they are bad, unacceptable, and deserving of emotional punishment. Some believe that if God and other people are not going to punish them, they should punish themselves. Sufferers spend a great deal of time and energy attempting to prove their unworthiness to God and others, adding new demeaning behaviors and experiences as proof for their deserved rejection, unkind treatment, and pain. Thus much of their emotional and spiritual pain is self-inflicted during this false crusade against themselves.

The spiritual consequence of this belief is that it makes the individual feel distant from all others, including God. They believe "even God could not love me," and so they stop trying to feel close to God. Such women become so busy proving themselves right about this pursuit of low self-image that there is no room for anyone to prove them wrong in their self-rejection. If they feel momentarily happy, hopeful, peaceful, or spiritual, they may chase these positive feelings away with their long list of personal negatives or personal putdowns.

False Belief 5: My Eating Disorder Will Make Me Perfect

Many women with eating disorders have deceived themselves into thinking that if they obtain perfection in their bodies, or in self-control over their bodies, somehow this perfection will make up for their perceived or felt inadequacies and failures. Many with eating disorders talk about how they need to be perfect "for everyone else." But even when they receive acceptance or approval, the best they can ever do is "break even"—in their own minds they never achieve perfection. Furthermore, any criticism or disapproval creates intense feelings of failure and imperfection, exacerbating the eating disorder cycle, making it more intense and rigid. In a sense, seeking perfection becomes a substitute for seeing love. Many women with eating disorders assume that if they can look perfect or perform perfectly, they will receive external validation from other people, which many of them equate with love.

The pursuit of perfection impedes the woman's spiritually because she neglects her spiritual growth and her relationship with God in pursuit of a kind of physical and literal justification for their existence: "If I obtain this perfection, I may have the right to be here." In some religious communities women with eating disorders can become very discouraged, feeling they cannot live perfectly in terms of certain religious precepts and principles. Instead of understanding self-improvement as ongoing and unfolding, they adopt an "all or nothing" approach, leaving mercy, compassion, and God out of their self-improvement pursuits.

False Belief 5: My Eating Disorder Will Give Me Comfort and Safety From Pain

Many use eating disorders to relieve anxiety and avoid painful emotions, but the sense of safety and comfort is artificial and temporary. Many of our clients, especially those with bulimia nervosa, describe bingeing and purging as attempts to find comfort and relief from their anxiety and tension. But because it is fleeting and unsatisfying, they are barely finished with one binge and purge episode before they find it necessary to begin another.

This sense of comfort, relief, and safety—although temporary—can lead them to depend on the eating disorder as the source of their comfort. One spiritual consequence of the immediate gratification and release provided by the eating disorder is that it distracts the sufferer from seeking the greater, more profound comfort that can come from God. A deep loss of hope is another spiritual consequence of giving up on the long-term comfort and healing of aid from God for the quick addictive fix for pain. The personal sacrifices, humility, and dedication needed over time to resolve the pain with the help of spiritual connections is considered too demanding, difficult, or even impossible to do. Some women who have an eating disorder lose all hope in themselves and in God to find a better way of bringing comfort into their lives. They feel hopeless in having their pain ever go away permanently so they settle for momentary breaks from it through the acts of the eating disorder.

False Belief 7: My Eating Disorder Will Give Me a Sense of Identity

Women with severe anorexia or bulimia often say that the eating disorder has become their identity. Losing their sense of self, they are frightened at the thought of giving up the eating disorder, asking, "Who will I be without it?" "This is me," they insist, "This is my life." Those with an underlying feeling of emptiness and void feel they cannot face these feelings without the false identity of their eating disorder. The shameful feelings associated with eating disorder behaviors, combined with self-rejection and underlying feelings of emptiness and unworthiness, can create a deep spiritual chasm. Spending the energy of one's mind, body, and soul on an eating disorder leaves no room for anything else, including a relationship with God.

For many patients, the eating disorder rules and "commandments" become a kind of pseudo-religion. They believe that the means of salvation for their pained souls is to be found in their obedience to the tenets of this nonspiritual pursuit. Commandments of the church of anorexia can be found on various eating disorder Web sites that promote the illness as the means to a higher level of being true to the cause. To lose their sense of identity by being better at living with an eating disorder can do devastating damage to women's spiritual self when the promised benefits and rewards for loyalty to the disorder do not bring the desired results.

We often say that it is very difficult to have an eating disorder and a life at the same time. Individuals have to pick one or the other. When an eating disorder is their life, it also becomes their sense of who they are. Their eating disorder impairs both their ability to see themselves as creations of God who are of inherent worth and their ability to connect spiritually with God.

In viewing the eating disorder as who they are rather than as something they do or as an illness they have, women with eating disorders may conclude, "God could never accept me. I *am* my eating disorder." Feeling spiritually hopeless, they may question, "If there is nothing else to me, how can God help me find the rest of me? How can God help me feel good about who I am if this is all I am? Is this all I'm good for?"

False Belief 8: My Eating Disorder Will Compensate or Atone for My Past

Sometimes an eating disorder becomes an attempt to compensate for childhood abuse or trauma, family problems, personal mistakes, or sins—a false pursuit of penance. This attempt to justify one's existence by trying to atone for the past becomes a driving force for some women with eating disorders. By denying themselves and suffering through the eating disorder, they self-justify past errors, failures, and suffering.

This attempt to compensate for the guilt, regret, or sorrows of the past greatly impedes spiritual and religious activity by putting the burden on the sufferer to do what only a higher influence can do to bring healing, forgiveness, and relief from past trauma, abuse, or errors. In punishing themselves as a way to resolve guilt and pain of the past, they too often overlook God as a source of the comfort, inspiration, and guidance that they need. They have difficulty trusting or accepting the counsel, encouragement, or comforting words of pastors, ministers, family, or friends because they feel that they must resolve the pain of the past alone instead of allowing God to help them. This ongoing crusade of self-punishment never leads to resolution, peace, or comfort; it may even reinforce the belief that no matter how much they suffer, they will always be unacceptable and unworthy.

False Belief 9: My Eating Disorder Will Allow Me to Avoid Personal Responsibility for Life

For some an eating disorder can become a justification for the absence of an abundant life, a reason to explain everything that is missing. It becomes an indirect and false attempt to avoid ownership of or responsibility for life choices, in essence saying, "My choice to have an eating disorder preempts all the other choices for which I am accountable." Blaming problems with relationships, feelings of inadequacy, and inability to function in life on an eating disorder exempts sufferers from accountability.

The spiritual impact of this false pursuit is an overall sense of hopelessness and futility, a sense of powerlessness that seems unreachable, even by God. Tragically, they feel they are the victims of God and life. The fact that God or loved ones do not instantly save the sufferer from her eating disorder seems to be further proof that she is powerless and thus not responsible for change. Some clients blame God and others for their struggles and consequently wait for them to "fix things."

This passive stance can create feelings of helplessness, abandonment, resentment, and anger toward God and toward people in their lives. Some clients can feel judged or blamed by God and others, yet at the same time they make God and others responsible for making needed changes. This pattern creates a roadblock to recovery: Without accountability for their choices and related consequences, they cannot be empowered to choose.

False Belief 10: My Eating Disorder Will Give Me Approval From Others

Many women with eating disorders pursue approval as a substitute for true acceptance and love, believing approval to be validation that they are acceptable. The eating disorder and all it brings with it, including public approval for external beauty and thinness, becomes almost an object of worship. Approval from others seems to become the primary purpose in life for these women. We have heard many with eating disorders talk about how positive, affirming, and congratulatory people were when they lost weight initially, a striking contrast to how negative they felt about themselves. Unfortunately, pursuing temporary expressions of approval becomes an obsession for some women.

In a spiritual context, we realize that approval from others for how we look or what we do is not sufficient to bring change and healing. It is not deep or lasting. The deep sense of acceptance that can be felt in relationship with God and with people who love us unconditionally can be a much more powerful source of healing and growth. Surface approval is an external, narrow, and short-sighted solution for pain. In contrast to the healing acceptance that comes from God, public approval leaves many feeling empty and starved.

ADDITIONAL SPIRITUAL ISSUES OF PATIENTS WITH EATING DISORDERS

In addition to the spiritual consequences of the 10 false beliefs there are a number of other spiritual issues that women with eating disorders may struggle with, including negative images of God, feelings of spiritual unworthiness and shame, fear of abandonment by God, guilt and shame about sexuality, reduced capacity to serve others, difficulty having faith, and dishonesty. Below we briefly describe each of these issues.

Negative Images of God

Eating disorder patients often struggle with a negative image of God. They may perceive God as angry—a judgmental and punishing figure. Believing that God views them as sinful, unworthy, and defective, they feel alienated and disconnected—undeserving of God's help. Thus, their relationship with God is filled with anxiety, guilt, and shame, rather than being a source of love, comfort, strength, and support.

Patients with eating disorders tend to perceive God much as they perceive their parents. For example, one patient, who considered her parents emotionally distant viewed God the same way. When an individual experiences her parents as rejecting, critical, controlling, angry, devaluing, or shaming, she is likely to project the same characteristics on God. Research has documented a common similarity between people's perceptions of their parents and of God (Wulff, 1991), so it is not surprising to find patients with eating disorders making this connection.

Feelings of Spiritual Unworthiness and Shame

Many individuals with eating disorders feel spiritually unworthy, defective, or ashamed. They believe that God (and everyone else) views them as unworthy. Instead of a healthy sense of their identity and self-worth, they have a cosmic sense of being spiritually and morally bad and sinful—undeserving of God's help.

Many patients with eating disorders attempt to compensate for their feelings of spiritual unworthiness through perfectionism, relentlessly striving to meet impossibly high standards—physically, morally, religiously, academically, and so on. Their failure to be perfect then confirms their belief that they are unworthy, reinforcing their feelings of shame and spiritual defectiveness. The patients' feelings of unworthiness and shame are often rooted in shaming experiences from their family of origin or their peers, or in other types of negative social experiences.

Fear of Abandonment by God

Many patients with eating disorders fear abandonment and disapproval from God. They want God and others to approve and take care of them. Their fear that they have displeased God and will be abandoned seems to be confirmed whenever they feel that God has not shown love by actively intervening in their lives. These patients have difficulty trusting in God's love and providence, viewing God as capricious and judgmental.

A high percentage of eating disorder patients were sexually abused as children and believe that God abandoned them during the abuse. They conclude, "A loving God would not have allowed me to be abused, but I was, and so God must not love me. I must be a very bad person because God didn't love and protect me." These patients often have great difficulty trusting and believing that God will support and help them. Because these patients' perceptions of God are often strongly connected to their perceptions of their parents, many fear God's abandonment because of physical or emotional neglect or abuse during their childhood.

Guilt and Shame About Sexuality

Patients with bulimia nervosa who were sexually abused as children or young adolescents can become sexually promiscuous. Society taught them that their needs for love and self-esteem can be fulfilled through sexual activity; thus, they confuse sex and love. They also believe that all they have of value to offer others is sex—or their bodies; paradoxically, they hate their bodies.

The guilt such patients experience seems to be intensified if they are religious, particularly if their religion has strong prohibitions against premarital or extramarital sex. We regard guilt as healthy when patients recognize that an act is harmful or morally wrong but do not condemn their whole selves as deficient or bad (Richards & Bergin, 2005). Some patients' guilt about their sexual promiscuity is dysfunctional, being so extreme that they are unable to separate the act from their worth as a person, resulting in deep feelings of shame, worthlessness, and deficiency. Guilt is also dysfunctional when it is compulsive and reoccurring and when it is not lessened by sincere efforts to confess, make restitution, and change.

Many eating disorder patients struggle with dysfunctional guilt, part of the pattern of feeling worthless and deficient. We have found that religious beliefs of patients with anorexia nervosa can intensify their inability to accept their developing sexuality, especially with patients whose religions have strict prohibitions about sexual behavior. In some cases, patients have received dysfunctional messages about sexuality from their parents that go well beyond the religious tradition. Thus, for many patients, their family's rigid and shaming messages about sex, not their religion, have been the cause of their sexuality problems.

Reduced Capacity to Love and Serve

Many patients with eating disorders seem to be deficient in their capacity to love and serve others in a healthy manner. During the development of their disorder, they learned to avoid feeling negative emotions, and in shutting down emotionally they also lose their ability to experience positive emotions such as love, empathy, and compassion for others. They also have less time to think about others because they are so preoccupied with their eating disorder. Many women with eating disorders also feel that their love is worth nothing, and so they are afraid to give love and service to others for fear of rejection. Thus, many eating disorder patients have lost the ability to connect with others and to love and serve because they have become so self-absorbed or they hold themselves back so much from others because they are afraid of exposing themselves.

In addition, many patients with eating disorders are codependent: To them, love and service means to "let people walk on you" or to "always please others at any cost." Having rarely experienced anything different, they seem unable to understand that they could love and serve others without giving up their identity, preferences, and needs. Some of our patients seem suspicious and fearful of love because the love they have experienced carries heavy expectations and obligations; thus, they tend to disqualify or avoid love, whether it is God's love or the love of others, often purposely remaining victims.

Patients who are religious may have added difficulty because of the expectations of their religious culture to "love and serve" others. Because of their issues, such expectations are uncomfortable for them. If they avoid acts of service, they often feel guilty and unworthy; if they ignore their anxieties and get involved in service, they often push themselves so hard they end up feeling used. We find that patients' difficulties with love and service, like those with fear of God and sexuality, most often originate in their families, where they have acquired the belief that loving and serving others requires giving up their own individuality and sacrificing their own needs. This unhealthy view of love and service may have been given a religious rationale.

Difficulty Surrendering and Having Faith

Many patients with eating disorders attempt to bring control into their lives by controlling their eating behavior and body weight. They attempt to control or "numb out" unpleasant feelings and emotions by restricting, bingeing, or purging behaviors (or a combination of these). Almost all women with eating disorders have difficulty surrendering their sense of control over their body and over food. Many patients also attempt to control their emotions and lives through perfectionism. Unfortunately, these efforts to control their emotions and behavior often become so extreme that they have a problem of overcontrol, which can impair their spiritual growth and well-being.

Many of our patients become so good at controlling or numbing out their emotions that they are unable to experience sensitive spiritual feelings. When they attend church, pray, read spiritual literature, or meditate, they still feel spiritually numb or dead. Feeling that something is wrong with them, they often attribute their lack of spiritual feelings to defectiveness or unworthiness.

Many patients also have difficulty surrendering their own will to have faith and trust in God. They seem so afraid of losing control that they are unable or unwilling to give up their control over their eating behavior and emotions. They fear and resist surrendering and having faith in God because they see that as "letting go" of control.

Dishonesty and Deception

Another important spiritual issue for eating disorder patients is that of dishonesty and deception. An eating disorder is founded on dishonesty—lies to self, others, and God. Most eating disorder patients, particularly those with bulimia nervosa, are secretive about their eating and weight control behaviors (i.e., bingeing, purging, food rules, laxative abuse, etc.) and experience a great deal of shame over their dishonesty. They often have a long history of lying to their families and friends to cover up and protect their addictive illness. Religious prohibitions may intensify the shame. A related problem is distrust: Because eating disorder patients are secretive and dishonest, they have difficulty believing others are honest; thus, they feel they cannot trust anybody, even God.

CONCLUSION

Identifying and finding healing solutions to the false pursuits and spiritual issues of patients with eating disorders requires patience; kindness; repetition; reassurance; inspiration; and emotional, family, and spiritual work over an extended period of time. The intense and personal worship of the eating disorder is difficult to give up because it is so deeply rooted in fear and self-contempt. For many, fear and shame are not only the root cause and sustaining force of the eating disorder but also barriers to spiritual reconnection (Lewis, 2001; Richards et al., 1997). Despite the challenges, we have found that spiritual discussions and interventions can greatly help women with eating disorders reconnect with themselves, with others, and with their God in healing and life-changing ways. We discuss treatment issues and intervention in the remaining chapters of this book.

4

A THEISTIC VIEW OF THERAPEUTIC CHANGE

In this chapter, we describe our view of the role of spirituality in healing and recovering from eating disorders. We begin by briefly summarizing prominent theories of therapeutic change and goals of treatment for patients with eating disorders. We describe the theistic view of therapeutic change on which we ground our understanding of recovery from eating disorders. We describe how we seek to help women with eating disorders learn to listen to their hearts reaffirm their eternal spiritual identity and worth. We offer suggestions for helping patients learn to place their faith in God, in significant others, and in their own divinely given capabilities instead of in the false pursuits of their eating disorder.

CONTEMPORARY THEORIES OF THERAPEUTIC CHANGE FOR EATING DISORDERS

Exhibits 4.1 and 4.2 briefly summarize some of the most prominent theories of therapeutic change along with goals and themes of treatment for eating disorders, in addition to our theistic perspective. According to the cognitive–behavioral perspective, therapeutic change occurs through the modification of dysfunctional or irrational cognitions and maladaptive behaviors that maintain the eating disorder. The objective of

EXHIBIT 4.1
Theories of Therapeutic Change for Eating Disorders

Cognitive–behavioral	Family systems	Interpersonal	Psychodynamic	Biological	Feminist	Theistic
Change occurs through modification of dysfunctional beliefs about food, weight, and body shape (e.g., worth is not based on body shape and weight) and by changing dysfunctional eating disorder behaviors.	Change occurs through healthy family interactions and patterns. Families are the most important resource in the healing process.	Change occurs when patients confront their need to please others, become sensitive to their own needs, and focus on underlying relationship issues, not symptoms.	As women gain insight into the source of their hatred of femininity and have positive experiences with their therapist, eating disorder symptoms diminish.	Correcting physiological disturbances or symptoms through medication and nutrition helps normalize weight and physiological functioning and reduces eating disorder thoughts and behaviors.	Change occurs by creating relational and dialogical space that counters adverse, widely sanctioned, oppressive conditions.	Change and recovery occur as women discover or regain their sense of spiritual identity and worthiness and reconnect with God and significant others. As women place their faith in God and in the loving support of significant others, they are able to quit relying on the eating disorder as their source of comfort and control.

EXHIBIT 4.2

Treatment Goals and Themes for the Treatment of Eating Disorders

Cognitive–behavioral	Family systems	Interpersonal	Psychodynamic	Biological	Feminist	Theistic
Modify automatic, negative thoughts and assumptions relating to food, weight, and shape. Break behavioral and psychological chains that maintain unhealthy eating behaviors and cognitions.	Encourage healthy family patterns and interactions. Encourage families to allow patients to have and share their feelings. Seek to reduce patient dependency and promote differentiation. Give families permission to quit trying to stop the disorder. Create an extrafamilial support network for the patient.	Short-term treatment is limited to treating one or two problem areas (grief, interpersonal role disputes, interpersonal deficits, role transitions). Facilitate the mourning process, modify expectations and faulty communication, reduce social isolation, and/or increase a sense of mastery regarding the demands of the new role.	Treatment focuses on working with transference. Patients inevitably react with defiance to therapists' interventions to defend against control by a powerful outside figure (e.g., mother). These transference reactions need to be analyzed and worked through so that the patient can understand her efforts to adapt.	Restore patients to healthier weight through feeding and nutrition. Medication is used (e.g., antidepressants) to treat patients' mood disturbance, minimize preoccupation with food and weight, and reduce binge and purge frequency.	Explore themes of power and role expectations in the family and in society. Give voice to pain and struggle. Focus on strengths and creative resistance. Encourage social transformation.	Explore patients' feelings of spiritual unworthiness and alienation from God and significant others. Help patients affirm their spiritual worth and identity as creations of God. Help patients turn to God and others for support and comfort in times of fear and stress. Help them place their faith in a "higher power" rather than the eating disorder.

cognitive–behavioral treatment is to modify spontaneous, negative thoughts and assumptions relating to food, weight, and shape and to break behavioral and psychological triggers and chains that maintain unhealthy eating behaviors and cognitions (Birmingham & Beumont, 2004; Wilson & Pike, 2001). Maladaptive schema are addressed by recording daily thoughts, keeping data logs, exploring and balancing dichotomous thinking, and monitoring eating behaviors in relation to external triggers. In addition, faulty thinking attached to the eating disorder is confronted and corrected through visual restructuring and visual rescripting (Pike, Devlin, & Loeb, 2004; Waller & Kennerley, 2003).

According to the family systems perspective, therapeutic change occurs through establishing healthy family interactions and patterns. Families are viewed as the most important resource in the healing process. A family systems objective for treating eating disorders is to encourage healthy family patterns and interactions, encourage families to allow for and share their feelings, reduce patient dependency, and promote differentiation. In addition, therapists strive to create an extrafamilial support network for the patient (Sargent, Liebman, & Silver, 1985). Some of the approaches for treatment include helping the family to set goals and work together to achieve them. The family therapist also strives to increase patients' awareness of thoughts, feelings, or familial interactions through role-playing, journaling, family symbolic food preparation, and family genograms (Eisler, le Grange, & Asen, 2003; Sargent et al., 1985). Another technique for the treatment of eating disorders is to have the family eat together in an inpatient context in the presence of the family therapist. Following the meal, the family and the therapist process through patterns and challenges experienced during the family mealtime (Eisler et al., 2003).

According to the interpersonal psychotherapy perspective, therapeutic change occurs when patients confront their need to please others and focus on their own needs and on underlying relationship issues not symptoms. An interpersonal perspective focuses on the short term, and treatment is limited to one or two problem areas (e.g., grief, interpersonal role disputes, interpersonal deficits, role transitions) that are assumed to underlie the symptoms of the eating disorders (Tantleff-Dunn, Gokee-LaRose, & Peterson, 2004). The therapist's role in treatment includes any one or a combination of the following: to facilitate the mourning process, help patients to modify expectations and faulty communication, encourage patients to find ways to include themselves in society, and help patients to gain a greater sense of mastery regarding the demands of the new role they are acquiring as a result of the treatment process (Wilfey, Stein, & Welch, 2003). Treatment strategies from an interpersonal perspective include exploring unresolved grief, becoming reinvolved in their lives, developing accurate perceptions of others, and creating more realistic expectations in their relationships with others. In addition, the patient is encouraged to assess realistically old and new roles, address any barriers that may interfere with the successful acquisition of new roles, and develop strategies for coping with the new role (Wilfey et al., 2003).

According to the psychodynamic perspective, therapeutic change occurs as patients gain insight into the source of their hatred of femininity and have positive experiences with their therapist (Herzog, 1995; C. Johnson, 1995). Treatment of eating disorders from a psychodynamic perspective focuses on working with transference that results from an attempt to defend against control by a powerful outside figure (e.g., mother). Transference reactions are analyzed and worked through so that the patient can understand previous dysfunctional efforts to adapt. Insight and positive relational experience with the therapist allow patients to pursue more adaptive coping strategies (Herzog, 1995; C. Johnson, 1995). The psychodynamic treatment approach includes offering patients specific symptom management strategies—for example, cognitive–behavioral, psychoeducational, psychopharmacological, and 12-steps (Herzog, 1995; C. Johnson, 1995).

According to the biological perspective, therapeutic change occurs as physiological disturbances or symptoms are corrected through medication and nutrition. The primary treatment goal of the biological perspective is to restore patients to a healthier weight and to restore proper physiological functioning. Medication is used (e.g., antidepressants) to treat patients' mood disturbance, minimize preoccupation with food and weight, and reduce binge and purge frequency. An intervention that may be offered from a biological perspective is administration of cyproheptadine, an antihistamine with antiserotonergic activity (Walsh, 2002). However, "the use of medication in anorexia nervosa is not dictated by the diagnosis of anorexia nervosa, but by other clinical features, and by the judgment of the responsible physician" (Walsh, 2002, p. 327).

According to the feminist perspective, therapeutic change that brings healing occurs by creating relational and dialogical space that counters adverse, widely sanctioned, oppressive conditions. A feminist approach to the treatment of eating disorders focuses on exploring themes of power and role expectations in the family and in society, giving voice to the pain and struggle associated with those themes. The strengths of the patients are emphasized, and their demonstrations of creative resistance are praised (Piran, Jasper, & Pinhas, 2004; Smolak & Murnen, 2004). The therapist may share examples of important women in history to help validate patient's experience as well as to facilitate a social connection to these women (Piran et al., 2003; Smolak & Murnen, 2004). Other important interventions include creating safety and empowerment in therapy, exploring how gender operates in culture, examining possible violations of personal boundaries, and helping patients recognize and assert their needs (Piran et al., 2004).

THERAPEUTIC CHANGE AND TREATMENT THEMES FROM A THEISTIC PERSPECTIVE

Our view of therapeutic change and healthy human functioning is based on the theistic view described by Richards and Bergin (2005), summarized in Exhibit 4.3. According to this view, pharmacological, behavioral, cognitive, social, emotional, and educational interventions may all be of assistance to patients. For many, however, healing that endures requires a spiritual process. Therapeutic change is easier and is often more profound and lasting when people heal and grow spiritually through God's inspiration and love (Richards & Bergin, 1997, 2005). To achieve complete therapeutic change and healing, patients need to get in touch with and affirm their eternal spiritual nature.

As patients uncover or move past the obscuring layers of the mortal overlay, they can recognize or reaffirm their divine worth, lovability, goodness, and potential. For many, spiritual practices and interventions such as praying, contemplating, meditating, reading sacred writings, journaling spiritual matters, listening to uplifting music, forgiving, repenting, worshipping, engaging in religious rituals, providing and receiving service and fellowship, seeking spiritual direction, and receiving moral clarification and in-

EXHIBIT 4.3
Theistic View of Therapeutic Change and Healthy Functioning

View of therapeutic change	View of healthy functioning
Therapeutic change and healing can be facilitated through a variety of means, including physiological (e.g., medications), familial (e.g., improving communication), social (e.g., preventative education), cognitive (e.g., modifying irrational beliefs), and spiritual (e.g., prayer, repentance, meditation). At the core, healing and change are spiritual processes. Psychological, relational, and even physical healing are facilitated and are more profound and lasting when people heal and grow spiritually.	Biological, social, psychological, and spiritual factors all influence personality development. People who believe in their eternal spiritual identity, follow the influence of God's spirit, and live in harmony with universal moral principles are more likely to develop in a healthy manner socially and psychologically. Spiritually healthy people have the capacity to enjoy loving, affirming relationships with others, have a clear sense of identity and values, and behave in harmony with their value system. They also feel a sense of closeness and harmony with God and experience a sense of strength, meaning, and fulfillment from their spiritual beliefs.

Note. Adapted from *A Spiritual Strategy for Counseling and Psychotherapy* (2nd ed., p. 113), by P. S. Richards and A. E. Bergin, 2005, Washington, DC: American Psychological Association. Copyright 2005 by the American Psychological Association.

struction can help facilitate this spiritual healing process (Richards & Bergin, 1997, 2005). Ultimately, God's loving and healing influence can help patients exercise the faith necessary to recognize and feel their eternal spiritual identity and worth.

Experiencing a deep affirmation of their eternal spiritual identity and worth during prayer or other spiritual experiences is a life-transforming event for many patients. They find it easier to feel and accept love and validation from their therapist, and from significant others. They begin to heal from the "inside out." Such experiences often increase patients' faith in God and in spiritual realities, change their identity (to that of an eternal being of great worth), heal their shame or feelings of being bad, and reorient their values (from a secular or materialistic value system to a more spiritual one). These inner changes in beliefs and values lead to outer changes in lifestyles, which lead to healthier behaviors and reductions in psychological and physical symptoms and problems (Richards, 1999). As patients regain their sense of spiritual identity and worthiness by reconnecting with God and significant others, change and recovery occurs. Through faith in God and in the loving support of significant others, patients stop relying on the eating disorder as their source of comfort and control.

Helping Patients Affirm Their Spiritual Identity

The primary goal of our theistic approach to treating women with eating disorders is to help them get in touch with and affirm their spiritual identity and worth as creations of God. As patients learn to listen to and discern spiritual feelings and impressions that can be accessed through their heart or spirit, they are able to discover or rediscover their sense of identity as spiritual beings. We refer to the heart as a metaphor for the eternal spiritual identity, which, according to the theistic perspective, is integrated with the physical body (Richards & Bergin, 2005). Helping patients get in touch with and affirm their spiritual selves through the metaphor of the heart is nonthreatening, easily understood, and well accepted. Patients with eating disorders readily acknowledge a lost or broken heart. The language of the heart is universal and ecumenical in nature. It invites patients of all religious backgrounds and spiritual traditions to open their hearts to themselves, God, and others.

We have observed that as patients progress through treatment and recovery, the artistic impressions and expressions of their hearts show a significant change. The artistic self-depictions show a healed heart, a complete and growing heart. For many, the heart is bigger and has a more profound presence in the drawing. Many hearts are radiating or glowing with vibrant colors and powerful words may be written on them. We have seen artwork in which the heart is the center of the body, and from that center beams of different colors or light diffuses through the rest of the body and mind. These new hearts show love, courage, strength, and hope.

These artistic expressions of the heart encourage us to believe in the importance of helping patients learn to listen to and follow their hearts. Therapists can help patients to discern their heartfelt impressions and desires and to follow and act on them with faith and courage. We know this process will help patients heal their hearts and get in touch again with their spiritual identity and inherent divine worth.

It is important for patients to know that listening to and trusting in the heart is a talent that can be developed and learned with experience and practice over time. Patients must understand that the problem is not that they have a defective heart or no heart at all, but trust that effective heart function requires listening and trust. To become aware of their own hearts as a source of information and a resource for self-direction is a process of positive self-development. Rediscovering their hearts can lead them to the center of both physical and spiritual well-being. We speak of the heart as the inner core of their beings, the deepest place for desires and emotions, and the receptor for spiritual feelings and impressions.

This validating and valuing of their own hearts and heartfelt desires and impressions is a gradual process that takes time, but it is a process that is possible for each of them. Too often, patients will believe what others say but will not listen to or believe themselves. If they cannot believe or trust themselves with what they know, they inevitably will feel a great inner hollowness or void. They go through the motions of living but do not fully experience or enjoy the clarity, empowerment, and goodness innate within themselves. For many the loss of flexibility and fluidity in adjusting to life, to relationships, and to life stressors and events may have more to do with a distant or disconnected heart than with lack of know-how or specific social skills. Intellect and emotions are important aspects of therapy, but for a patient to understand what she knows in the quiet depths of the heart and to trust and act on those impressions can become one of the most powerful relationship and life skills she can possess.

Learning to trust the heart is a process of discovery for patients—not a quick fix or simply a therapeutic intervention, but an ongoing development of an inner understanding, a sense of purpose and direction for themselves. When patients are engaged in the false beliefs of an eating disorder (see chap. 3) they are no longer paying attention to their hearts. These intense, false pursuits shift the patients' focus away from the heart and spiritual influences while they consume all of the patients' thoughts, energies, and time. Addressing the false beliefs and helping patients find ways to break out of these negative cycles frees these patients to pay attention to and care for their hearts. We say more about how to help patients heal and listen to their hearts, or eternal spirits, in chapter 6.

Reconnecting With God and Significant Others: Challenging the 10 False Beliefs of Eating Disorders

In chapter 3, we described 10 false or dysfunctional beliefs commonly held by women with eating disorders and discussed how the pursuit of these beliefs undermines the individual's spirituality, relationships with God and significant others, and psychosocial well-being. We have found that during the treatment process, we must identify and address the specific false beliefs of each patient. Not every woman with an eating disorder accepts and pursues all 10 of the false beliefs; typically, a woman will be devoted to only 3 or 4. So it is necessary to assess which of the specific beliefs are problematic for each patient and to help the individual recognize how the pursuit of these beliefs contributes to her emotional distress and relationship problems with God and with others. We help our clients understand why their beliefs are false. We also help them challenge their false beliefs and replace them with more healthy perspectives. Exhibit 4.4 summarizes 10 therapeutic goals along with our clinical suggestions for helping patients achieve them.

Help Patients Give Up Control

Women with eating disorders must experience vulnerability and learn to trust in safe relationships. They can learn that it is acceptable to feel hurt, sadness, or pain in relation to other people or even to God and that these feelings won't destroy them. They can learn that they are strong enough to be vulnerable.

We help patients understand that they can "take their wall down" and allow themselves to be vulnerable without giving up their choices. They can learn that being genuine in relationships is more rewarding and healthy than putting up walls and seeking to control all relationship outcomes. They can acquire a sense of healthy control by allowing God and significant others to be a part of their decision process rather than trying to make all decisions by themselves. Patients can learn to be aware, honest, open, and vulnerable in relationships with their counselor, with significant others, and with God.

We urge patients to give up controlling through their negative self-perceptions by helping them consider that others' positive perceptions of them may be accurate. We encourage them to start trusting God and other people by giving up their rigid expectations and allowing themselves to

EXHIBIT 4.4
Therapeutic Goals and Suggestions for Challenging the 10 False Beliefs of Eating Disorders

Therapeutic goal	Suggestions
1. *Help patients give up control.*	Help patients understand that they can "take their wall down" and be vulnerable without giving up their choices. Help patients acquire a healthy sense of control by allowing God and significant others into their hearts and lives. Help patients learn to recognize and accept divine will rather than thinking they can control when and how God intervenes in their lives.
2. *Help patients more effectively communicate their pain and suffering.*	Help patients clarify and share the messages communicated by the behavior and symptoms of their eating disorder. Help patients clarify what they want God, their loved ones, and the world to understand about their pain, needs, and desires. Help patients find more direct and open ways to express their pain and their needs to God and others, leaving out their self-judgments and self-punishment.
3. *Help patients accept their inherent uniqueness.*	Help patients understand and internalize that they are no better and no worse than any other person and that there are no special rules that apply only to them. Help patients recognize that other women with this disorder have the same perception of being "the exception," but that none of them really is exceptional or different in bad or shameful ways. Help patients learn that positive self-esteem comes from being genuinely oneself, not from being exactly the same as or radically different from everyone else. Help patients learn to accept God's and others' loving perceptions.
4. *Help patients accept their goodness and worth.*	Help patients affirm their inherent worth as creations of God and as members of the human family. Help patients recognize that their self-rejection prevents them from feeling love and kindness. Help patients understand that their eating disorder and other weaknesses and difficulties do not keep God from loving them. Help patients find the good in themselves and share it with others.
5. *Help patients accept their human limitations.*	Help patients learn that making mistakes is unavoidable and that mistakes can help us learn and grow. Help patients understand that safety can be found in recognition of God's perfection, not in pursuit of their own. Help patients understand that humility is what brings us closer to God, not striving for unrealistic standards of perfection.

(continued)

EXHIBIT 4.4 *(Continued)*

Therapeutic goal	Suggestions
6. *Help patients seek comfort and safety from others and God.*	Help patients learn that true comfort and safety come from loving relationships with God and others. Help patients grow in faith that they are not alone. Help patients learn to recognize how God and others extend comfort and support to them.
7. *Help patients affirm their spiritual identity.*	Help patients recognize that who they *are* is more than what they *do.* Help patients recognize that the part of them that struggles with an eating disorder is not their complete identity. Encourage patients to seek spiritual confirmation of their worth as a creation of God and member of the human family.
8. *Help patients seek forgiveness.*	Help patients understand the distinction between *repentance*, with its healing corrections, and *self-atonement*, with its devastating punishments. Help patients understand that only God can atone and compensate for the past. Help patients seek forgiveness and give away to God what they cannot correct from the past, asking for help in making good choices in the present and future.
9. *Help patients accept responsibility for their lives.*	Help patients understand that accepting responsibility is different from imposing blame, judgment, or fault. Help patients accept responsibility for their lives without blaming and condemning themselves. Encourage patients to ask for help from God and others to make new, healthier choices. Encourage patients to be kind and patient with themselves as they assume personal responsibility and learn from their choices during recovery.
10. *Help patients recognize and accept love from God and others.*	Help patients understand the difference between worldly approval for appearance and performance versus Godly acceptance and love, which is unconditional. Help patients understand that love changes lives but approval for appearance or performance does not. Help patients give up their desires for approval based on appearance or performance. Help patients learn to recognize and accept unconditional love and acceptance from God and others.

Note. From "Spirituality and Ten False Beliefs and Pursuits of Women With Eating Disorders: Implications for Counselors," by R. K. Hardman, M. E. Berrett, and P. S. Richards, 2003, *Counseling and Values, 48,* pp. 75–76.

experience love for what it is and how it is manifest in their lives. We help them understand the importance of learning to recognize and accept God's will, rather than thinking that they can control exactly when and how God intervenes in their lives. Looking for providence and recognizing that God is part of their lives can aid them in relinquishing the obsession to control.

Help Patients More Effectively Communicate Their Pain and Suffering

We help patients explore, clarify, understand, and share the nonverbal messages communicated by the behavior and symptoms of their eating disorder. Doing this can help patients clarify what they want God, their loved ones, and the world to understand about their pain, suffering, needs, and desires. We help patients find more direct and open ways (e.g., through writing, discussing, sharing) to express their pain and their needs, leaving out their self-judgments, self-defenses, and self-punishment. As patients begin to understand that having painful feelings does not mean that they are bad or flawed, they become more honest in sharing their feelings and allow God and significant others to validate their painful emotions and experiences.

For many women suffering with anorexia nervosa, the illness has become a question of life and death. To regain their ability to live, patients must be willing to face their emotional pain. We also discuss with patients the need to pray directly, specifically, and accurately rather than attempting to communicate with God through the self-contempt of their eating disorder. We teach patients that God and loving people can help them find positive meaning, belonging, and purpose in their suffering. The pain and suffering they experience and express can promote healing by helping them feel connected to themselves, to others, and to God. Their emotional pain creates a fellowship with other women suffering with similar pain and creates a sense of togetherness and belonging rather than aloneness. It is impossible to release their pain to God and hold on to it at the same time. Their pain can be given to God so that it no longer only belongs to them. It becomes a shared pain.

Help Patients Accept Their Inherent Uniqueness

Each patient needs to internalize that she is no better or no worse than any other person. We explain to each that there are no special rules that apply only to her, that her view of herself as exceptional originated in her mind and hurt her heart when she was emotionally wounded as a child.

Women with eating disorders benefit from recognizing that other women who have the same disorder have the same perception of being "the exception," but none of them really is exceptional or different in these shaming ways. Through opportunities to take risks and be themselves, they can discover that strong self-esteem comes from being genuinely oneself, not from being exactly the same as or radically different from everyone else.

Learning that true love is unconditional and a gift that does not have to be bought or earned with performance, achievement, or any specific exceptionality is a powerful insight. Patients can learn to accept God's and others' loving perceptions of them. We encourage them to reexamine their rigid beliefs that God thinks or feels negatively toward them, because these beliefs impair their ability to accept God's love. We help patients understand that the negative thoughts they have about themselves are their thoughts alone, not God's thoughts or the thoughts of their loved ones.

Help Patients Accept Their Goodness and Worth

As women with eating disorders begin to affirm their inherent value and spiritual identity, they can begin to give up this false crusade against themselves. We have found it helpful to affirm to patients their inherent worth as creations of God and as members of the human family. We help them recognize that their self-punishment and self-rejection prevent them from feeling love and kindness from God and others. Patients also need to understand the importance of kindness to self in thought and deed, overcoming the intensity of their negative feelings. Self-kindness and compassion, along with their ability to view the self in the more complete context of both strengths and weaknesses, can interrupt the cycle of self-punishment, opening the door to God's love and to the love of other people.

We seek to help patients recognize that healing from intense feelings of shame comes best from a spiritual source. We teach that God does not allow our humanness, including an eating disorder, to get in the way of divine love. Our weaknesses and difficulties do not stop God's interest and involvement in our lives. We ask patients to look for and find the good in themselves so that they may share with others a more honest and balanced accounting of their strengths and weaknesses.

Help Patients Accept Their Human Limitations

To change the course of this pursuit of perfection, women with eating disorders must learn that it is acceptable to make mistakes. By recognizing and correcting their mistakes, they will make the improvements in themselves that, over time, lead to a significant difference in their lives. They must also come to understand that their specific pursuit of perfection in their eating disorder is why they often end up feeling imperfect, unsatisfied, and unhappy. Change and growth can become a positive journey when patients learn to let spiritual and loving influences help them make corrections, learn from their experiences, and accept themselves as being in the process of positive growth.

Patients also benefit from the belief that God can help them overcome and transcend their human limitations. This spiritual empowerment can replace an unhealthy pursuit of perfection if they understand that they do not need to be perfect, only humble so that God can help them do what they cannot do on their own. Reverencing God as perfect can take away the pressure to be perfect themselves. Safety can be found in God's perfection, not pursuit of their own. We have found it helpful to emphasize that humility is what brings us closer to God, not striving for unrealistic standards of perfection.

Help Patients Seek Comfort and Safety From Others and God

True safety and comfort for those with eating disorders comes from participating in loving and accepting relationships and from knowing that they are not alone in facing the ups and downs of life. Through prayer and meditation, patients can learn that God is available to them. Through talking and listening, patients can also learn that significant others are available to them. This knowledge can be a great comfort in facing life's challenges.

We have also found it helpful to teach patients that God is a "partner" who can be included in all that they go through. Safety comes from feeling that they are not alone, that they are connected to and supported by God and by other people who care for them. Recognizing the various ways that God and others extend comfort to them can help them let go of rigid and specific expectations of how comfort should look or feel. Helping patients recognize God's hand in their lives can give them hope and strength.

Help Patients Affirm Their Spiritual Identity

Part of a spiritual reawakening for patients is the discovery that who they are is more than what they do. What anyone does, including those with eating disorders, can never fully express the unique person or her individual personal qualities and characteristics. We help patients recognize that who they are is much bigger and more complex than the eating disorder. The eating disorder can never be all of their identity. Helping patients identify and affirm their many positive qualities and traits can help broaden their sense of identity and facilitate the healing process.

Most patients' false identity is based on a deep shame that they feel about themselves. The therapist can encourage patients to listen during conversations, prayers, sacred music, and quiet, reflective moments for spiritual confirmation of their worth as a creation of God and a member of the human family. Challenging the truthfulness of patients' feelings of shame from within a spiritual framework can lead to a more peaceful connection with the true self.

Feeling peaceful with God and with significant others can allow patients to value every aspect of themselves, rather than reject themselves in entirety. Learning self-acceptance helps a person discover that negative qualities or limitations do not make her less of a person, but rather a "real" and "whole" person. A patient who believes that God or others can accept all of her—with her strengths, weaknesses, "pluses and minuses"—and do so unconditionally, with love and kindness, is going through a spiritual experience that can be fundamental in the recovery process.

Help Patients Seek Forgiveness

We help patients understand the emotional and spiritual distinctions between *repentance*, with its healing corrections, and *self-atonement*, with its devastating punishments and constrictions. When people try to make up for past wrongs, mistakes, or injustices for themselves or for other people through the self-atonement or self-punishment that occurs through their eating disorder, they are attempting to control circumstances that they do not have the power to change by themselves.

In helping patients understand the difference between self-atonement and repentance, the therapist may need to discuss the differences between real and false guilt. We help our patients understand that real guilt is caused by the recognition that they have done something wrong and that is incongruent with their inner belief system. They have an inner sense (conscience) that the action was wrong, and they feel guilt, regret, discomfort, or sadness in reaction to it. They do not take on self-blame or condemnation but rather make an honest appraisal and accept ownership for the misdeed. The feelings of guilt at that time tend to be brief and intense, motivating them toward corrections such as repenting, asking forgiveness, making restitution, and resolving not to repeat the wrongdoing.

False guilt, however, is a painful counterfeit. We help our patients understand that false guilt makes them feel that they are bad, worthless, stupid, weak, and flawed. The shameful feelings of false guilt make it extremely difficult for them to separate their actions from their core self. Their core self feels bad and flawed. False guilt is chronic and long lasting; it can rarely be resolved, and the pain from the self-condemnation and internal attempts to "atone" for past wrongdoings and shortcomings can be intense. For these and other reasons, the differences between real and false guilt need to be clarified with patients so that they can begin to differentiate for themselves the difference between the self-induced suffering of false guilt and the corrective influences of real guilt.

Helping patients see God as the healer can open them up to healing. In cases of past mistakes, we encourage patients to see repentance as a process by which they make loving changes and corrections in their perceptions and behavior, with God and trusted people as active partners in that process. Their feelings that they are undeserving can be replaced with feelings of gratitude for the loving kindness of God and others toward them. Regardless of the original events, letting go of the past can become a spiritual process in which patients give away to God what they cannot correct from the past, asking for help in the present and future to make good choices and to deal effectively with adversity.

Help Patients Accept Responsibility for Their Lives

Many women in the severe stages of an eating disorder no longer have much control of their emotions, behavior, and lives. Such patients need physicians and mental health professionals to take initial control, providing much direction in the physical and emotional recovery process. Once patients are stabilized and begin to function at a higher level, they can begin to take more responsibility for their lives and recovery. At this point, they may be ready to address the false pursuit of avoiding responsibility for life.

One cannot change or let go of something without first assuming ownership for it. Patients cannot heal and change if they have not first taken full responsibility for their lives, being honest and open with themselves about their mistakes, weaknesses, and poor choices. We teach patients that *responsibility* is different from self-blame, judgment, or criticism. Responsibility accepts the fact that much of the eating disorder behavior, pursuits, and coping strategies are learned, admitting, "I learned it, I have choices about it, and it is mine to change."

Many women who suffer with eating disorders have difficulty understanding that being honest and accepting responsibility for themselves must be done without self-contempt, self-criticism, or self-rejection. For example, one of our patients, Diane, a talented, bright woman who had devoted 15 years to bulimia, came to realize during treatment that she needed to stop lying to herself and others. As she courageously worked at becoming more honest and responsible for her behavior, Diane would often become negative and hurtful toward herself as she experienced shame and self-contempt with increasing awareness of her past dishonesty. Her therapist pointed out her self-condemnation and pleaded with her to quit hurting herself in that way. He asked her to show kindness and compassion toward herself as she courageously continued her efforts to have a more honest heart.

When women with eating disorders leave blame and fault out of the concept of personal responsibility, they create an agent for positive change and learn to be honest with themselves about the consequences of their choices. This honesty is important if they are to escape their self-contempt or feelings of despair and hopelessness. Holding themselves accountable without judgment, they can approach God and others with more faith and with confidence in their own ability to make positive choices with the loving support of God and of the people around them.

Once proper ownership is assumed, one can ask for help from God and others to make new choices. We encourage patients to choose to be kind and patient with themselves as they assume personal responsibility and learn from their choices. They must face their lives directly and without blame so that they can begin to see options beyond their eating disorder.

For many women with eating disorders, responsibility means having to be perfect in everything they do, satisfying more and more performance expectations that they attribute to God and others. To most of them, responsibility means failure; thus, in avoiding responsibility, they avoid failure. Disconnecting perfection and failure from responsibility can assist them in accepting responsibility for their choices. Asking God and others for help becomes a positive experience in recovery as patients begin to see God and their loved ones as allies rather than enemies.

Help Patients Recognize and Accept Love From God and Others

We seek to help patients understand that God's acceptance is not encumbered by the damaging, external conditions or expectations so often found in human relationships (e.g., based on performance and appearance). Godly acceptance can bring peace, comfort, and hope rather than anxiety and pressure to please other people. When patients feel this confirming acceptance from God, they feel encouraged to become kinder toward and more accepting of themselves. Acceptance and love are worth working for when people develop honest and congruent connections with God and with other people. Love is an agent for change; approval for appearance or performance is not. Love changes lives; approval does not.

When people understand the difference between worldly approval for appearance and performance and Godly acceptance and love, they tend to take more positive risks in relationships with others. They become warmer and friendlier; they show more compassion to the people around them. They become less self-absorbed and competitive in their relationships. In a spiritual sense, as women stop seeking external approval and become less self-absorbed, they desire to be closer to God and to other people. Their relationships feel more positive and loving, less threatening or scary. They are better able to give up their self-imposed isolation.

Through developing a sense of God's and others' unconditional love of her, a patient more easily senses herself as a whole person, not "just a body." With this sense of self-acceptance, occasional disappointments, disapproval, or rejections can be worked through and resolved, rather than allowing them to generate shame and depression. Many women discover healthy friendships for the first time in their lives, being better able to give love and service to others. Giving love and service, being concerned for the welfare of others, helps open the door to a spiritual recovery and a fulfilling life journey.

WORKING THERAPEUTICALLY WITH ADDITIONAL SPIRITUAL ISSUES

In chapter 3, we briefly described a number of additional spiritual issues with which many patients with eating disorders struggle, including negative images of God, feelings of spiritual unworthiness and shame, fear of abandonment by God, guilt and shame about sexuality, reduced capacity to love and serve, difficulty surrendering to and having faith, and dishonesty and deception. These issues are virtually always intertwined with deficits in spiritual identity and with their false beliefs and worship of the eating disorder. Hence, as we work therapeutically to address the spiritual identity issues and false beliefs of the eating disorder, we also address these seven spiritual issues when pertinent. In the following sections, we offer some therapeutic suggestions for addressing them.

Help Patients Examine and Modify Images of God

Negative images of God usually develop at an early age through the influence of parents, religious leaders, and significant others. We ask our patients to talk about how they believed their parents viewed them and reacted to their mistakes and struggles. Then we ask them to talk about their image of who God is, what God is like, and how God feels about them when they make mistakes or have struggles. Sometimes we ask patients probing questions such as the following: "What rules did your parents play by? What rules do you believe God plays by? How did your parents respond to your honesty? How do you think God responds to your honesty?"

We invite our patients to consider possible parallels between their image of God and their view of their parents so that they can explicitly consider these connections. Sometimes our patients project their own negative self-image on God and assume that God will view them and respond to them in the same way they view themselves. We invite our patients to consider the possibility that God views and responds to them differently from how their parents did or more mercifully from the way they judge themselves.

We encourage our patients, "Let God be God—do not make God into the image of your parents." Sometimes we find it helpful to ask our patients to revisit and recall what it felt like as a little girl to be in the presence of their parents. Then we ask them to visualize and imagine who they think

God might be, who they wish God could be, and what it might be like to be in God's presence. We find that over the course of treatment, as we help patients examine and modify their negative assumptions and images of God, they begin to soften their hearts and feel God's love, kindness, and influence in their lives.

Help Patients Heal Their Shame

We seek to help our patients understand what shame is, how it feels, and where it comes from. We help them recognize that the feelings of unworthiness, deficiency, and unloveableness associated with shame are based on lies—false beliefs about themselves that they internalized earlier in their lives. We help patients recognize that shame is a spiritual ailment that prevents them from feeling spiritual influences and love.

We find that acceptance helps patients heal from shame—acceptance from their therapist, acceptance from the treatment staff, acceptance from significant others, and acceptance from God. Shame says, "I don't deserve to be accepted" and so receiving acceptance from caring people helps challenge this lie. Group therapy can provide acceptance from peers, going beyond what patients can experience in individual therapy. Letting others get to know them and accept them with all of their imperfections and past mistakes helps heal shame.

We also help our patients understand the difference between real guilt and false guilt. False guilt is fed by shame; thus, patients must differentiate shame and false guilt from real guilt so that they can begin to separate their behaviors, which are sometimes wrong, from their core self, which is lovable and of divine worth.

Healing from shame requires that the individual learn to listen to her heart and learn who she really is without the shame—a creation of God with divine worth and inherent goodness. We sometimes say to our patients, "How about letting God have a vote on who you are! See what God has to say!" Prayer, meditation, and uplifting or sacred music, as well as listening to one's heart, are spiritual practices that can help patients feel their inherent lovability, worth, and goodness.

Help Patients Overcome Fears of Abandonment

We encourage patients to talk about times in their lives they have felt abandoned by others. We help our patients understand that true abandonment is something that can happen to children through abuse, neglect, loss, divorce, and so on. Abandonment can be devastating to children and threaten their very existence because they do not have the power to care fully for themselves. In addition, children assume that they were abandoned because something was wrong with them. Adults can experience intense loss, but they are more capable of taking care of themselves physically and emotionally, and so the loss rarely threatens their survival. We seek to help our patients affirm their ability to take care of themselves physically and emotionally.

Because abandonment and loss make people feel empty and alone, we find that helping patients learn to receive love, comfort, and support from their therapist, from other members of the treatment staff, from other patients, and from significant others can help them feel more secure and thus promote healing. When people feel they have been abandoned in the past, they do not want to risk being abandoned again, and so they do not allow themselves to be close to others in fear of being vulnerable to hurt again. Believing that God might abandon them can be an ultimate fear for some religious patients. We also find that some patients abandon themselves emotionally and then conclude that other people and God have abandoned them. We seek to help our patients understand that allowing themselves to take the risk of growing close to others, including God, is a wise choice because it opens up the doors to love and joy.

Helping Patients Deal With Guilt and Shame About Sexuality

In our work with patients who have eating disorders, we find it important to take a careful body image and sexual history during the assessment phase of treatment. Did the patient get messages that sexuality is shameful, bad, and dirty? Does she feel guilt and shame about her sexual life? Inability to accept her body and sexuality can contribute to a patient's shame.

If a patient has been sexually exploited or abused, it is important for her to talk to her therapist about what happened so that she can confront and talk about the shame she feels about it. As a patient feels accepted, loved, and valued by her therapist—regardless of what she has done or experienced in her sexual life—this acceptance can be a healing experience. Group therapy helps participants feel accepted and less ashamed about their sexuality. Often they find out that they are not alone in what they have experienced and felt.

We often invite our religious patients to explore how they think God views them regarding their sexuality and sexual experiences. If patients feel real guilt and remorse over past sexual activities that have violated their moral beliefs, we invite them to consider God's role in repentance and forgiveness. If patients believe that confession to clergy is a necessary part of the repentance process, we support them in doing this. We encourage them to take the steps they feel are needed to find peace in their hearts.

Helping Patients Learn to Love and Serve

We ask our patients to begin watching for evidences of love in their lives, even if they may not feel love in their hearts. We also ask them to begin expressing love in treatment of others, even when they may not have fully loving feelings in their hearts. We find that if our patients begin to notice and express love, their hearts may be more fully open to loving feelings.

We also seek to help our patients understand the difference between love and service or dependency and caretaking. Caretaking involves feelings of dependency, deficiency, and obligation, whereas service flows from feelings of concern, love, and self-respect. Some patients fear serving because they are afraid that those served will take advantage of them. We help them understand that they can provide loving service without losing their boundaries or their ability to keep themselves safe in relationships.

Many religious patients consider service a part of living their religion, so if they are not serving, they feel selfish and out of harmony with God. Feelings of selfishness can exacerbate an eating disorder, so we provide opportunities for patients to serve each other or provide help to those with needs in the community so that they feel less selfish and better about themselves. We also seek to help our patients recognize that giving is a reciprocal process—that giving and serving can help them learn to receive good gifts from others. Receiving and accepting service from others is also a form of giving and loving.

Helping Patients Learn to Surrender and Live With Faith

We seek to help our patients understand how their intense fears and self-doubts are the underlying dynamics of their need to control their bodies and their food intake. Women with eating disorders live in constant fear of rejection. They live in fear of being vulnerable, of being rejected, and of being viewed as stupid or bad by others and by God.

We seek to help our patients learn to trust themselves, their hearts, their goodness, and others' goodness. We encourage them to take risks, be vulnerable, and open their hearts to the possibility of love and acceptance. We invite them to be receptive to the love of other people and of God. We encourage them to listen to their hearts, and we help them understand that the false beliefs and pursuits of an eating disorder are destructive to their well-being.

We ask our patients to remember when they lived their life based more on faith. We help them understand that faith is believing in things that are true even though we may not be able see them or prove them. We teach our patients that they cannot wait until they have absolute proof before they risk opening their hearts to trust and love. We encourage them to have faith that God has their welfare in mind. We ask them to "give God good intent." If a patient has been abused, we find it is important to help her separate the bad intent of the abuser from God and other people and not to see others as a projection of her fears. We encourage patients to gather evidence to support their faith, not evidence to refute it. Both kinds of evidence are available, but overgeneralizing or blowing the negative out of proportion distorts reality, which is not helpful.

Helping Patients Be More Honest and Congruent

We seek to help our patients understand that truth sets people free, whereas lies and dishonesty keep them in bondage. As stated in the previous chapter, an eating disorder is based on dishonesty—lies to self, to others, and to God. We help our patients understand that they might at times succeed at deceiving others, and even themselves, but they cannot deceive God. We invite them to consider why they spend so much time trying to deceive or hide from others. We find that most patients attempt to hide who they are because they feel that who they are is unacceptable, and so they lie to avoid judgment by others and by themselves.

We encourage our patients to listen to their hearts about what is true. We help them separate who they are from what they have done. We help them see during individual and group therapy that telling the truth feels better than lying. We encourage them to extend this understanding to their relationships with family members, with religious leaders, and with God. We help them understand that they cannot change if they do not first own responsibility and tell the truth about their actions. We help them understand that telling the truth about their eating disorder will help them find a way to heal from it.

CONCLUSION

The overall spiritual goals of our theistic approach to working with patients with eating disorders is to help them learn to (a) listen again to their hearts; (b) reclaim their sense of spiritual identity; (c) give up the false pursuits of their eating disorder; (d) resolve other spiritual issues with which they may be struggling; and (e) reconnect with themselves, others, and God. Despite the challenges involved, we have found that spiritual discussions and interventions can greatly help patients in healing and life-changing ways. In the remaining chapters, we say more about our spiritual treatment approach and the interventions we use to assist patients with their healing and recovery process.

5

MULTIDIMENSIONAL THEISTIC TREATMENT FOR EATING DISORDERS

In this chapter, we describe the theistic spiritual view of treatment on which we base our eating disorder treatment approach, in the context of contemporary treatment recommendations. We describe our theistic approach and how it contributes to a multidimensional treatment strategy. We offer some general recommendations for working with patients who have eating disorders, as well as some process guidelines and suggestions integrating spiritual perspectives and interventions into eating disorder treatment. We conclude by describing some structured spiritual interventions that can be used in inpatient and residential treatment settings.

CONTEMPORARY TREATMENT RECOMMENDATIONS FOR EATING DISORDERS

The American Psychiatric Association (2000b) has published practice guidelines for the treatment of patients with eating disorders. In general, these guidelines recommend a multidisciplinary and multidimensional approach to treatment. Physicians, psychiatrists, psychologists, family therapists, nutritionists, nurses, and other health professionals should normally all be part of the treatment team. Medical management; nutrition and weight stabilization; medication; and individual, group, and family psychotherapies are viewed as necessary interventions. Here we briefly summarize some of the general guidelines for treatment recommended by the American Psychiatric Association (2000b). Tables 5.1 and 5.2 summarize some of the specific treatment recommendations unique to anorexia nervosa and bulimia nervosa.

Choosing a Site of Treatment

When deciding on the best setting for treatment of a patient with an eating disorder, a number of factors should be taken into account; in particular, the weight and cardiac and metabolic status of the patient should be considered. If a patient's weight is less than about 85% of her healthy weight, she will probably recover best in a highly structured program. Patients weighing less than about 75% of their healthy weight will likely require a 24-hour hospital program. If a patient experiences a decline in weight despite outpatient treatment interventions, rapid or consistent declines in oral intake and weight, or other stressors (viral illness) that are interfering with her ability to eat, hospitalization should be considered.

Patients should be admitted to a hospital immediately if they are experiencing marked hypotension with an increase in pulse of more than 20 beats per minute (bpm), a drop in blood pressure of more than 20 mm Hg per minute standing, bradycardia below 40 bpm, tachycardia over 110 bpm, or inability to sustain core body temperature above 97° Fahrenheit. Most patients with uncomplicated bulimia nervosa do not require hospitalization, but if a patient with this disorder exhibits severe debilitating symptoms that have not responded adequately to outpatient treatment or if she has serious comorbid medical problems, suicidality, substance abuse (drug or alcohol), or other severely debilitating psychiatric disturbances, hospitalization should be considered.

Other options for treatment include partial hospitalization and day hospitals. These sites are appropriate for milder cases, but likely will not be effective for patients with initial weights at or below 75% of average weight for height. In addition to this consideration, patients' level of motivation and ability to participate in a group setting should be assessed. Those with strong motivation for recovery, supportive families, and brief symptom duration and who are less than 20% below their healthy body weight may be treated effectively in outpatient settings. Patients who qualify for this option should be monitored carefully and reminded that if they fail to progress, they may need to be moved to a more restrictive setting. When deciding on the best treatment setting for patients, the advantages of outpatient treatment (e.g., staying in school, living with the family, maintaining employment) should be weighed against the risks of failure to recover.

TABLE 5.1
Practice Guidelines for the Treatment of Patients With Anorexia Nervosa

	Goals	Efficacy	Implementation
Nutritional rehabilitation	The primary goal is to restore weight, normalize eating patterns, achieve normal perceptions of hunger and satiety, correct biological and psychological consequences of malnutrition, provide ongoing support, and help patients deal with concerns about weight gain and body image changes.	Weight gain for severely underweight patients is typically achieved in inpatient settings. In inpatient settings, .5 to 3 pounds a week can be obtained. As weight is restored, other eating disorder symptoms typically diminish or alter (e.g., alterations in mood and anxiety symptoms, and cessation of lethargy).	Rehabilitation occurs in an emotionally nurturing environment in which some positive and negative reinforcements have been built into the program. Temporary use of liquid food supplements; nasogastric feedings are preferable to intravenous feedings. Physical activity should be adapted to food intake and energy expenditure initially, moving toward a focus on physical fitness once a safe weight is achieved. Staff should help patients cope with concerns over weight and body shape changes.
Medication	Medication is typically used to maintain weight after it has been restored and to treat psychiatric symptoms associated with anorexia nervosa.	Antidepressants seem to be most effective in treating symptoms that remain after weight has been restored (as opposed to contributing to weight restoration). Serotonin reuptake inhibitors (SSRIs) may be helpful for patients who continue to exhibit depressive, obsessive, or compulsive symptoms after weight is restored. Low-dose neuroleptics used in conjunction with SSRIs may be helpful for obsessionality, anxiety, and psychotic-like thinking. Studies indicate that lithium carbonate and pimozide are not significantly beneficial. There is no strong evidence supporting the use of estrogen replacement therapy to restore bone health.	The decision to use medication and the type of medication to be used should be postponed until weight has been restored so medication can be selected based on the remaining symptoms.

(continued)

TABLE 5.1 *(Continued)*

	Goals	Efficacy	Implementation
Psychosocial treatments	Understand and participate in patients' nutritional and physical rehabilitation, understand and alter dysfunctional behaviors and attitudes associated with the eating disorder, improve interpersonal and social functioning. Address pathologies and psychological conflicts that reinforce the eating disorder.	Behavioral programs often produce good short-term therapy outcomes. Individual therapy alone is not sufficient during the acute stage, but it can be helpful when implemented in conjunction with other supports and when it is conducted from a psychodynamically informed perspective that provides empathic understanding, explanations, praise, coaching, support, encouragement, and other reinforcements. Once malnutrition has been corrected, individual therapy seems to be effective in improving mood, enhancing cognitive functioning, and clarifying thought processes. Family therapy seems to be effective in reducing relational problems that may contribute to the disorder. Twelve-step programs seem to be most effective when accompanied by other treatment approaches. Support groups or programs can be helpful but should be monitored to determine accuracy of the information being distributed.	Treatment is implemented within an interdisciplinary model. All personnel must work together, maintain open communication, and respect one another to avoid contributing to patients' tendency to "split the staff."

Note. Summarized from *Practice Guideline for the Treatment of Patients With Eating Disorders* (2nd ed.), by the American Psychiatric Association, 2000b, Arlington, VA: Author.

TABLE 5.2
Practice Guidelines for the Treatment of Patients With Bulimia Nervosa

	Goals	Efficacy	Implementation
Nutritional rehabilitation	Reduce binge eating, purging, and other behaviors related to the disorder.	There is some evidence that treatments that include dietary management and counseling are more effective than those that do not include both treatments.	Nutritional counseling is provided to help minimize food restriction, correct nutritional deficiencies, encourage healthy exercise patterns, and establish a pattern of nonbinge meals.
Medication	Medications are used to reduce the frequency of dysfunctional eating behaviors and to treat symptoms that may accompany disordered eating behaviors.	Antidepressants are often effective in treating associated comorbid symptoms of the disorder and have been shown to be effective in increasing interpersonal functioning. Antidepressants may reduce binge eating and vomiting by 50% to 70%.	Several antidepressants may need to be tried to find the most effective treatment. Many clinicians recommend continuing antidepressant therapy for 6 to 12 months during the maintenance phase.
Psychosocial treatments	Goals may include elimination or reduction of binge-eating and purging behaviors, improvement in attitude about the disorder, minimization of food restrictions, increased variety of foods eaten, establishment of healthy exercise patterns, addressing underlying themes of the disorder, and treating comorbid conditions.	A variety of individual approaches seem to be effective for treating the comorbid mood, anxiety, personality, interpersonal, and trauma/abuse-related disorders that frequently accompany the eating disorder. Group therapy may provide patients with peer feedback and help them deal with feelings of shame. Family therapy seems to be effective in reducing relational problems that may contribute to the disorder. Some patients find 12-step programs helpful in addition to other treatments and for preventing relapse.	Twice-weekly psychotherapy sessions early in treatment and once- or twice-weekly sessions are recommended throughout treatment. Clinicians may want to use cognitive–behavioral treatment manuals as a guide for implementing their own approach for treatment.

Note. Summarized from *Practice Guideline for the Treatment of Patients With Eating Disorders* (2nd ed.), by the American Psychiatric Association, 2000b, Arlington, VA: Author. Copyright 2000 by the American Psychiatric Association. Adapted with permission.

Psychiatric Management

Psychiatric management is an integral part of treatment for patients with eating disorders. All treatment programs should include psychiatric treatment in conjunction with other treatment modalities. Some of the responsibilities of psychiatric management are to (a) establish and maintain a therapeutic alliance (e.g., clinicians should create a environment of safety, trust, and mutual respect); (b) coordinate care and collaborate with other clinicians; (c) assess and monitor eating disorder symptoms and behaviors; (d) assess and monitor the patient's general medical condition; (e) assess and monitor the patient's psychiatric status and safety; and (f) provide family assessment and treatment.

Choice of Specific Treatments for Anorexia Nervosa

The aims of treatment for patients with anorexia nervosa are as follows: (a) restore patients to healthy weights; (b) treat physical complications; (c) enhance patients' motivations to cooperate in the treatment program; (d) provide didactic support for healthy eating patterns; (e) correct maladaptive thoughts, attitudes, and feelings related to the eating disorder; (f) treat associated symptoms; (g) enlist family support and provide family counseling and therapy where appropriate; and (h) prevent relapse.

Three global treatment strategies can be used to achieve these aims: (a) nutritional management, (b) psychosocial interventions, and (c) medication. A nutritional program that includes target weights and rate of progress should be implemented for patients who are significantly underweight. Medical monitoring during refeeding is essential. Psychotherapy is another important element in the recovery process. Ongoing psychotherapy intervention is usually needed for at least 1 year and may be needed for up to 6 years because of the persistent nature of many of the psychopathological symptoms of anorexia nervosa. Family or couple therapy (or both) is often used to help alleviate eating disorder symptoms as well as to address patterns in the family that may be contributing to and maintaining the disorder. Psychotropic medication should be used in combination with other forms of treatment. Antidepressants can be helpful for preventing relapse and treating comorbid symptoms of the eating disorder.

Choice of Specific Treatment for Bulimia Nervosa

The aims of treatment for patients with bulimia nervosa include the following: (a) monitoring and correcting patterns of binge eating and purging, (b) increasing the variety of foods eaten, (c) encouraging healthy exercise patterns, and (d) reducing associated symptoms of the eating disorder. The same general treatment strategies are used for the treatment of bulimia nervosa as for anorexia nervosa. Nutritional counseling can help reduce unhealthy behaviors related to bulimia nervosa. In addition, this form of treatment may help increase the variety of foods eaten and encourage healthy, balanced exercise patterns.

Choice of psychosocial intervention should be based on individual patient's cognitive and developmental features, psychodynamic issues, preference, family dynamics, and associated symptoms. Family therapy should be considered for all patients, but particularly for adolescent patients still living with their parents. Psychotropic medication should be considered in combination with other forms of treatment. Antidepressants may help reduce symptoms associated with bulimia (e.g., obsessions, depression, and anxiety). Recent studies indicate that the combination of medication and psychosocial interventions yield higher remission rates than that of either form of treatment alone.

TREATING EATING DISORDER PATIENTS FROM A THEISTIC PERSPECTIVE

We believe that a spiritual component is an essential part of a multidimensional, multidisciplinary treatment approach for women with eating disorders. We help patients actively use their spirituality in recovery. In doing so, we integrate theistic spiritual perspectives and interventions with standard medical and psychological treatment methods. This approach is consistent with the recommendations of numerous professionals that spiritual interventions should not be used alone but should be integrated with standard psychological and medical interventions (Richards & Bergin, 1997; Richards & Potts, 1995; Shafranske, 1996). We do not use spiritual interventions rigidly or uniformly with all patients but in a flexible, treatment-tailoring manner.

Exhibit 5.1 summarizes some of the distinctive characteristics of the theistic approach of treatment on which our approach to treating eating disorders is based (Richards & Bergin, 1997, 2005). The most unique contribution of this perspective is that it affirms that God can intervene in the lives of human beings (Richards & Bergin, 2004, 2005). Patients who have faith in God and draw on the spiritual resources in their lives during eating disorder treatment may receive added strength and power to cope, heal, and grow.

Another distinctive element of this approach is that it asserts that a theistic moral framework for treatment is possible and desirable. According to this perspective, general moral values regulate healthy human development and functioning, and these can be used to guide and evaluate

EXHIBIT 5.1
Distinctive Features of Theistic Psychological Treatment

Goals of therapy	Therapist's role in therapy	Role of spiritual techniques	Patient's role in therapy	Nature of the therapy relationship
A spiritual perspective is part of an eclectic, multisystemic view of humans, thus therapy goals depend on the patient's issues. Goals directly relevant to the spiritual dimension include the following: (a) help patients affirm their eternal spiritual identity and live in harmony with the Spirit of Truth; (b) assess what impact religious and spiritual beliefs have in patients' lives and whether they have unmet spiritual needs; (c) help patients use religious and spiritual resources to help them in their efforts to cope, change, and grow; (d) help patients resolve spiritual concerns and doubts and make choices about the role of spirituality in their lives; and (e) help patients examine their spirituality and continue their quest for spiritual growth.	The therapist (a) adopts an ecumenical therapeutic stance and, when appropriate, a denominational stance; (b) establishes a warm, supportive environment in which patients know it is safe and acceptable to explore their religious and spiritual beliefs, doubts, and concerns; (c) assesses whether patients' religious and spiritual beliefs and activities are affecting their mental health and interpersonal relationships; (d) implements religious and spiritual interventions to help patients use their religious and spiritual resources more effectively in their coping and growth process; (e) models and endorses healthy values; and (f) seeks spiritual guidance and enlightenment on how best to help patients.	Interventions are viewed as important to help patients gain more faith in their spiritual identity and worth; understand and work through their religious and spiritual concerns; and draw on the religious and spiritual resources in their lives to assist them in coping, healing, and changing. Examples of major interventions include cognitive restructuring of irrational religious beliefs, the transitional figure technique, forgiveness, meditation and prayer, Scripture study, blessings, participating in religious services, spiritual imagery, journaling about spiritual feelings, repentance, and using patients' religious support systems.	Patients examine how their religious and spiritual beliefs and activities affect their behavior, emotions, and relationships. They make choices about what role religion and spirituality will play in their lives. They set goals and carry out spiritual interventions designed to facilitate their spiritual and emotional growth. They seek to use the religious and spiritual resources in their lives to assist them in their efforts to heal and change. They seek God's guidance and enlightenment about how to better cope, heal, and change.	Unconditional positive regard, warmth, genuineness, and empathy are regarded as an essential foundation for therapy. Therapists also seek to have charity or brotherly and sisterly love for patients and to affirm their eternal spiritual identity and worth. Patients are expected to form a working alliance and share in the work of change. Patients must trust the therapist and believe that it is safe to share their religious and spiritual beliefs and heritage with the therapist. Patients must know that the therapist values and respects their autonomy and freedom of choice. Patients know it is safe to differ from the therapist in their beliefs and values, even though the therapist may at times disagree and confront them about unhealthy values and lifestyle choices.

Note. Adapted from *A Spiritual Strategy for Counseling and Psychotherapy* (2nd ed., p. 182), by P. S. Richards and A. E. Bergin, 2005, Washington, DC: American Psychological Association. Copyright 2005 by the American Psychological Association.

psychotherapy (Bergin, 1980, 1985, 1991; Richards & Bergin, 1997; Richards, Rector, & Tjeltveit, 1999). These include values and principles such as integrity, honesty, kindness, respect, forgiveness, repentance, spirituality, religious devotion, marital and sexual fidelity, family loyalty and kinship, the benevolent use of power, respect for agency, humbleness, and lovingness (Bergin, 1985, 2002; Richards & Bergin, 1997). Of course, therapists who use a theistic approach are careful not to engage in value imposition, but encourage patients to examine and live congruently with their own beliefs and values (Richards et al., 1999).

A third distinctive aspect of the theistic treatment approach is that it provides a body of theistic spiritual interventions that professionals can use to help treat those with eating disorders. No mainstream psychotherapy tradition has interventions designed for this purpose. Spiritual interventions that psychotherapists may use include praying for patients, encouraging patients to pray, discussing theological concepts, making reference to scriptures, using spiritual relaxation and imagery techniques, using sacred or uplifting music, encouraging repentance and forgiveness, helping patients live congruently with their spiritual values, self-disclosing spiritual beliefs or experiences, consulting with religious leaders, supporting attendance at religious services, recommending religious bibliotherapy, and helping patients recognize and seek inspiration (Richards & Bergin, 1997; Richards & Potts, 1995). Research indicates that there is significant healing potential in many of these spiritual practices (e.g., Benson, 1996; Miller, 1999; Richards & Bergin, 1997, 2000).

A fourth distinctive view of the theistic treatment approach is that it asserts that therapists and patients may seek, and on occasion obtain, spiritual enlightenment to assist with the healing process (Richards & Bergin, 1997, 2005). Through meditation and prayer, therapists may experience inspired insights that go beyond ordinary clinical hypothesizing. Spiritual insights and impressions can give therapists important insight into patients' problems and perhaps lead to effective interventions. Therapists can also encourage patients to seek inspiration to help them better understand their challenges and how to resolve them.

PROCESS GUIDELINES FOR INCORPORATING SPIRITUALITY INTO TREATMENT

Several important process issues and principles need to be kept in mind when implementing a theistic approach in treating women with eating disorders. The following process recommendations are based in part on recommendations made by Richards and Bergin (1997, 2005), as well as on our own clinical experience.

Adopt an Ecumenical Therapeutic Stance

We recommend that therapists adopt an ecumenical therapeutic stance—one that is sensitive and open to diverse spiritual perspectives—when working with patients with eating disorders (Richards & Bergin, 2005). The foundations of an ecumenical therapeutic stance are the attitudes and skills of an effective multicultural therapist (e.g., Sue & Sue, 1990; Sue, Zane, & Young, 1994). Ecumenically sensitive therapists are aware of their own spiritual heritage and values and are sensitive to how these could affect their work with patients from different traditions. Such therapists communicate understanding and respect to patients who have spiritual beliefs that are different from their own. They seek to establish trusting relationships with leaders in their patients' religious communities and consult with and refer to them when it seems appropriate. During treatment they use spiritual interventions that are in harmony with patients' beliefs when it appears appropriate and helpful. They also tailor their treatment approach in a denominationally specific manner when appropriate to address more fully the fine nuances of their patients' spiritual issues (Richards & Bergin, 2005).

Establish a Spiritually Open and Safe Relationship

Establishing a spiritually safe and open therapeutic relationship is crucial for the effective and ethical exploration of spiritual issues with patients. We recommend therapists let their patients know it is permissible and appropriate to explore spiritual issues should they so desire. This can be done in the written informed consent documents that are given to patients at the beginning of treatment and verbally at appropriate times during the course of treatment. Questions about patients' religious and spiritual backgrounds can also be included on an intake questionnaire (Richards & Bergin, 2005).

We think it is important for treatment centers that admit patients from a diversity of religious and spiritual traditions to adhere to a nondenominational treatment approach that is sensitive to and respectful of all patients. Therapists and staff should avoid disclosing details about their own religious affiliation unless patients directly ask for such information. By communicating willingness to explore spiritual issues without attempting to promote their own religious beliefs, therapists can establish trust with a wider range of patients.

Establishing a spiritually safe environment involves in part helping patients understand what spirituality is and why it may be important to address in treatment. We recommend that therapists define spirituality broadly to patients with the hope that they will more clearly recognize the many ways spirituality can be manifested and evident in their lives. Many patients view themselves as unspiritual—they don't believe they are able to have spiritual feelings, but if the definition of spirituality is broadened to include things such as love, kindness, forgiveness, compassion, and hope, it helps them affirm that they are more spiritually attuned than they previously believed.

Some patients also refuse to acknowledge their spirituality because they have labeled themselves unworthy based on perceived failures to live up to unrealistically high religious or behavioral standards and expectations. Religious people who have a traditional religious upbringing sometimes define worthiness so narrowly or negatively that there is no way they can live up to it and be worthy. Helping patients understand that part of being human is that they are not perfect and that many people fluctuate in their efforts to have a close relationship with God. This does not mean they have to give up or devalue their core religious beliefs or values. Encouraging them to honor and respect their core religious beliefs and values and to understand that developing their spirituality is a process, not an outcome or a destination. It can also be helpful to encourage patients to look beyond their behavior to their intentions and to examine what they believe in and what they truly desire.

Be Alert to Potential Ethical Concerns

Implementing spiritual interventions in treatment may raise a number of potentially difficult ethical questions and challenges, such as dual relationships (religious and professional), displacing or usurping religious authority, imposing religious values on patients, violating work setting (church–state) boundaries, and practicing outside of the boundaries of professional competence (Richards & Bergin, 1997, 2005). It is beyond the scope of this book to discuss these issues in detail, but we refer readers to other books and articles that have done so (Richards & Bergin, 1997, 2005; Tan, 1994, 2003).

Spiritual interventions should not be used with patients until their psychological functioning, spiritual background and beliefs, and attitude about exploring spiritual issues during treatment have been carefully assessed and understood. Therapists should work within the value frameworks of their patients, making sure that the interventions used are in harmony with patients' religious beliefs. Spiritual interventions should be used in a respectful manner, remembering that many patients regard these interventions as sacred religious practices (Richards & Bergin, 1997).

We encourage therapists to permit patients to take the lead in their own spiritual journey and recovery. When incorporating a spiritual perspective into recovery from eating disorders, therapists must respect each patient's perspective and simply encourage her to open the door to spiritual influences within the context of what she believes (Kelly, 1995; Lewis, 2001; Richards & Bergin, 1997, 2000).

Spiritual interventions are usually contraindicated in a number of situations: (a) when patients make it clear they do not wish to participate in them; (b) when patients are delusional or psychotic; (c) when spiritual issues are clearly not relevant to a patient's presenting problems; and (d) when patients are minors and their parents have asked the treatment staff not to use spiritual interventions. Spiritual interventions must also be used cautiously, or not at all, when patients are antireligious or nonreligious, spiritually disinterested, or perceive God as distant and condemning.

Conduct a Spiritual Assessment

In our view, an assessment of the religious background and spirituality of patients with eating disorders is an essential part of a comprehensive assessment strategy. When patients are admitted for eating disorder treatment, a thorough assessment of their functioning should be conducted, including their physical, nutritional, psychological, social, and spiritual functioning. The overall goal of the spiritual assessment is to gain a clear understanding of each patient's current spiritual framework so that the treatment staff can work within the patient's belief system in a sensitive and respectful manner. Information about patients' spirituality can be gathered through written intake questionnaires, clinical interviews, and standardized measures of religious orientation and spirituality.

When gathering information about patients' history and family background, therapists may wish to inquire about patients' childhood religious affiliations and experiences. Therapists also may wish to ask patients to describe the role religion currently plays in their lives. Possible conflicts and resentments concerning religion can be identified and explored. Therapists may also wish to inquire whether patients view their faith and spirituality as a potential resource in their treatment and whether they are open to discussions about faith and spirituality during treatment. We provide more information about conducting religious and spiritual assessments in chapter 6.

Establish Spiritual Goals for Treatment

We assume that every person has several important emotional and spiritual needs. We seek to address these needs during treatment in the ways we relate with the patients and through the interventions we use. The needs are as follows:

1. Having a sense of acceptance and belonging in a social sphere and in relation to God.
2. Having a sense of being important and valued in one's family.
3. Having a sense of spirituality, purpose, hope, and meaning in life.
4. Having a sense of self through identification, individuation, self-awareness, and self-understanding.
5. Having a set of principles and values in which one's life is anchored.

Therapists can help patients decide whether and how they want to use their faith and spirituality in treatment. Many patients feel that they have lost their spirituality during the development of their eating disorder and wish to set goals to rediscover their faith and spirituality. Some patients say that spirituality has never been important to them but that they would like to learn more about the possible role it could play in their recovery. Some patients say that they do not wish to include discussions about spirituality in their treatment, and such requests should of course be respected. Therapists and treatment staff should affirm the right of each patient to decide for herself what role faith and spirituality will play in her treatment and recovery and then seek to support and encourage patients in their spiritual goals.

Richards and Bergin (1997, 2005) have suggested that the following general spiritual goals may be appropriate for psychotherapy. We often pursue one or more of these goals during eating disorder treatment depending on the unique concerns and issues of the patient. Of course, we do not impose any of these goals on patients who do not wish to pursue them.

1. Help patients experience and affirm their eternal spiritual identity and live in harmony with God's spirit.
2. Help patients examine and better understand what, if any, impact their religious and spiritual beliefs have on their eating disorder and on their lives in general.
3. Help patients identify and use the religious or spiritual resources in their lives to assist them in their efforts to engage in treatment and to recover from their eating disorder.
4. Help patients to examine and resolve religious and spiritual concerns that are pertinent to their eating disorder and to make choices about what role religion and spirituality will play in their lives.
5. Help patients examine how they feel about their spiritual growth and well-being and, if they desire, help them to determine how they can continue their quest for spiritual growth and well-being.

Regardless of their own spiritual beliefs, therapists can assist eating disorder patients with these important goals if they are willing to seek competency in religious and spiritual aspects of diversity (Richards & Bergin, 2000). We often find it helpful to tailor these general goals so that they more specifically address the spiritual issues and needs of our patients. Once spiritual goals have been established with patients, we also help them formulate an action plan for how they will work toward accomplishing their goals.

IMPLEMENTING SPIRITUAL INTERVENTIONS IN TREATMENT

Spiritual interventions can be integrated into virtually every treatment modality, including individual, group, and family therapy. Such interventions are easiest to tailor to meet patient needs in individual therapy, although they can also be appropriately used in group and family therapy. Spiritual interventions can also be used in inpatient, residential, and outpatient treatment settings. In inpatient and residential settings, some spiritual interventions must be approached in a structured programmatic manner, although there is still usually room for some individual adaptation. Before describing specific spiritual interventions that can be used in various treatment settings and modalities, we first offer some general treatment guidelines for inpatient and residential treatment settings that we think can also be important when working from a theistic perspective with patients with eating disorders.

Involve the Family System

Families should be involved in treatment where possible, unless the family is on the farthest extreme of dysfunction and unhealthiness. It is important to find resources within the family to help meet the patient's needs. The therapist should seek to help the patient make emotional and spiritual connections within the family, increase empathy and compassion within the family, and help the patient individuate from the family in a healthy way that allows family connections to remain intact. It is important to join the family as a team in fighting the real enemy—the illness.

Be Directive and Specific

The therapist should take responsibility in treatment to be active, to create energy in sessions, and to direct the process. Doing so will help the patient who has less experience to draw on and whose lifestyle has been based more on approval and peer acceptance rather than self-definition and internalized principles.

Use Activity-Based Sessions

It is helpful to use more activity-based, and fewer "talking only," sessions when treating patients with eating disorders. Activity-based sessions give the therapist a chance to join patients in their worlds because many individuals with eating disorders use externalization as their approach to life, a process that includes a constant search for external approval. The "active" style of therapy is particularly important for adolescents because they have difficulty learning from others' experiences and seem focused on learning only from their own. Experiential interventions teach lessons that are more easily internalized and set the stage for later learning from insight and from others' experiences.

Provide Structures for Therapy

Nebulous and unguided therapy can create additional confusion and insecurity for patients with eating disorders. It is helpful to give them information on the processes of therapy and change. Predicting struggles and helping patients to anticipate the ups and downs of recovery and prepare for those times can provide a sense of security. Explain to patients what will happen, the sequence of events, why you are doing what you are doing, what they can expect, and the changes they will go through during therapy. This increases their trust in your understanding of them and in your ability to help them.

Provide Immediate Encouragement and Support

Without hope for overcoming these devastating illnesses, movement in recovery is minimal at best. It is the therapist's job to attempt to provide, create, and nurture hope in the patient. Tell patients about your vision of their future, because they often cannot see this for themselves. Remind them that their illness can be temporary and that their feelings of hopelessness are temporary. Point out their progress and their successes. Help them recognize and label improvements, no matter how small these steps forward may be. Help them set short-term, sometimes very short-term goals, and help them find evidence of progress. Teach the concept and value of the small steps of change, and help them see the progress in specific moments along the way. Help them see not only what they are doing differently but also the internal process taking place inside of them as well.

Explore the Differences Between Love and Acceptance Versus Approval

People with eating disorders have often learned to believe that "approval is everything and disapproval is the end of everything." They often have minimized and compartmentalized themselves into one or two explicit parts of themselves. Often these are their body, their external performance, or what others think of them. Therapists should stress that what they do and who they are, are not the same. Acceptance of "all of the self," taking the focus off what others think, and helping patients turn inside to find value are important themes in therapy. Helping patients find language and labels to understand the differences among love, acceptance, and approval can help them notice these experiences.

Emphasize Having Feelings Without Self-Judgment

Helping patients feel, label, understand, accept, and express their own emotion without making emotional judgments about who they are and what kind of person they are is important in the creation of an environment of self-acceptance. Many individuals with eating disorders are tender-hearted, sensitive people who have become "shut down," numb, and avoidant because having feelings lead to secondary and consequent feelings of guilt, shame, selfishness, or "badness." Helping patients enlarge their ability to notice and experience their feelings without self-judgment is critical throughout the therapy process.

Make Honesty and Congruence Ongoing Themes

Helping patients become more honest and congruent without self-criticism is necessary for recovery. Stress the need for patients to stop pretending, hiding, or lying and the need for being genuine and open with themselves and other people. Achieve honesty and openness in the therapeutic relationship by building trust and creating safety in the relationship and by helping patients understand the expectation of honesty. This honesty includes helping the patient reveal secrets so that they can process their beliefs and feelings out loud, begin to allow help from others in overcoming shame, and break the childlike cycle of "hiding under the blanket of shame." Secrets to be told may include past trauma and abuse from long ago. It may include discussing mistakes made or thoughts or feelings that seem unthinkable and unforgivable. It may also include telling the whole truth about their eating disorder. Telling secrets helps in being "grown up" as opposed to feeling the fear of "being little." "Sweeping out all the corners" in the private stash of misery can bring relief and peace.

Teach Patients to Avoid Only One Thing—Avoidance

Eating disorders are disorders of avoidance. Help patients learn about avoidance, its many faces, its damaging consequences, its seductive yet short-lived rewards, and its relationship to eating disorders and other addictive patterns. Help the patients understand their fears, their unhealthy responses to fear, and the need to face their fears in healthy ways. Discuss with the patients their fears of failure and the all too common patterns of failing to avoid failure. Give patients challenges and urge them to take risks and to face their pain and help them understand that avoidance maintains low self-esteem. Teach and help them to experience vulnerability as a healthy precursor to growth within oneself and emotional intimacy within relationships.

Persistently Show Nurturance, Kindness, and Caring

Those with eating disorders most often have had an absence of nurturing and care, at least during the history of their eating disorder, because they have withdrawn from it in their primary relationships; they often feel unworthy of love and therefore have difficulty "letting it in." Some have lacked nurturance throughout their lives or have actively resisted the caring shown to them because they have deemed themselves undeserving of it. It can help to make this pattern explicit by pointing out the reality of care, love, concern, and acceptance within relationships; these are available to them not only from the therapist but also from others who love them as well. As they learn to notice and label it and are encouraged to receive it, they prepare to again accept nurturing connections with others important to them in their social and family circles.

Make Unhealthy Behavior and Relationship Patterns Explicit

As patterns of dishonesty, manipulation, pushing away others, justifying unhealthy choices, helplessness, powerlessness, and food and behavioral rituals show up in the therapeutic relationship by report or observation, make them an issue in therapy. This can be done by pointing them out, labeling them, and dismantling their justification. Have patients look at the negative effects of such patterns and help them to risk choosing new ways to live. The self-deception, justification, and rationalization of an eating disorder builds a strong wall that needs to be directly addressed and carefully dismantled.

Help Patients Separate Themselves From Their Disorder

In the later stages of an eating disorder, the disorder becomes the person's identity. These individuals begin to perceive and live congruently with that perception; they believe they are their eating disorder. This self-definition brings with it fear, disgust, self-contempt, hopelessness, withdrawal, and guilt. In the later stages of the illness, individuals truly lose some conscious control over their behavior and choices. They need help to understand that much of their behavior is due to the illness of the eating disorder and that it is not the result of personal deficiency or flawed willpower. Again, a theme here is that "you are not your illness, and you are not simply the sum of your behaviors, thoughts, or feelings." As patients begin to view their illness as linked to well-intended yet self-harming coping strategies and begin to have understanding and compassion for their painful journey into the eating disorder, they can feel a sense of hope and self-empowerment. They can assume an increase in personal responsibility for their choices and have the power to change self-defeating choices.

Help Patients Affirm Their Spiritual Identity and Heal Their Hearts

As discussed in chapter 4, a major goal of our theistic treatment approach is to help patients discover or rediscover their sense of spiritual identity and worth. We do this in part by helping patients learn to listen to the impressions and understandings of their hearts, in other words, their core spiritual self. We now describe several therapeutic strategies and interventions that we have found to help patients heal their hearts and reaffirm their spiritual identity and worth.

Giving and Receiving Love

One of the things we say to our patients is that to regain their hearts, they need to let love in and out. In sessions, we begin to talk about how the patients resist and refuse love and what they can do to open up their hearts to receiving love from others. We talk about ways to show love for others. We also talk about ways to increase the expression of their loving and heartfelt desires, either through word or action. We talk of how they can "heartfully" respond to someone else's loving actions toward them. The key to this process is to begin labeling love as an expression of the heart and to see love from others as a gift from the heart. They can begin to increase their awareness of how much love there really is around them and how much love there really is inside of themselves. We talk with our patients about how love touched their hearts today or during the past week and how their love reached somebody else's heart. In chapter 7, we give an example of a group exercise that can help a patient connect with her heart.

What Speaks to the Heart

Another suggestion that can help create a context for listening to the heart is to encourage discussions and awareness of the experiences that patients know have spoken to their hearts before they became numb, disconnected, or lost in the eating disorder. We generate a "before list" of the kinds of things that spoke to their hearts, impressed their souls, or touched them deeply in a positive way. One of the things we communicate with our patients is that if they are going to begin to listen to their hearts again, they have to know what they are looking for in life. We want their life experiences to begin to speak to their hearts again.

We have learned over the years that the experiences that speak to a person's heart are often the simple but profound expressions of what is the best in all of us and in life. Tenderness and warmth speak to the heart. Gentleness speaks to the heart. Compassion and understanding in the face of difficulty speak to the heart. Kindness, especially unconditional kindness, speaks to the heart. Beauty and wonder speak to the heart. Patriotism can speak to the heart. Generosity with no strings attached can speak to the heart. Genuineness and honest laughter speak to the heart. Love speaks to the heart. Faith speaks to the heart. The greatness of God can speak to the heart. Forgiveness and mercy speak to the heart. Courage speaks to the heart. Light can speak to the heart. The key is to help patients give up some of their focus on their "wrongness" and help them begin to look for those things that speak to their hearts. We have asked some religious patients to look for God's providence in their daily lives and to begin to see this as God speaking to their hearts.

We can acknowledge and nurture patients' awareness of those things that speak to their hearts, including what is true inside themselves and their own lives. We help them understand that fear does not speak to the heart. We explain that when they give in to fear, they are running from their hearts and trying to rely on their minds alone. We encourage our patients to look beyond themselves and beyond their fears, to find what speaks to their hearts, and to learn to listen to their hearts instead of blinding themselves to these impressions. Sometimes patients with eating disorders are so afraid to feel pain, sorrow, happiness, and joy that they go through life—through the motions of life—without feeling alive. Life can speak to the heart—if they allow themselves to feel.

Positive Expectancy of Heart

A third therapy emphasis that develops a talent for listening to the heart is for patients to create a positive general and internal expectancy for themselves. One of us attended a conference in which the presenter Michael D. Yapko (1997) asked, "What is the word in your heart?" He went on to say that if the word in someone's heart is "yes," then that person's expectancy will be optimistic, trusting, open, positive, and receptive. If the word in their heart is "no," then that person's expectancy will be full of skepticism, pessimism, doubt, mistrust, and negativity.

With this focus on their hearts, we can nurture a shift toward hearts that are filled with "yes" about themselves and about their lives. To begin to nurture this "yes" in their hearts, we need to help patients to recognize the narrow and specific mind-held expectations that get in the way of their hearts. We need to reduce the expectations that they carry for themselves, other people, and life events so that they have more room to listen to themselves and respond to life experiences.

Often when patients have emotional and behavioral expectations that are very specific or self-driven, they are disappointed with the outcomes. Patients are able to make long lists of all of their disappointed expectations. We seek to broaden their expectations to create an approach of positive self-expectancy that is simpler, one that has more emphasis on general internal qualities such as, "I want to be trustworthy," "I want to be kind," "I want to be respectful," "I want to listen," and so on. If the word in the heart is "yes," then patients can face ambiguity in their lives with a deeper sense of optimism and hope. Hope is like having a big "yes" in their hearts. We see this positive expectancy as patients being on "their own side" and "being for themselves" in life.

As patients broaden this positive expectancy and make decisions or choices, there should be no second-guessing. Second-guessing and doubting create a painful self- or double bind. The message needs to be "once a 'yes,' it stays a 'yes'" for at least some significant period of time before the decision can be reconsidered. "Once a 'no,' it stays a 'no.'" This idea of staying with the "yes" or staying with the "no" becomes a way for them to begin to trust their own impressions, decisions, and conclusions. We help patients make self-directed corrections as they go along and to avoid that internal debate and confusion that leads them to seek the decision from someone else. One of us recently experienced an example of this positive self-expectancy when a patient said during a session, "I know I can face hard things now, and I can face the unknown because I know what is in me and in my heart, and I can trust me to come up with good answers for myself." This is the same patient who 6 months earlier relied on everyone else to tell her what to do because she was terrified of making a mistake. This same patient had to get permission from as many people as possible before she could go ahead and decide that it was all right to do something. This patient fortunately reached the point in her recovery where she could say, "I am a 'yes' for me. What is in my heart is 'yes.' I can listen and trust myself." Her self-expectancy became broader and more positive, and she was more able to be herself and to listen to her own impressions.

When patients develop this positive self-expectancy of heart, we often see that, along the way, they come to know that God is a "yes" for their heart as well. This is a powerful realization. Prayer can help build positive self-expectancy. Most spiritually minded women who have lost their hearts to eating disorders have stopped praying. One of the ways to help regain that positive expectancy back in the heart is to invite patients to pray again, and especially to pray for themselves. We invite patients to pray, listen, and not prejudge or presume God's answers. We encourage patients to listen to what God has to say to them in their hearts to understand God's positive expectancy of them.

Written Impressions of the Heart

A fourth suggestion that can be helpful in listening to the heart is to develop a journal that may be titled, "The Writings of My Heart." In this assignment, we often ask patients to write down, over the course of months, first impressions, inspirations, spiritual promptings, and personal intuitions that have come to them in specific situations, as well as insights or reflections that have come to them in quiet moments. Then we have them take this rather raw list of impressions and compile or rewrite them in one place so that they can return often to review their intuitions, understandings, and spiritual impressions. These writings of the heart become a personal reminder of how the individuals want to be and to live and help them know that they can follow their own hearts. Sometimes patients need some help to clarify and sort out what these messages are, but once they are written down in their journal, they become personal revelations and reminders—not those of another person. These writings can become a personal means to self-empowerment and self-trust.

We once worked with a 19-year-old woman, Jean, who had had an eating disorder since she was 14. During treatment, we encouraged Jean to write down the impressions of her heart during her solo times in the treatment center. Jean spent considerable time writing down the feelings, inspirations, and impressions that came into her heart at these times. During these quiet moments, Jean reported that she often felt loved, sustained, and lifted up by God and that impressions and that insights came to her. During the course of treatment, Jean's writings and spiritual understandings helped her develop a personal code of living. She used this to comfort and encourage herself during the recovery process. As Jean followed the impressions and writings of her heart, her self-trust and self-confidence grew.

Quiet Answers From the Heart

The fifth suggestion that can strengthen awareness of heart is to create ongoing therapeutic discussions with patients that are consistent over time, even if they only last for a few minutes in each session. It is helpful to have them respond to questions that emphasize listening to or knowing what their hearts are telling them. For example: "What does your heart already know about how you want to handle this situation?" "What does your heart already know that your head has not yet figured out?" "What are the quiet impressions about how to view, feel, or respond to a dilemma that have come to you since our last discussion about it?" "Before you started thinking about this problem, what was your sense of what needed to happen?" "What was your intuition about what would be best for you?" Patients should have permission to guess at and explore these heartfelt promptings. For those who are religiously minded, therapists could ask, "What impressions came to you in your prayers?" "As you were reading sacred writ, what else came up inside of you in response to what you read?" Religiously and spiritually minded patients believe that God can bring answers to their hearts and that God knows the intents of their hearts. As therapists we should respect these spiritual concepts in our clarifications.

Dr. Hardman once worked with a Christian woman, Marge, who had been engulfed in her eating disorder for nearly 29 years. At 5′10″, she weighed 79 pounds. Marge's thinking was not clear or coherent because of malnutrition. She seemed totally unable to connect with herself with any kind of clarity, insight, or understanding. She believed she was bad. As Dr. Hardman visited with her, he had his own "searching in his heart." In his heart, he asked, "What will help? What will make a difference to help Marge begin her process of recovery?" An impression came to Dr. Hardman. In an earlier session, Marge had told him of her love for God and her sorrow for how she had treated herself. He asked Marge, "If God was here tonight, sitting here with us, what would He do?"

Marge, who normally had such a hard time expressing herself, said without hesitation, "He would feed me." She knew in her heart the answer to that question, and so Dr. Hardman asked Marge if she was willing to have Him feed her. That was the beginning of Marge's long recovery. Dr. Hardman saw Marge recently after many years. She is a very different woman. There is light in her eyes and brightness to her countenance. She smiles, feels happy, and is contented. Marge told Dr. Hardman that letting God's spiritual influences in to feed her made it possible for her finally to feed, care for, and nourish herself.

It is important to help patients understand that the heart is more than feelings or thoughts. It is deeper and quieter. It does not speak in long sentences but conveys a sense of knowing and understanding or an impression. Another important emphasis in therapy is that the desires and motives of patients' hearts can be the most powerful resource in redirecting their lives. If they understand what their internal motives are and if they understand the intent behind their words, choices, and behaviors, they can develop a powerful self-awareness that can help them to correct their course. Knowing and discovering the desires of their hearts can help patients clarify not only how they want to live but also where they want to go in their lives. If vision of mind can lead to commitment, then trusting of their hearts' intent can help patients keep their most important promises both to themselves and to others.

True to the Heart

As a patient listens and understands the quiet messages of the heart, another important theme that emerges for discussion in therapy is what it means to the patient to be true to her heart. The therapist helps the patient explore for herself the significance of the statement, "What will it mean for me to be true to my heart?" Invariably through discussions about this aspect of heart, patients come to recognize that they do have a sense of right or wrong about things in their life and that their heart is a great resource in knowing, in an intuitive or spiritual way, whether something will be good or harmful for them. In being true, in being consistent, and in following through with these impressions of their heart and the inner truths that they believe originate there, they can move forward with increased confidence. Patients experience the healing that comes from being congruent within themselves. Despite the external consequences of their choices, patients begin to feel empowered internally if they are true to their inside convictions and heartfelt truths. Being true to the heart is the step between clarifying questions and courageous acts of the heart. It is a commitment or promise to stay true to their deepest selves. The deep desire that is apparent in many spiritually minded women is the desire to live in harmony with spiritual laws or spiritual truths.

Being true to the heart generates an inner strength in the patient that is expressed through dignity and self-respect. Dignity of self is expressed by increased confidence, faith, and determination to live life with real purpose and meaning. One of the greatest losses patients experience is that of dignity and self-respect related to the deprecating pursuits of their eating disorders. They often feel they have sacrificed their dignity to addictive urges, to please other people, and to try to find acceptance through the eating disorder.

Patients like the "taste" or "sense" of being true to themselves. They like being able to look in the mirror and feel pleased that they handled a situation with dignity and respect. Being true to the inner convictions and truths of their hearts resonates with them, and they want to keep the important commitments that they have ignored or neglected in the past.

An additional benefit that comes from being true to their hearts is that patients experience more of the enabling power of love, acceptance, inspiration, or spiritual influence. It deepens their understandings of who they are and helps bring a sense of higher purpose to their lives. Instead of simply getting through the day or finding temporary relief from their pain or discomforts through the eating disorder, they can allow their inner convictions to carry them over the rough times during recovery. They can remain firm in their resolve to take the higher road in difficult situations, to be forgiving in the face of rejection, to be giving in times of scarcity, to have faith in God even in the face adversity and difficulties, or to be kind and decent when others have mistreated them. There is great power in learning these important lessons of the heart.

Just as there are benefits that come from honoring their hearts, when patients betray their hearts, they naturally experience painful consequences. When patients know a course of action to be true or best for them yet chose not to pursue it, they harm themselves. As patients come to understand how to honor their inner convictions, they experience feelings of empowerment and self-enhancement. They feel empowered to put commitments ahead of impulses, faith ahead of fear, and love ahead of hurt. Patients can learn that living true to the heart is a dignifying and affirming process. Helping patients return to their hearts and come to understand the messages, truths, and desires of their heart, as well as supporting patients as they strive to keep the convictions of their heart in the course of recovery is a powerful spiritual intervention.

A Courageous Heart

The seventh suggestion for listening to the heart is to recognize that it takes courage to listen and to act on the heart. Once patients know what their heart is telling them, they need to trust and to act on it. It is important to have discussions about courage and bravery in the honest expression of their hearts. Patients then must have the courage to learn from their experiences of the heart and make positive corrections and adjustments along the way to help to strengthen their trust in themselves and their hearts. It is impossible to take a stand for something important to them if their hearts are not in it. It will not last. Being courageous means having their words and actions become congruent with the desires and intentions of their hearts. This congruence between the internal and external self becomes an acquired and powerful way of being and living. It feels good to them, and other people in their lives will recognize and respond to them in ways different from the past.

Spiritual Interventions for Inpatient and Residential Treatment Settings

To help facilitate spiritual exploration and healing in inpatient and residential treatment settings, structured, programmatic spiritual interventions can be integrated into treatment in a variety of ways, including the following: (a) spirituality groups, (b) 12-step groups, (c) opportunities for worship and ritual (nondenominational weekly devotionals and opportunities to attend religious services in the community), (d) opportunities for altruistic service, and (e) providing opportunities for spiritual direction (e.g., visits from religious leaders). Here we briefly describe these interventions. In chapter 7, we describe a variety of additional spiritual interventions that can be used during individual, group, and family therapies in both inpatient and outpatient settings.

Spirituality Groups

We invite all of our patients to participate in weekly 60-minute spiritual exploration and growth groups and to read a self-help spirituality workbook (Richards, Hardman, & Berrett, 2000). We have found that this group provides patients with a safe and consistent opportunity to engage in spiritual exploration and growth. Patients are able to take insights from the spirituality group and use them during other aspects of their treatment, including individual, group, recreational, art, movement, and family therapies. The spirituality workbook is grounded in the Judeo-Christian tradition but is nondenominational in nature and includes readings and educational materials about topics such as faith in God, spiritual identity, grace, forgiveness, repentance, faith, prayer, and meditation.

Patients use the structure of the workbook and support of the group to help them come to an understanding of their own spiritual beliefs and convictions and to include those understandings in their recovery program. The spirituality group and workbook are described in more detail in chapter 8, along with an outcome study that investigated whether adding this group to an inpatient treatment program enhanced treatment outcomes.

Twelve-Step Groups

We also invite patients to participate in a weekly 12-step group that uses traditional 12-step principles from Alcoholics Anonymous that have been adapted specifically for use with those with an eating disorder (C. L. Johnson & Sansone, 1993). Twelve-step groups provide a tried and tested method for including spirituality in treatment and allow patients from diverse religious and spiritual backgrounds to come together in an accepting atmosphere. The 12-step approach can also help instill hope and faith for recovery, give women a common language for discussing spirituality, provide a concrete action plan for using one's faith in recovery, and offer a support network that can help prevent relapse (C. L. Johnson & Sansone, 1993). Twelve-step groups can also provide learning experiences that patients can take to individual, group, and family therapy where they can do more focused, in-depth work on their spiritual issues. We describe how we use 12-step groups in more detail in chapter 9.

Opportunities for Worship and Ritual

All the major world religious traditions encourage their followers to engage in various acts of private and public worship and ritual (Smart, 1983). Benson (1996) suggested that opportunities for worship and ritual might be "full of potentially therapeutic elements" (pp. 176–177) that can help promote physical and psychological healing and health. We think that forms of worship and ritual that help patients affirm their spiritual identity and worth, sense of life purpose, and involvement with their religious community are often helpful for patients with eating disorders.

One way to provide patients in inpatient and residential treatment settings with opportunities to engage in worship and ritual is for the treatment staff to transport patients who wish to attend worship services to local places of worship. We find it is not feasible to transport each patient to her preferred place of worship on every occasion. At our treatment center, we give patients the option of attending religious services each week as a group from a selected denomination—not necessarily their own. The following week, patients are invited to attend worship services of another denomination, and the following week another. The overall goals of this activity are to help patients develop a greater awareness of and appreciation for those who belong to religious traditions that differ from their own and to provide opportunities for worship and ritual for all patients.

In inpatient and residential treatment settings, nondenominational devotionals can provide opportunities for worship. At our treatment center, a weekly nondenominational devotional is held and is optional for patients who wish to attend. The devotional is designed and led by the patients. Patients share spiritually inspiring stories, poems, experiences, thoughts, and readings. This devotional also helps promote understanding and tolerance among patients from diverse religious backgrounds and gives them an opportunity to join together in an ecumenical form of worship.

Opportunities for Altruistic Service

All the major world religious traditions encourage their followers to perform (and be the recipients of) acts of altruistic service (Smart, 1993, 1994). Altruistic service can take many forms, including, for example, giving food to the hungry, clothing and money to the poor, visiting the sick, providing emotional support to those who are discouraged or grieving, and serving in volunteer positions in one's community. There is considerable evidence that altruistic service can have beneficial physical and psychological effects. For example, in *The Healing Power of Doing Good*, Luks (1993) reported the results of a survey of thousands of volunteers across the United States. He found that people who helped other people consistently reported better health than other people and that many believed their health improved when they began doing volunteer work. The vast majority of those surveyed said that helping others gave them a physical sensation or rush, including a sudden warmth, increased energy, a sense of euphoria, and greater calm and relaxation.

Opportunities for patients in inpatient and residential treatment settings to engage in acts of service within the community can be arranged by treatment professionals. For example, patients can be invited to participate in community service, such as planting flowers, delivering care packages, and so on. We have found that when patients engage in altruistic service, they grow in their capacity for unselfish empathy and love (Richards & Bergin, 1997).

Providing Opportunities for Spiritual Direction

Ganje-Fling and McCarthy (1991) described spiritual direction as "a relationship which has as its major objective the on-going development of the spiritual self" (p. 104). Worthington, Kurusu, McCullough, and Sanders (1996) defined it as "guided reflection about the spiritual aspect's of one's life" (p. 465). Believers in all the world religious traditions at times seek guidance and direction from their religious and spiritual leaders, such as their priest, minister, pastor, rabbi, bishop, guru, spiritual director, elder, or prophet. Religious personnel often can be of great help to patients and to the therapy process. They can provide meaningful spiritual and emotional guidance and comfort. It is often helpful for patients with eating disorders to experience a leader's caring and support during their treatment. When inpatient treatment is completed, religious leaders can significantly assist in relapse prevention by mobilizing social and emotional support in the patient's religious community.

We inform our patients that, on appropriate occasions, it is their right to invite religious leaders or other members of their religious community to visit them at the treatment center. When patients request this, specific appointments are made with the religious leader or member to visit. Adolescent patients must have parental permission for such visits. The visits take place in a room at the treatment center that has a window so that a treatment staff member is able to provide visual oversight of the visit to ensure patient safety.

CONCLUSION

In chapter 8, we report the findings of a study conducted in our treatment center that provides empirical support for our belief that multidimensional theistic treatment can be effective in reducing eating disorder symptoms and enhancing patients' psychological and spiritual well-being. It remains to be seen whether spiritually oriented eating disorder treatment programs and approaches lead to better treatment outcomes than do programs that do not view patients' faith and spirituality as resources in treatment and recovery. We hope that such comparative studies will eventually be conducted.

III

THEISTIC TREATMENT GUIDELINES AND INTERVENTIONS FOR EATING DISORDERS

6

RELIGIOUS AND SPIRITUAL ASSESSMENT OF PATIENTS WITH EATING DISORDERS

In this chapter, we describe a theistic view of religious and spiritual assessment in the treatment of women with eating disorders. We briefly describe contemporary medical and psychological assessment approaches for eating disorder patients. We describe our theistic approach and how it contributes to a comprehensive multidimensional assessment strategy for women with eating disorders. We describe religious and spiritual assessment techniques, including intake questionnaires, clinical interviews, and standardized assessment measures.

CONTEMPORARY ASSESSMENT APPROACHES FOR EATING DISORDERS

There is widespread agreement in the eating disorders field regarding whether patients should be assessed in a multidimensional manner. Much has been written about the assessment of patients' medical, nutritional, and psychosocial functioning. Here we briefly summarize some of the main contemporary assessment guidelines and procedures.

Medical and Nutritional Assessment

The medical consequences of eating disorders, and the attendant starvation, weight loss, and bingeing and purging, are numerous; thus, a thorough medical and nutritional assessment is necessary with these patients. A medical assessment should include a physical examination by a physician to assess all organ systems including dermatologic, gastrointestinal, and cardiovascular, as well as endocrine function (Kaplan & Garfinkel, 1993; Mehler & Andersen, 1999). Laboratory tests should also be conducted and routinely include serum electrolytes, creatinine, blood urea nitrogen, and a complete blood count. An electrocardiogram may be indicated for some patients, including those with significant weight loss and cardiovascular symptoms. Liver enzymes should be checked for patients who have lost weight rapidly or who are chronically emaciated. Radiographic or endoscopic assessment procedures may be needed for patients with gastrointestinal bleeding. A serum amylase may be needed for patients with significant abdominal symptoms. Serum calcium and phosphate should be conducted for patients with chronic amenorrhea and emaciation. Bone density studies may be needed for patients with repeated fractures (Kaplan & Garfinkel, 1993; Mehler & Andersen, 1999). Referral for a dental consultation and treatment may also be necessary for bulimic patients whose tooth enamel is eroded (Mehler & Andersen, 1999).

A nutritional assessment should include a weight history, including patients' current, highest, and lowest body mass index. For patients who may be severely malnourished, the risk of refeeding syndrome should be assessed during the first meeting. Patients' premorbid weight should also be established, if possible, as well as the weight at which amenorrhea occurs (Kaplan & Garfinkel, 1993; Mehler & Andersen, 1999). Patients' medically preferred or ideal weight should also be estimated as well as their protein, energy, and calorie needs. Patients' typical food intake should be assessed by documenting the number of meals and snacks engaged in each day as well as patients' daily calorie intake. Patients' methods of weight control should also be ascertained, including the frequency of bingeing, purging, exercising, and the use of laxatives and diet pills. Patients' beliefs about food should also be assessed. A nutritional assessment may also include an evaluation of patients' attitudes and perceptions about their body, including the size and shape of it overall as well as specific body parts (Kaplan & Garfinkel, 1993; Mehler & Andersen, 1999).

Psychosocial Assessment

Because a variety of psychological and social influences may be implicated in the development and maintenance of eating disorders, a comprehensive psychosocial assessment of patients with eating disorders is needed to understand and treat them. A psychosocial assessment should be multidimensional and typically includes taking patients' life history, eating disorder history, family history, and sexual history. It also includes an assessment of patients' current psychological and social functioning, as well as an assessment of related disorders that may co-occur with the eating disorder, including affective disorders (e.g., depression, anxiety), personality disorders, substance abuse, obsessive–compulsive behaviors, and interpersonal and family problems (C. Johnson, 1985; Williamson, 1990). Inquiring about patients' perceptions and feelings about sociocultural pressures to be thin may also be helpful. Essentially, the overall purpose of the psychosocial assessment is to give treatment professionals a comprehensive understanding of patients and their eating disorder, including when and how the eating disorder developed, possible precipitating influences, psychological and social issues that may be contributing to its maintenance, and patient strengths and resources that may assist in treatment and recovery.

Assessment Methods

A number of methods to assess patients with eating disorders are available, including medical and nutritional examinations, laboratory testing (e.g., blood samples), clinical interviews, structured assessment interviews, written assessment questionnaires, and standardized psychological testing. We refer readers who would like more information about medical and nutritional examinations and laboratory testing to literature devoted to these topics (e.g., Kaplan & Garfinkel, 1993). In the following sections, we briefly comment on methods that are typically used in conducting a psychosocial assessment, including structured assessment interviews, standardized psychological tests, and clinical interviews.

Structured Interviews

A number of structured interview guides have been designed to assist clinicians in diagnosing and assessing patients with eating disorders. For example, the Eating Disorder Examination is a semistructured clinical interview developed to measure behavioral and cognitive features of eating disorders, including subscales that assess eating concern, shape concern, dietary restraint, and weight concern (Fairburn & Cooper, 1993). It can be used to discriminate between women who have anorexia and bulimia, although it is not intended to be used alone in making a diagnosis.

Another structured interview guide is the Interview for Diagnosis of Eating Disorders, developed to help clinicians diagnose anorexia nervosa, bulimia nervosa, compulsive overeating, and obesity (Williamson, 1990).

The open-ended interview questions are divided into four categories: general assessment and history, anorexia nervosa, bulimia nervosa, and compulsive overeating.

Another interview guide is the Structured Clinical Interview for Axis I *DSM–IV* Disorders (SCID) for Module H (Eating Disorders; First, Spitzer, Gibbon, Gibbon, & Williams, 1994). Interviewers ask questions that are based on *Diagnostic and Statistical Manual of Mental Disorders* (4th ed.; *DSM–IV*; American Psychiatric Association, 1994) criteria for eating disorders. The SCID can help clinicians discriminate among the eating disorders.

Finally, another interview guide is the Diagnostic Survey for Eating Disorders (DSED), a multi-item survey that focuses on various aspects of anorexia nervosa and bulimia nervosa (C. Johnson, 1985). The questions are divided into 12 sections, including questions about patient demographics, weight history and body image, dieting behavior, binge eating and purging behavior, exercise, sexual functioning, menstruation, medical and psychiatric history, life adjustment, and family history. The DSED can be used either as a self-report instrument or as a semistructured interview guide.

Structured interview guides are helpful because they offer clinicians a systematic way to gather interview assessment data in a manner that can maximize comprehensiveness and diagnostic reliability. Unfortunately, from our theistic viewpoint, none of the existing interview guides adequately assess the religious and spiritual dimensions of patients' lives, although some of them do briefly inquire about limited aspects of it (e.g., religious affiliation).

Standardized Assessment Instruments

A large number of standardized self-report instruments have been developed to assess eating disorder symptoms. Such instruments are often useful because they are inexpensive and more convenient to administer than an interview. For example, the Eating Disorder Inventory—2 (EDI–2) is a frequently used 91-item measure that assesses the cognitive and behavioral symptoms of anorexia nervosa and bulimia nervosa (Garner, 1991). The EDI–2 has 11 subscales: Drive for Thinness, Bulimia, Body Dissatisfaction, Ineffectiveness, Perfectionism, Interpersonal Distrust, Interoceptive Awareness, Maturity Fears, Asceticism, Impulse Regulation, and Social Insecurity. In general, the EDI–2 has been shown to have adequate reliability and validity and is useful for assessing patients' symptoms and to aid in treatment planning, although it should not be used alone as a diagnostic instrument.

Another widely used eating disorder self-report measure is the Eating Attitudes Test (EAT-40; Garner & Garfinkel, 1979). It contains 40 items that assess behaviors and attitudes associated with anorexia nervosa and bulimia nervosa. An abbreviated 26-item version that is highly correlated with the EAT-40 is also available (EAT-26). Both the EAT-40 and EAT-26 have been found to be relatively reliable and valid measures, successfully identifying people with abnormal eating attitudes and behaviors from normal control subjects. However, these instruments do not appear to discriminate between those with anorexia nervosa and bulimia nervosa.

Another frequently used self-report eating disorder measure is the Bulimia Test—Revised (BULIT–R), which assesses the behavioral, physiological, and cognitive symptoms of bulimia nervosa (Thelen, Mintz, & Vander Wal, 1996). It contains 36 items that inquire about binge eating, purging behavior, negative affect, and weight fluctuations. The BULIT–R has been shown to be reliable and valid for identifying those who may suffer from bulimia nervosa and is recommended as a screening instrument.

Many other standardized self-report measures assess various aspects of eating disorder symptoms—too many to discuss here. We refer interested readers to other sources devoted to the topic of eating disorder assessment (e.g., Kashubeck-West & Saunders, 2001; Mitchell & Peterson, 2005; Williamson, 1990). Let it suffice to say that there is a broad range of standardized eating disorder assessment measures available to clinicians; however, none attempts to assess how the religious and spiritual aspects of patients' functioning may be related to eating disorder symptomatology.

Clinical Interviews

For many clinicians, unstructured clinical interviews are the primary method used to assess eating disorder symptomatology. Such interviews are flexible and can be conveniently used during both individual and group therapy, thereby allowing assessment to be an ongoing process throughout the course of treatment. Effective clinical interviews require good communication skills and in-depth knowledge and skills concerning diagnosis, assessment, and case and treatment conceptualization. We regard unstructured clinical interviews as the primary method for clinicians to assess the religious and spiritual dimensions of patients' functioning. We say more about how to use clinical interviews for this purpose later in this chapter.

A THEISTIC VIEW OF RELIGIOUS AND SPIRITUAL ASSESSMENT

From a theistic perspective, contemporary approaches to assessing eating disorders are valuable but incomplete because they give little systematic or explicit attention to the religious and spiritual dimensions of patients' lives. Faith and spirituality are extremely important to the majority of people in North America and throughout most of the world (Richards & Bergin, 2005). If helping professionals do not adequately assess patients' faith and spirituality, they may overlook an aspect of patients' lives that is central to their sense of identity, lifestyle, eating disorder, and recovery.

The overall goal of a religious and spiritual assessment is to gain a clear understanding of each patient's current spiritual framework so that treatment professionals can work within the patient's belief system in a sensitive and respectful manner. Richards and Bergin (2005) suggested that there are at least five reasons therapists should assess their patients' religious and spiritual backgrounds, beliefs, and lifestyle.

1. Conducting a religious–spiritual assessment can help therapists better understand their patients' worldviews and thus increase their capacity to empathize and work with each patient sensitively.
2. Conducting a religious–spiritual assessment can help therapists determine whether a patient's religious–spiritual orientation is healthy or unhealthy and what impact it is having on the presenting problems and disturbance.
3. Conducting a religious–spiritual assessment can help therapists determine whether patients' religious and spiritual beliefs and community could be used as a resource to help them cope, heal, and grow.
4. Conducting a religious–spiritual assessment can help therapists determine which spiritual interventions could be used in therapy.
5. Conducting a religious–spiritual assessment can help therapists determine whether patients have unresolved spiritual doubts, concerns, or needs that should be addressed in therapy.

From a theistic perspective, a religious–spiritual assessment should be embedded in a multilevel, multisystemic assessment strategy (Richards & Bergin, 2005). Figure 6.1 helps illustrate what this means. The divisions within the circle represent the various systems that therapists should assess: the physical, social, behavioral, intellectual, educational–occupational, psychological–emotional, and religious–spiritual systems. When therapists begin working with a new patient, they need to do a brief global assessment of all the major systems mentioned earlier. Richards and Bergin (2005) referred to this as a *Level 1 multisystemic assessment.* During a Level 1 assessment, therapists rely primarily on patients' perceptions and self-descriptions of how they are functioning in each system of their lives.

Depending on the patient's presenting problems and goals, along with the information obtained during the Level 1 assessment, therapists then proceed with more in-depth assessments of the systems that seem clinically warranted. The more focused, in-depth assessments are referred to as *Level 2 assessments* (Richards & Bergin, 2005). More focused, probing questions

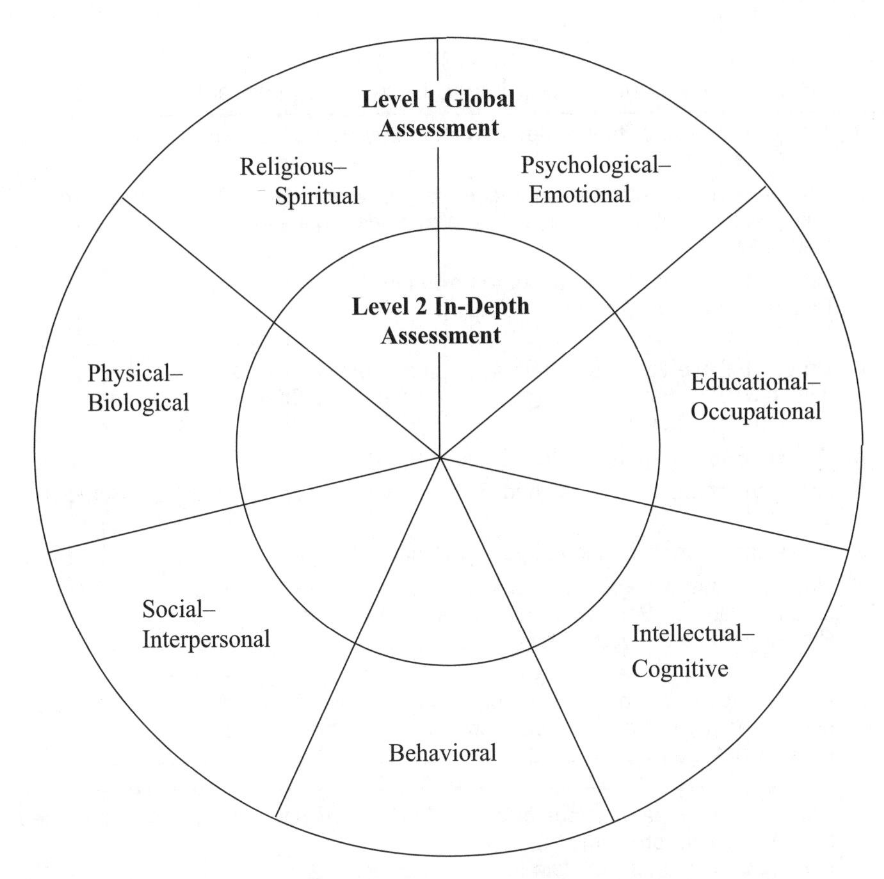

Figure 6.1. A multilevel, multidimensional assessment strategy. Adapted from *A Spiritual Strategy for Counseling and Psychotherapy* (2nd ed., p. 235), by P. S. Richards and A. E. Bergin, 2005, Washington, DC: American Psychological Association. Copyright 2005 by the American Psychological Association.

would be asked during clinical interviews. Exhibit 6.1 provides examples of religious and spiritual assessment questions that can be asked on a written intake questionnaire to assess whether religion or spirituality is important to a patient and whether she would like to include it in her treatment. Exhibits 6.2 and 6.3 provide lists of possible questions we have formulated that can be asked in clinical interviews to help therapists explore patients' faith and spirituality in greater depth. We find that the questions in Exhibit 6.2 are often more suitable for patients who are affiliated with a religion. The questions in Exhibit 6.3 often seem more suitable for patients who are not affiliated with a religious denomination.

Another assessment activity we have found to be valuable with teenagers and adults is to give patients a handout that has a variety of spiritual

EXHIBIT 6.1
Religious–Spiritual Patient Intake Level 1 Assessment Questions

1. Are religious or spiritual issues important in your life? ___ Yes ___ No ___ Somewhat
2. Do you wish to discuss them in counseling, when relevant? ___ Yes ___ No
   If not, you do not need to answer the remaining questions about religion and spirituality.
3. Do you believe in God or a Supreme Being? ___ Yes ___ No
   Please elaborate if you wish. ____
   ____
4. Do you believe you can experience spiritual guidance? ___ Yes ___ No
   If so, how often have you had such experiences: ___ Often ___ Occasionally ___ Rarely ___ Never
5. What is your current religious affiliation (if any)? ____________________
6. Are you committed to it and actively involved? ___ Yes ___ Somewhat ___ No
7. What was your childhood religious affiliation (if any)? ____________________
8. How important was religion or spiritual beliefs to you as a child and adolescent?
   ___ Important ___ Somewhat important ___ Unimportant
   Please elaborate if you wish. ____
   ____
9. Are you aware of any religious or spiritual resources in your life that could be used to help you overcome your problems? ___ Yes ___ No
   If yes, what are they? ____
   ____
10. Do you believe that religious or spiritual influences have hurt you or contributed to some of your problems? ___ Yes ___ No
    If yes, can you briefly explain how? ____
    ____
11. Would you like your counselor to consult with your religious leader if it appears this could be helpful to you? ___ Yes ___ No ___ Maybe
    If yes, a permission and confidentiality form will be provided for you to sign.
12. Are you willing to consider trying religious or spiritual suggestions from your counselor if it appears that they could be helpful to you? ___ Yes ___ No

Note. Adapted from *A Spiritual Strategy for Counseling and Psychotherapy* (2nd ed., p. 238), by P. S. Richards and A. E. Bergin, 2005, Washington, DC: American Psychological Association. Copyright 2005 by the American Psychological Association.

thoughts from wise people and leaders from different religions and spiritual traditions. The handout helps patients think about different ways of seeing the world, recovery, and spirituality. After passing out the handout of spiritual quotes, therapists can ask patients to read the quotes and to pay attention to what strikes them in their heart or in their mind as important. Before they read, the therapist can ask patients to pay attention to how they feel and what they think when they read each quote and to ask themselves questions such as, "Which quote did you connect with the most?" "Which quote touched your heart in a special way?" "Which quote caused inspira-

EXHIBIT 6.2
Level 2 Religious–Spiritual Assessment Questions for Patients With Eating Disorders Who Are Affiliated With a Religious Denomination

1. Do you belong to any organized religion?
2. Are you formerly a member of any religion?
3. Do you attend religious services of that organization or cause to which you belong?
4. Do you engage in any spiritual or worship practices? If so, can you tell me what they are?
5. Do you spend time in nature for spiritual reasons? If so, how often?
6. Do you ever engage in meditation or contemplation? If so, how often?
7. Do you pray? If so, how often?
8. Do you ever pray for yourself? If so, how often?
9. Do you ever participate in yoga? If so, how frequently?
10. Do you ever read sacred, uplifting writings, whether they are books, articles, poetry of a sacred nature, or scriptures? If so, what do you read and how often?
11. Do you believe in forgiveness?
12. Do you believe in repentance?
13. Do you actively involve yourself in the process of repentance and spiritual change from that perspective?
14. Do you have any worship rituals or practices? If so, what are they?
15. Do you believe in confession and telling the truth? If so, who do you feel you need to confess to when you make mistakes?
16. Do you take advantage of the opportunities of fellowship from your religious organization or social network?
17. Do you participate in service of others, and if so, what kind of things do you do and how often?
18. Do you seek spiritual direction in your life to guide you in decisions?
19. Do you seek spiritual influences to help you through rough times? If so, explain.
20. How does your spirituality show up in your life every day?
21. How do you keep connected to your spiritual nature and your spiritual beliefs every day?
22. How would you like your spiritual life to look in the future?
23. What kind of roadblocks are getting in the way of living your religion the way you would really like to?
24. Do your parents or grandparents belong to any spiritual or religious organization? If so, which one?
25. How actively do they participate in that religious doctrine and/or organization?
26. How actively do you participate?
27. How do you feel about your participation in your religious or spiritual activities?
28. Do you do any religious or spiritual activities in private, when you are all alone and no one else would know? If so, what are they?
29. Have you ever had a negative spiritual or religious experience with God or a higher power?
30. Have you ever had any negative experiences with what some may call "the dark side"? If so, please explain.
31. Have you ever had a negative experience with a religious leader, clergy, ecclesiastical leader, or member of your religion? If so, what was it, and what was its impact on your faith, your practice of religious doctrine, or your participation in activities of your religious organization?
32. If you make a mistake, what do you have to do to make things right or to be at peace?
33. If you commit a sin, what do you have to do to make things right or to be at peace?

EXHIBIT 6.3
Level 2 Religious–Spiritual Assessment Questions for Patients With Eating Disorders Who Are Not Affiliated With a Religious Denomination

1. Tell me your beliefs of what laws govern the universe.
2. Tell me a little bit about your beliefs of the creation of the world.
3. Please talk for a minute about your beliefs about the relationship between mother earth, nature, and humankind.
4. What were the core values taught and lived by in your home growing up?
5. What do you respect the most about your mother?
6. What do you respect the most about your father?
7. What do you respect the most about your grandparents or other influential family members?
8. Who is your best friend, and what do you most respect about him or her?
9. Who do you view as a spiritual person, and why do you view him or her as spiritual? In what way do you think this person is spiritual?
10. Who do you view as a "really good person?" What is it about him or her that you view as "really good?" What is it that you see, feel, or admire about this person?
12. What kind of a person are you? Please describe this as best you can. You can use different characteristics if you would like.
13. What kind of a person would you like to become in the future?
14. In what ways would you like to develop in character over time?
15. What qualities are you most looking for in a friend?
16. What qualities are you most looking for in a marital partner or companion?
17. Out of all the priorities that one could have about life, what are the three most important things to you?
18. Tell me your beliefs about how people should be treated by others?
19. Tell me your beliefs about universal laws that we, as humans, have to live by.
20. Where do those universal laws come from?
21. Tell me your beliefs and thoughts about the concept of a "higher power."
22. Do you believe in God?
23. If you believe in God, tell me your concept of who or what God is.

(continued)

tional thoughts to come into your mind?" "Which quote resonated with you as something that is true or something that you believe in?" "Which quote seemed most important to you?" Patients are then asked to read the quote that resonated with them or with which they connected the most to the group or to their therapist. They then explain why the quote they selected had resonance for them. Several examples of the quotes are the following:

> We are all children of the Great Spirit. We all belong to mother earth. Our planet is in great trouble. If we keep carrying old grudges and do not work together, we will all die.
>
> —*Chief Seattle*

> From what I've found, there is just too much noise in modern life, and because of this, many people are afraid of silence. As God speaks only in silence, this is a big problem for those who are searching for God.

EXHIBIT 6.3 *(Continued)*

24. What are your beliefs about human nature and the purpose and meaning of life?
25. Tell me your beliefs about the purpose and meaning of adversity in your life?
26. Do you believe in divine intervention in human life?
27. Have you ever had a negative religious or spiritual experience?
28. If a person were spiritual, what would he or she be like?
29. Name a person whom you view as very spiritual whom you respect. What is that person like? What makes that person spiritual?
30. Have you ever experienced a miracle or providence? If so, explain.
31. Have you ever noticed God's "hand" in your life?
32. How can you know whether you are doing the right thing?
33. What do you think is the meaning or purpose of life generally?
34. What do you think the meaning or purpose of your life is?
35. What spiritual goals are you working on? And what goals do you want to work on over the next little while?
36. How do your spiritual beliefs show up in your life every day?
37. Do you have any religious or spiritual practices? If so, what are they?
38. Do you believe in intuition? If so, explain.
39. Do you believe in inspiration? If so, explain.
40. Do you believe in the concept of "conscience"? What is the role of conscience in your life?
41. What main principles do you live by?
42. When you go against the principles that you live by, how do you feel and what do you need to do about it?
43. Do you believe in the concept of a spirit, soul, or "heart"?
44. Do you believe that listening to your spirit or "heart" is important?

> Many young people, for instance, don't know how to reflect and just act instinctively.
>
> —*Mother Teresa*

> We are not human beings having a spiritual experience; we are spiritual beings having a human experience.
>
> —*Teilhard de Chardin*

As patients talk about how and why they resonated with the quote they selected, therapists can gain some insight into their spirituality without asking patients to describe their belief system directly or explicitly. This assessment activity allows therapists to do some spiritual assessment either individually or as a group. It can also help patients talk about their spirituality with others because it gives them permission to examine, share, accept, and embrace their own spiritual beliefs, as well as the spiritual beliefs of other patients.

In addition to the information gathered on intake questionnaires, in clinical interviews, and in experiential activities such as the one just described, therapists may also wish to assess patients' religious beliefs and spirituality in more depth by asking them to complete one or more standardized religious and spirituality measures. A recent handbook, *Measures of*

Religiosity, contains copies and critical reviews of more than 120 measures of various types of religiousness, including religious beliefs, practices, and attitudes; religious orientation; religious development; religious commitment and involvement; religious experience; religious and moral values; religious coping and problem solving; spirituality and mysticism; God concept; religious fundamentalism; views about death and the afterlife; religious attributions; and forgiveness (Hill & Hood, 1999). This resource has helped make religious and spiritual measures more easily accessible to clinicians. In addition, increasing numbers of book chapters and journal articles providing helpful perspectives and guidelines for clinicians about religious and spiritual assessment have been published in recent years (e.g., Chirban, 2001; Gorsuch & Miller, 1999; Hill & Pargament, 2003; Richards & Bergin, 1997, 2005).

In our own work, we sometimes supplement our clinical interview assessments by administering measures of intrinsic and extrinsic religious orientation (Gorsuch & McPherson, 1989) and spiritual well-being (Ellison & Smith, 1991). These give us a quick standardized indication of patients' general levels of religious and spiritual maturity and well-being. Copies of these measures are available in Hill and Hood (1999). Several other religious and spiritual measures have recently been developed, that we think are important from a theistic perspective with potential for clinical settings, including the Religious Commitment Inventory (Worthington et al., 2003), Index of Core Spiritual Experiences (Kass, Friedman, Lesserman, Zuttermeister, & Benson, 1991), and Spiritual Transcendence Scale (Piedmont, 1999). Copies and brief descriptions of the Religious Commitment Inventory and Spiritual Transcendence Scale measures are provided in Exhibits 6.4 and 6.5.

Because most religious and spiritual measures have not been adequately validated in clinical situations, therapists should use such measures only after carefully examining them and personally verifying the measure's suitability for their patients. Even then, therapists should interpret these measures tentatively. Normative data are so limited for most of these measures that sharing normative comparisons with patients should be avoided. At most, these measures should be used only to give therapists some tentative insights into their patients and perhaps as a tool to help patients engage in exploration and self-discovery. Additional research is needed with most of these measures to ensure their validity for non-Christian patients. Further information about conducting religious and spiritual assessments is provided in Richards and Bergin (1997, 2005).

Clinically Important Dimensions of Spirituality

What dimensions of religiosity and spirituality should therapists assess? Consistent with Richards and Bergin (2005), we have found that the follow-

EXHIBIT 6.4
Religious Commitment Inventory

Directions: The following items deal with various types of religious ideas and social opinions. Please indicate the response you prefer, or most closely agree with, by circling the number corresponding to your choice in the right margin (e.g., 1 = *not at all true of me,* 2 = *somewhat true of me,* 3 = *moderately true of me,* 4 = *mostly true of me,* 5 = *totally true of me*).

Scale	Item	
Intrapersonal	1. I often read books and magazines about my faith.	1 2 3 4 5
Interpersonal	2. I make financial contributions to my religious organization.	1 2 3 4 5
Intrapersonal	3. I spend time trying to grow in understanding of my faith.	1 2 3 4 5
Intrapersonal	4. Religion is especially important to me because it answers many questions about the meaning of life.	1 2 3 4 5
Intrapersonal	5. My religious beliefs lie behind my whole approach to life.	1 2 3 4 5
Interpersonal	6. I enjoy spending time with others of my religious affiliation.	1 2 3 4 5
Intrapersonal	7. Religious beliefs influence all my dealings in life.	1 2 3 4 5
Intrapersonal	8. It is important to me to spend periods of time in private religious thought and reflection.	1 2 3 4 5
Interpersonal	9. I enjoy working in the activities of my religious affiliation.	1 2 3 4 5
Interpersonal	10. I keep well informed about my local religious group and have some influence in its decisions.	1 2 3 4 5

Note. Description and Evaluation: The Religious Commitment Inventory—10 was developed to be used in research, counseling, and health psychology and purports to measure "the degree to which a person adheres to his or her religious values, beliefs, and practices and uses them in daily living" (Worthington et al., 2003, p. 85). From "The Religious Commitment Inventory—10: Development, Refinement, and Validation of a Brief Scale for Research and Counseling," by E. L. Worthington Jr., N. G. Wade, T. L. Hight, J. S. Ripley, M. E. McCullough, J. W. Berry, et al., 2003, *Journal of Counseling Psychology, 50,* p. 87. Copyright 2003 by the American Psychological Association.

ing dimensions are often important to assess when working with eating disorder patients.

1. *Metaphysical Worldview.* A metaphysical worldview comprises the beliefs a patient holds about the universe and the nature of reality. Is the patient atheistic, agnostic, theistic, or polytheistic? What are her views about human nature, the meaning of life, spirituality, morality, and life after death?
2. *Religious Affiliation.* Does the patient affiliate with any religious organization, religious movement, or religious cause?
3. *Religious Orthodoxy.* Does the patient believe in and adhere to the traditional doctrines and moral teachings of her religion?

How orthodox is the patient in her beliefs and how orthodox is she in practice? Does the patient accept and believe in the doctrines and teachings of her religion? Does the patient go to church? Does she get involved in a religious study group or in doing service with the church organization? Does she take part in religious ordinances, ceremonies, or rituals?

4. *Religious Problem-Solving Style*. A patient's religious beliefs can influence the manner in which she seeks to cope with and solve life's problems and difficulties. Does the patient believe that God is a source of support and guidance in her life? How does the patient use her religion to solve problems? Does she pray? Does she read scriptures or other religious books? Does she seek guidance and support from ecclesiastical or church leaders? Does she fellowship with and provide service to members of her religious community?
5. *Spiritual Identity*. Spiritual identity refers to a patient's sense of identity and worth in relation to God and her place in the universe. Does the patient feel that she has a connection or relationship with God? Does the patient feel that she has divinity within her? Does she believe she is a creation or daughter of God? Does the patient believe that her life has spiritual purpose and meaning?
6. *God Image*. God image refers to a patient's perceptions or representations of God. God is perceived by some patients as loving, kind, and forgiving but by others as wrathful, vindictive, and impersonal. What does the patient believe about the nature of God, including God's personality, characteristics, and willingness to have a relationship with humans? Many patients have an image of God that is in the image of their parents or primary caretakers.
7. *Value–Lifestyle Congruence*. Value–lifestyle congruence is the degree to which a patient's lifestyle and behaviors are congruent with her professed moral, religious, and spiritual values (Richards & Bergin, 2005). It is important to assess the major tenets that patients believe they should be practicing or being obedient to and how congruent they are at living those tenets. It is also helpful to assess the emotional impact on patients if they are not living congruently with their religious or spiritual beliefs.
8. *Doctrinal Knowledge*. Doctrinal knowledge involves patients' understanding and knowledge of the doctrines and theology of their religious tradition (Richards & Bergin, 2005). It is important to assess whether a patient truly understands the

EXHIBIT 6.5
Spiritual Transcendence Scale

Scale	Item
C	1. Although dead, images of some of my relatives continue to influence my current life.
PF	2. I meditate and/or pray so that I can reach a higher spiritual plane of consciousness.
PF	3. I have had at least one "peak" experience.
U	4. I feel that on a higher level all of us share a common bond.
U	5. All life is interconnected.
U	6. There is a higher plane of consciousness or spirituality that binds all people.
C	7. It is important for me to give something back to my community.
C	8. I am a link in the chain of my family's heritage, a bridge between past and future.
C	9. I am concerned about those who will come after me in life.
PF	10. I have been able to step outside of my ambitions and failures, pain and joy, to experience a larger sense of fulfillment.
U	11. Although individual people may be difficult, I feel an emotional bond with all of humanity.
C	12. I still have strong emotional ties with someone who has died.
U	13. I believe that there is a larger meaning to life.
PF	14. I find inner strength and/or peace from my prayers or meditations.
U	15. I believe that death is a doorway to another plane of existence.
U	16. I believe there is a larger plan to life.
PF	17. Sometimes I find the details of my life to be a distraction from my prayers and/or meditations.
PF	18. When in prayer or meditation, I have become oblivious to the events of this world.
PF	19. I have experienced deep fulfillment and bliss through my prayers or meditations.
PF	20. I have had a spiritual experience where I lost track of where I was or the passage of time.
PF	21. The desires of my body do not keep me from my prayers or meditations.
C	22. Although there is good and bad in people, I believe that humanity as a whole is basically good.
U	23. There is an order to the universe that transcends human thinking.
U	24. I believe that on some level my life is intimately tied to all of humankind.

Note. The Spiritual Transcendence Scale purports to measure "the capacity of individuals to stand outside of their immediate sense of time and place to view life from a larger, more objective perspective. . . . a person sees a fundamental unity underlying the diverse strivings of nature and finds a bonding with others that cannot be severed, not even by death" (Piedmont, 1999, p. 988). PF = prayer fulfillment; C = connectedness; U = universality. From "Does Spirituality Represent the Sixth Factor of Personality? Spiritual Transcendence and the Five-Factor Model," by R. L. Piedmont, 1999, *Journal of Personality, 67,* 985–1013. Copyright 1999 by Ralph L. Piedmont. Reprinted with permission.

doctrines of her religious tradition and whether any of her spiritual struggles and issues are related to a lack of understanding of the doctrine or to disagreements with it.

9. *Spiritual Maturity*. A number of theorists and researchers have proposed theories of religious and spiritual well-being,

development, and maturity that could prove useful for helping professionals conceptualize the maturity of eating disorder patients' spiritual orientations, including Allport's (1966; Allport & Ross, 1967) theory of intrinsic and extrinsic religious orientation; Fowler's (1981) six-stage model of faith development; Paloutzian and Ellison's (Ellison, 1983; Paloutzian & Ellison, 1991) two-dimensional model of spiritual well-being; Malony's (1985) eight-dimensional model of Christian maturity; Pargament's model of religious coping (Pargament et al., 1988); and Richards and Bergin's (2005) psychospiritual themes model of spiritual maturity. A description of Richards and Bergin's model and an assessment guide based on it is provided in Table 6.1.

Metaempathy and Assessment

From a theistic perspective, a religious and spiritual assessment also includes making an effort to seek and remain open to spiritual impressions and insights about patients and their problems that may come from the divine source. Metaempathy is the capacity to receive impressions and insights about patients that go beyond ordinary clinical hypothesizing or hunches (Richards & Bergin, 2005). As treatment professionals engage in patient assessment and conceptualization, we encourage them to pray and contemplate about their patients. As they do, professionals may experience spiritual impressions and insights that clarify and deepen their understanding of their patients' issues and how to help them.

PROCESS SUGGESTIONS FOR ASSESSING SPIRITUALITY IN PATIENTS WITH EATING DISORDERS

When conducting a religious and spiritual assessment, it is important for therapists to communicate to patients a desire to be respectful of their religious and spiritual views. Therapists may wish to ask patients to help them understand and use their spiritual views and religious beliefs during the course of treatment. Therapists may find it helpful to say something such as, "Is it okay if we include your spirituality and religiosity as one aspect of what we are doing in trying to help you overcome the eating disorder?" Patients typically are happy and relieved that spirituality is something they can talk about openly and something that will be explored and included in their treatment. If patients say they are uncomfortable or unwilling to discuss spiritual issues this should be respected, and treatment can proceed without a spiritual focus.

TABLE 6.1
Psychospiritual Themes of a Theistic Personality Theory: An Interview and Assessment Guide

Assessment question	Adaptive–healthy faith and spirituality	Maladaptive–unhealthy faith and spirituality
1. Do my client's faith and spirituality promote a mature sense of spiritual identity and purpose or obscure divine potential?	1A. Eternal spiritual identity Love and reverence of God Divine image and worth Meaning and purpose in life Love of humanity God inspired	1B. Negative aspects of mortal overlay Preoccupation with self Materialistic self-image Nihilism Selfish individualism Hyperspiritual or evil inspired
2. Do my client's faith and spirituality promote agency and choice or impairment and loss of self-control?	2A. Agency Internal locus of control Long-term goals and strivings Acceptance of responsibility Anticipation of consequences Self-regulation Good reality testing	2B. Impairment External locus of control Immediate gratification Denial of responsibility Inability to foresee consequences Addictions Poor reality testing
3. Do my client's faith and spirituality promote moral responsibility or relativism and immorality?	3A. Moral responsibility Belief in moral universals Attunement to Spirit of Truth Moral behavior Moral self-esteem	3B. Relativism and uncertainty Belief in moral relativism God-controlled (externalizing or deferring) Immoral behavior Shame
4. Do my client's faith and spirituality promote integrity and congruence or deception?	4A. Integrity Intrinsic personal faith Truthfulness Sincerity Congruence Authenticity–integrity	4B. Deception Extrinsic normative faith Deceitfulness Role-playing Incongruence Manipulation–deception

(continued)

TABLE 6.1 *(Continued)*

Assessment question	Adaptive–healthy faith and spirituality	Maladaptive–unhealthy faith and spirituality
5. Do my client's faith and spirituality promote faithful intimacy or infidelity and self-focus?	5A. Faithful intimacy Nurturing Tender–protective Warm–faithful–intimate Caring Empathic Forgiving Humble Assertive	5B. Infidelity and self-focus Neglectful Angry–abusive–violent Antisocial-unfaithful Sadistic Insensitive Unforgiving Compliant–masochistic Aggressive or passive
6. Do my client's faith and spirituality promote healthy concern for family and community or selfish individualism?	6A. Marriage, Family and Community Interpersonal social orientation Networking–familial kinship Cooperation Mature self-sacrifice Altruistic	6B. Alienation and isolation Narcissistic Self-aggrandizing Competitive or individualistic Self-gratifying Hedonistic
7. Do my client's faith and spirituality promote benevolent uses of power and influence or authoritarian abuses?	7A. Benevolent power Authoritative–affirming Tolerant Egalitarian Facilitating growth	7B. Authoritarian Dogmatic–absolutistic–critical Intolerant–prejudiced Controlling–dominating Power-seeking
8. Do my client's faith and spirituality promote personal growth and change or stagnation?	8A. Growth and change Actualizing Growth-oriented Change-oriented Self-renewing–repentant Experiential–creative Integrates ambiguity and paradox	8B. Stagnation Perfectionistic Righteous performances Rigid Self-punitive–depressed Ritualistic–stagnant Anxious about the unanticipated

Note. From *A Spiritual Strategy for Counseling and Psychotherapy* (2nd ed., pp. 230–231), by P. S. Richards and A. E. Bergin, 2005, Washington, DC: American Psychological Association.

Most clients are willing to discuss and explore their spirituality and religious convictions with a therapist if they believe that the therapist is accepting and not negating, judgmental, dismissing, or surprised by their religious and spiritual beliefs and observances. Some patients may initially be reluctant or hesitant to share this personal, private part of their lives because they have previously encountered psychologists, psychiatrists, or therapists who have treated religiosity or spirituality as insignificant or not pertinent to treatment. Patients have sometimes reported to us that helping professionals have made comments to them about their spiritual beliefs that felt disqualifying, negating, mocking, or critical.

When patients have had such experiences, it may be important to invite them to share their feelings about it and to validate that such cultural insensitivity on the part of helping professionals is inappropriate. Communicating respect and tolerance for patients' religious and spiritual beliefs is an essential part of the assessment process. Information that patients disclose about their religion and spirituality is often viewed as sacred to the patient, and trivializing it in any way can be extremely painful for patients and undermine the therapeutic relationship.

We encourage therapists to not be afraid to ask questions about patients' religious background and spirituality. Being afraid to ask about these topics may teach patients that they should be ashamed of it or that professionals are ashamed of it. Silence or refusal to talk about spiritual things may also send a message to patients that their therapist thinks it is unimportant, thereby making patients feel that it is unsafe to talk about spirituality during treatment.

We encourage therapists to do a thorough and specific history of the religious and spiritual background of every patient with an eating disorder whom they treat. We encourage them to explore in some depth the tenets and beliefs of their patients' religion, their patients' adherence to those beliefs, the positive and negative experiences in their patients' religious backgrounds, and the personal preferences that their patients may have in response to denominational requirements or religious doctrines. It is important to explore with patients what is meaningful to them in spiritual matters and what is not meaningful and to find out how much time and energy they devote to religious study, prayer, church attendance, meditation, private religious experiences, service, and so on.

Every question about spiritual or religious matters can lead to many other questions that can assist the therapist in understanding the underlying spiritual aspects of the eating disorder. By asking questions, inviting patients to elaborate, and then asking more questions that build on patients' initial responses, therapists can gain this in-depth understanding. Patients' spirituality often cannot be adequately assessed by simply going through a list of questions. Rather, a well-crafted and clinically mature interview process is needed in which patients are invited in a safe environment to share more and more about their true thoughts, feelings, and beliefs about spirituality and the role of it in their lives and eating disorder.

To expand and enlarge their insight into how patients' spirituality may be intertwined with emotional, psychological, and relationship issues, therapists may need to probe deeper than the short or obvious answers patients may give initially. There is often a need to continue gathering information about patients' spirituality over the course of treatment so that it can be used to facilitate treatment. Assessment is ongoing, and clarifications can continue throughout the course of treatment, whether psychological or spiritual.

The other important part of doing a religious and spiritual assessment lies in the uncovering and clarification of the possibilities, hopes, and desires about what patients truly want, how they want their spiritual life to be, and how they might want to incorporate spirituality into their treatment and recovery. Therapists should clarify patients' strengths and resources and then tap into them during the course of treatment. Therapists may wish to ask patients questions such as the following: "How might your faith help you as you look ahead in the pursuit of recovery?" "How do your religious beliefs provide encouragement, comfort, and aid as you face this difficult problem?" Therapists need to seek understanding about how patients' religious beliefs and background may contribute to their conflicts, impasses, and difficulties, but it is also often helpful to understand the positive, the uplifting, and the strengthening aspects of patients' spirituality and religiosity that may assist patients in recovery.

When conducting a religious and spiritual assessment, we also recommend that therapists assess patients' spiritual goals. It is common practice for therapists to assess the goals patients have for treatment, whether these be to overcome depression, decrease anxiety, or improve relationships. We find it is also usually helpful to help patients set goals about faith and spirituality. We ask patients, "What do you want to do in your spiritual life?" "What do you want to change or improve about your spirituality?" "What would you like to be different about your spirituality when you walk out of treatment?"

We think it is also important for therapists to assess in what patients are placing their faith. Women with eating disorders have often placed their faith in the eating disorder. They have faith that their eating disorder is a way to deal with life and negative emotions and to find some kind of safety or contentment in their identity. In treatment, we encourage patients to put faith in better things: faith in themselves, faith in God, faith in those who love them, and faith in a hopeful future. We assume that everyone has faith in something. If therapists assess in what patients put their faith, they can help patients put faith in something besides their eating disorder.

We encourage patients to have faith in something hopeful, inspiring, transcendent, or character building.

Another benefit of spiritually assessing patients with eating disorders is that therapists can use the information obtained during the assessment to help them affirm patients' goodness, courage, and congruency. When therapists understand patients' spiritual beliefs and values, they can watch for occasions when patients are demonstrating faithfulness, hard work, their endurance, humility, congruence, and other signs of good character and strength. When this occurs, they can point it out in an affirming way to their patients. Many patients with eating disorders have a hard time seeing the good in themselves and so affirming their goodness and spirituality by providing feedback about specific occasions when patients have behaved congruently, courageously, and honorably can have a positive impact. By doing so, therapists can be the mirror to the positive aspects that patients often have a hard time seeing in themselves.

CONCLUSION

Compared with the medical, nutritional, and psychological assessment of eating disorders on which much has been published and for which numerous standardized, commercially published tests are available, the religious and spiritual assessment of patients with these disorders is in its infancy. Much more theoretical, clinical, and research work is needed on this topic. Nevertheless, sufficient clinical and scholarly work has been done to enable helping professionals who treat women with eating disorders to include a religious and spiritual assessment as part of a comprehensive assessment strategy. We hope that the ideas and resources provided in this chapter will assist those who treat women with eating disorders in doing so. We hope that conducting religious and spiritual assessments of patients with eating disorders will soon become an accepted, standard practice among helping professionals.

7

SPIRITUAL INTERVENTIONS FOR INDIVIDUAL, GROUP, AND FAMILY THERAPY

In this chapter, we describe a variety of interventions that we use when conducting individual, group, and family therapy with patients with eating disorders. The interventions described in this chapter are often useful for helping patients to (a) challenge and modify unhealthy and inaccurate perceptions of God and self, (b) overcome feelings of shame and unworthiness, (c) alter distorted body image, (d) affirm their spiritual nature, and (e) gain a clearer sense of life's purpose and meaning. Ultimately, these interventions can help patients learn to listen again to their hearts, reaffirm their sense of spiritual identity and worth, and reconnect with God and significant others.

INDIVIDUAL THERAPY INTERVENTIONS FOR PATIENTS WITH EATING DISORDERS

During individual therapy with patients who have expressed interest in exploring their spirituality, we encourage a variety of spiritual practices that may help promote their spiritual growth and well-being, thereby helping them to better cope with and overcome their eating disorder. We find it important to work within the patient's belief system and to avoid prescribing interventions that may conflict with her religious beliefs and values.

Spiritual Discussions and Education

Some patients with eating disorders have acquired distorted and dysfunctional religious and spiritual beliefs from their families of origin; thus, a major therapeutic task is to help them become aware of, examine, and modify these cognitions. In this cognitive restructuring process, we frequently discuss patients' religious and spiritual conceptions with the goal of helping them examine whether their beliefs are consistent with their own theology and are having a healthy impact on their lives. Sometimes we share our spiritual beliefs and understandings about an issue, and at other times, we encourage patients to study the sacred writings of their religious tradition or consult with religious leaders from their tradition to clarify doctrinal misunderstandings that are contributing to her emotional distress.

We discuss a wide variety of spiritual concepts with our patients depending on their issues and religious beliefs. For example, we often have discussions about God's love and grace, forgiveness, prayer, love and service, honesty, human suffering, imperfections, and so on. Many patients with eating disorders are developmentally delayed in emotional and spiritual matters due to the negative spiritual impact of their eating disorder, and giving them opportunities to discuss emotional and spiritual concepts is often helpful to them.

Sacred Writings

One way that we teach our patients spiritual concepts is by asking them to read scriptures (e.g., Bible, Koran) and other spiritual literature about topics such as forgiveness, grace, love, guilt, trust, spiritual identity and worth, the role of suffering and pain, and transcending parental transgression. Spiritual literature may help patients challenge and modify dysfunctional religious beliefs as they explore the consistency or inconsistency between their beliefs and the core teachings of their religious tradition as set forth in scripture or other authoritative writings.

In addition, many spiritual writings are laced with powerful stories and metaphors about the human condition from which patients can gain insight and inspiration. Some patients find that reading and pondering spiritual writings helps them feel an inner harmony and peace, giving them comfort, perspective, meaning, and strength. Some patients report feeling more secure and grounded spiritually in their feelings of identity and self-esteem after reading such literature.

Prayer

We often pray privately for our patients and encourage them to pray privately for themselves and for others outside of therapy sessions, according to the patient's belief in, comfort with, and desire for prayer. Because praying with patients in-session can cause role boundary confusion and transference issues (Richards & Bergin, 1997; Richards & Potts, 1995), we avoid this practice.

Many of our patients do not know how to pray specifically and directly about their needs and concerns; some feel that they don't deserve to pray or pray for themselves. We encourage our patients to pray according to their beliefs, referring those who do not share our religious beliefs to their spiritual leaders for guidance. In praying for themselves and others, we encourage our patients to be specific, direct, and honest, looking to God for guidance and for validation instead of seeking validation exclusively from other people.

Prayer can be a powerful resource to assist religious patients in their coping, healing, and growth. Much evidence indicates that people who pray feel better, both physically and emotionally (Dossey, 1993). We have found prayer to be a powerful practice for helping patients with eating disorders learn to accept their body image. Some of our patients have told us that the only way they could see their body differently, or accept it as God-given, was by praying that their distorted body image would leave them. Prayer also seems to help our patients feel less isolated and more hopeful, accepting, and optimistic. At times our patients have reported powerful experiences of insight and healing during moments of prayer.

Imagery

Using imagery in therapy can be powerful not only in helping clients talk about experiences in their past, people in their lives, and their vision for the future, but also in seeing these things and feeling them inside their minds and hearts. Imagery can be used in many ways and for many issues: finding understanding and compassion for the "little child" of their past, visiting with a "wise man or woman" and receiving advice and counsel, using imagery in conjunction with empty-chair techniques for resolving issues with significant others, creating safe places, and having vivid remembrances of successes and positive experiences in life. Imagery should only be done if the therapist is trained or experienced in using such techniques. It may be contraindicated for patients with severe trauma, severe dissociative symptoms, or psychotic features unless the therapist has expertise or expert supervision. Imagery allows patients to see and understand in ways for which words can be insufficient.

Imagery with patients can be spiritual as well as emotional. Imagery is guided by the inside inclinations of the patient in response to the directions of the therapist. Spiritual places, people, or messages can be included in these imagery journeys. Seeing themselves or their lives with "new eyes" can be motivating, healing, and self-correcting as emotional and spiritual interventions.

Uplifting and Sacred Music

Sacred or uplifting music can speak to patients' minds and hearts in powerful ways and give them hope, comfort, direction, and inspiration. It can soften their hearts and lift their spirits. Encouraging clients to find an uplifting song and share the lyrics and its personal meaning or impact with their therapist can help validate the role of music as a healing and spiritual resource. Sometimes we ask patients to choose a song that represents for them the way they want to live during a period of time. We then encourage them to listen to this song often, so that the lyrics and music can serve as a regular reminder of how they want to be. Often patients will share with us sacred or spiritual experiences that they have had in response to sacred or life-confirming music.

Encouraging Forgiveness

Much has been written recently about the importance of forgiveness in healing and therapy. Research indicates it to be one of the most frequently used spiritual interventions in psychotherapy (Richards & Bergin, 1997). Helping our patients with eating disorders to forgive others, themselves, and God is important in the healing process. Many patients find it hard to forgive parents or others who have hurt or abused them or to acknowledge that they feel disappointment, resentment, and anger toward God; thus, it is often helpful to frame forgiveness as a gift or choice, not a requirement or condition.

Some patients have particular difficulty with self-forgiveness because feelings of shame and spiritual unworthiness cause them to believe they do not deserve to be forgiven. We try to help these patients receive God's forgiveness and mercy instead of denying it. All of the major Western religious traditions include teachings about the love and mercy of God, so when it seems relevant, we emphasize such teachings to our patients to help them understand self-forgiveness as a healing process that includes responsibility and accountability but not self-punishment.

Forgiveness should not be rushed: Intense feelings of hurt, disappointment, anger, and rage must often be acknowledged, re-experienced, and worked through before patients are ready to forgive. To "foreclose" on these emotions and prematurely forgive gets many patients into trouble emotionally because they must deny their feelings of hurt, disappointment, resentment, and anger over what they have suffered. Because many of our patients with eating disorders are already repressing their emotions, prematurely encouraging them to forgive others would exacerbate this problem. Once patients have worked through the difficult emotions associated with their abuse or severe neglect (i.e., shock, denial, awareness and recognition, hurt, shame, grief, anger, and rage), forgiveness becomes possible. A profound healing and peace occurs when patients are able to forgive themselves and others.

Carrying the Burden

This activity can help patients experience the physical sensations of carrying a heavy emotional burden and help them get in touch with deeper feelings about carrying such burdens. The burden might be their eating disorder, guilt for some act in the past, shame, self-hatred, or responsibility for someone else's life or happiness. The therapist may give the patient a rock, a box, or another heavy or awkward object and ask her to carry it with her everywhere she goes for the next few days or weeks. She should be encouraged to notice the ways that the burden interferes with her daily life and to talk honestly about what she is learning and feeling as she carries it. (The therapist should be sure that the burden is not heavy or awkward enough to cause any physical damage to the patient from carrying it.)

Carrying heavy burdens internally is an experience that many women with eating disorders have become well acquainted with over the course of the illness. The burdens of grief, regret, sadness, shame, disappointment, and other heartaches need to be lifted and resolved but the patient's patterns of avoidance and numbness prevent the healing that needs to occur. Giving up or letting go of their burdens to a higher power can bring relief, a sensation of lightness, and healing.

Wearing a Sign: Making the Implicit Explicit

As themes emerge in therapy about core messages the patient may communicate in her relationships with others that either push others away or prevent her from allowing their love and support into her life, she can write these and other messages on a card and wear the card in an obvious place (e.g., worn as a necklace). Discussions in therapy sessions can be focused around the messages: what she really wants to say, how she might make direct communication, how she might meet needs in a healthy way, and what she desires to change. As she becomes acutely aware of a negative message and gets tired of giving the same old message, she can begin to replace old messages with new ones.

The signs may be used alternatively to help change inside messages. The patient can write down self-rejecting messages she constantly gives herself—for example "I'm no good," "I'm afraid to look stupid," "No one can accept me, I don't deserve it," "I'll let everybody down," "I am weak"—and put out the appropriate sign to fit the inside messages occurring in any given situation. These messages can be assessed and discussed until the patient is ready to change them to more self-affirming or kind internal statements. The therapist can ask the patient to wear and act on new positive signs for a period of time.

To create positive self-expectancy and hope, the patient must stop negating core messages of self-contempt. Listening to the heart may require a patient first to increase her awareness and honestly appraise the negative messages she is sending to herself, God, and significant others. The process of changing or replacing the negative messages can be a matter of trusting her heart again and being "on her side" with self-affirming, kind, and respectful inner messages.

General Letter Writing

Therapeutic writing assignments can be powerful in helping clients clarify, understand, and face their feelings toward themselves, others, and their eating disorder. The completed letters can be read in session and processed, and they can, in certain circumstances, be read to individuals, families, or groups. The letters can be framed for the patient not only as symbols of her work and growth but as preparation for further therapeutic work. Letters to perpetrators or hurtful significant others can also be a part of a healing process. Letters to self can be a part of self-forgiveness and preparation for imagery or other self-messages to aid in the healing childhood hurts or in changing unhealthy childhood beliefs.

Letters of the heart to self, God, and others open the door to truth. Asking patients to write down everything they know in their hearts that needs to be said is a powerful validating message. They can stop lying, hiding, or minimizing the messages of their honest hearts, and, in giving voice to their deepest truths and desires, they can find their true selves.

Letters to the Eating Disorder

Writing letters to the eating disorder can elicit powerful feelings and increase awareness and recognition of the roles and functions of the eating disorder in the patient's life. It is also helpful to have family members write honest and descriptive letters to their loved one's eating disorder and to have them read these in family therapy. Such letters reveal the intensity of the relationship between the individual and the disorder and reflect the pain and suffering of all family members and for everyone else involved in the illness. These letters can move patients emotionally toward a desire to let go of the illness. Reading letters out loud in session can increase the impact of this intervention.

The eating disorder is not who the patient is no matter how true that belief may feel inside her mind. Those letters reveal how patients have lost their sense of identity to the rules and demands of their anorexia and bulimia. Hearing and seeing what their parents, husbands, and other family members have to say to their eating disorder can be a painful awakening. In a spiritual sense, coming to know that their God does not see them as the eating disorder nor want them to have an eating disorder can be a powerful incentive to move toward recovery.

Solo Time

Creating structural opportunities for clients to spend time alone for a 1- to 4-hour period can be helpful to patients who are stable and not in danger of self-harm. This is a time in which they can focus on the internal aspects of self and spiritual understandings without distractions from the outside. During this solo time they can self-reflect, listen to themselves, and write down the quiet insights, feelings, or impressions that come to them. They can also, if desired, pray or meditate and later share their written insights and experiences in therapy. Solo time can be a powerful intervention to help them learn to listen to themselves and trust what they sense and hear.

Being alone in a secluded place with the only motive being to listen to the quiet impressions of the heart or the whisperings of spiritual influences is both calming and uplifting. The writings of the heart from these solo times are inspiring and powerful messages and guidance to aid in recovery. Most patients report that they get better at this listening process as time goes on.

Creating a Help Sheet

Some patients need extra help and reminders in times of stress, difficulty, or emotional upset. Writing down and compiling several pages of helpful hints, thoughts, or strategies that have come out of therapy sessions over time can become a supportive structure to them. When in doubt, they can review the help sheets and remind themselves of better choices or responses they might use to face a situation, an eating disorder trigger, or a dilemma they may face at a given moment. Following the suggestions or hints on the help sheet reminds them of their power to make choices and it can empower them to choose positive or "self-care" strategies to deal with their current stressors.

Everyone needs reminders, and everyone needs help recovering from an eating disorder. In stressful and triggering moments, a patient may be tempted to return to what she knew in the past. Asking a patient to "delay or pause" in these moments and to use the help sheet to remember what she truly wants to do differently is supportive. For a religious patient, scriptures, holy writ, books, recited prayers, and other spiritual reminders can serve the same important purpose.

"How I'm Doing" Letters

A therapist may ask a client to write short weekly or biweekly letters honestly and candidly discussing her fears, struggles, secrets, experiences, and needs without the pressure of having to say these out loud. The client can mail or bring these letters to session to discuss the content in a nonthreatening way. Discussing some of the information revealed in the letters can build rapport and open up therapeutic communication. As time goes on, patients can add "what I'm going to do" or "what I am doing" segments to these update letters.

Prayer is a most important form of communicating the "how I'm doing" messages for spiritual or religious patients. Checking in regularly with God to give updates on difficulties, challenges, progress, special requests, and gratitude provides comfort and a defense against feeling alone in recovery. Many patients report how good it feels to be back in communication with their God or a higher power.

Journaling

Having clients journal at bedtime or at another regular time can provide time for them to listen to themselves and pay attention to internal experiences they had during the day. In the beginning stages of therapy, journaling can help patients pay attention to eating disorder patterns, their emotional experiences, and the important connection between emotions and an eating disorder. This can help patients come to a better understanding of eating disorder triggers, thoughts, and behaviors and the issues for which the disorder becomes the distraction. Reading journal entries from the past can also give patients a sense of the progress they are making in recovery over the course of treatment. Therapists can ask patients to write down daily "miracles" that they have noticed or three things about themselves that they feel proud of or good about from that day.

A patient willing to write down her thoughts and feelings on paper is opening her heart to learn new things about herself. A willingness to learn or to be taught is a humble approach to change and recovery. Writing down spiritual or uplifting experiences in a journal shows a patient how far she has come and how much she has learned or grown on her road to recovery. Journals can be used for promoting spiritual understanding, challenging negative thoughts and feelings, keeping track of learning, and many other therapeutic purposes.

GROUP INTERVENTIONS FOR PATIENTS WITH EATING DISORDERS

When using spiritual interventions during group therapy, a therapist must be careful to respect patients' unique religious beliefs so that they do not feel coerced into discussions or practices that make them uncomfortable. We frequently remind group members about the importance of respecting each other and seeking to understand and tolerate differences in religious and spiritual beliefs and practices. We encourage them to learn from their differences and to support each other in their own personal spiritual journeys. We emphasize that they have the right of refusal—the right to decline participation in spiritual discussions or practices with which they do not feel comfortable.

Kneeling at the Shrine of the Eating Disorder

An object representing the eating disorder is placed in the center of the room on a chair or table, and each group member is asked to kneel at the shrine and talk to the eating disorder about why it has been the most important thing in her life and what it has cost her. All group members participate to express their deep and honest feelings toward their eating disorder. Each member participates in this typically intense and emotional activity. Following individual sharing, the group processes the experience.

Sometimes when using this intervention, we have asked a religious or spiritual woman, "What have you given up to worship anorexia and bulimia?" Through many tears and soul-wrenching expressions, we have heard over and over: "I have lost the ability to think; I have lost the ability to care and to feel warmth for others; I have lost love of my family; I have lost hope; I have lost faith; I have lost God; I have lost the ability to do what I love to do; I have lost peace." And then we may ask her to be honest and tell what worshiping the eating disorder has given her. Almost always, the woman will say, "Misery, pain, numbness, feeling out of control, loss of dignity, isolation, nothing good."

At other times, we may have a group member give voice to the eating disorder shrine and interact with the woman kneeling before it. Issues connected to resisting temptation, confronting messages of the devil, fighting between the light and darkness, and so on can come up in these interchanges. On occasion, we have had parents and siblings witness and also participate in this group activity of talking to the eating disorder, with powerful results including spiritual messages.

Body Image Exercise

A group member struggling with unrelenting self-hatred and loathing of her body is invited to the center to stand in the middle of a small group. With her eyes closed, she is guided to imagine everyone in the group staring at her body, especially the parts of her body she dislikes. As the person gets in touch with her painful feelings about her body, she can be guided to examine where those feelings came from, discover what beliefs and decisions were born in those early painful experiences of childhood, and make new decisions, commitments, and promises from that point onward. Self-compassion and compassion from others can often be felt and then used in self-healing as well as healing within the group. A patient's experience with rejection, pain, and body hatred can begin to heal.

Some patients have reported a spiritual awareness of God's compassion for them in relation to the painful events and feelings of body hatred. Others have talked about giving up their self-hatred toward their "little-girl self" and feeling love and compassion for her in her times of confusion and distress, saying that this compassion brought feelings of spiritual peace and comfort to them. By the end of the activity, they have reported that they felt like God was encouraging them to see their little-girl self for who she really was and to love and accept her.

Hiding Behind the Wall

This group activity can be done with a few members of the group inside the larger group circle, or it can be done by having every group member participate throughout the room. The facilitator can bring in large pieces of cardboard (3 × 4 feet) or large cushion pillows to be used as props to represent the wall. Group members break up into dyads and sit facing their partner with one member of the dyad holding the cardboard or pillow in front of her in a protective and self-hiding fashion. The partner behind the barrier tells her partner honestly why she is hiding what she is hiding, what she does not want other people to see, why she is afraid to show her real self, what she is trying to protect herself from with this wall, and why she put up the wall in the first place, for example. Her partner can ask clarifying questions and give feedback about how it feels to be on the outside of the wall. We process the experiences, observations, and emotions that have emerged during the activity as a group. At times, the facilitator can ask individual group members to create from behind the wall, for the group to witness, past relationship scenes with family members and friends. Participants then return to dyads and explore ways to take down the wall, revealing themselves honestly to their partners. Questions can be asked again to facilitate the sharing without the wall.

The protective wall is intended to keep hurt and rejection from occurring in their relationships. The problem is that the wall keeps them in and alone and keeps out honesty, love, and support from others. In a spiritual sense, some patients have come to feel so negative about themselves that the wall is meant to keep God out or to keep them away from God as a form of self-punishment (e.g., "I don't deserve God's love or kindness" or "I am afraid that God will reject me, too"). If spiritual content comes up in the activity with patients, it is a powerful intervention to role-play their relationship with God with the wall up between the patient and God and then with the wall down. Patients can give awareness and insights into how they are keeping the wall up between self and God.

Enactment of the Negative Mind

Patients who are struggling with strong negative voices in their minds take the middle position in a triad. When cued, the other two members begin to talk into the central patient's ears. One voice represents the negative mind; the other speaks as the positive or validating mind. The central patient listens to the voices and experiences the intense conflict of what they tell her; she expresses her feelings, explores her ability to quiet the negative mind, and exercises her power to embrace the messages of the positive mind.

The goal of both voices is to convince the center patient that her messages are true and accurate. For the negative side, we ask the patients to tell the woman in the middle all of the painful and negative messages that they constantly tell themselves. The positive messages are to be (a) the affirming and validating messages they want to hear and believe, (b) messages spoken to others that they have heard and rejected or minimized in their lives, or (c) all the beliefs and messages they personally hold for the person in the middle of the triad.

In processing this activity, some patients talk about how it felt like an inner battle for their soul and spirit or a battle between God and the devil, light and darkness, or good and evil. Some express the sense of despair and hopelessness they felt listening to the negative mind and the hope and peace they felt listening to the positive mind. Some have even described the positive messages to be like the voice of their guardian angel.

The Tree of Life

A live tree is placed in the middle of the group room on the floor. The therapist gives a brief statement about life, growth, energy, development, the choice to live or be alive, and choices about "living" versus "surviving." The patients are invited as a group to create a live spatial and nonverbal sculpture of their commitment to living, recovering, and giving up their eating disorder, each representing the nature of her commitment by the way she places herself in proximity to the "tree of life." Each patient in the group is asked to share her feelings and self-assessment of her commitment to live and to let go of her eating disorder.

The visual and spatial images of patients' commitment to life bring them out of their denial or avoidance of responsibility and choice. They can see and feel where they are and what they are choosing. This realization for some women has resulted in deep emotional and spiritual grief and mourning over the loss of living caused by the eating disorder. Many religious-minded women associate life and the tree of life with spiritual significance and meaning. Some have shared how it felt as if they were choosing between spiritual life or worldly death through the eating disorder rather than embracing the aliveness that comes from being close and in tune with God who is the giver of life, for example. There is often an outpouring of love and support among group members as they struggle in the pursuit of life rather than succumbing to fears of their eating disorder.

The Creation of a Horse: Who I Am Versus What I Do

Group members are given a blank piece of unlined paper and instructed to stand in a circle as a group, facing each other with their hands behind their backs and both hands holding the piece of paper. They are then instructed to tear out a horse, with their hands behind their back, being unable to see and only feel with their hands what they are doing. When all participants are done creating their horse, they are asked to put the horse in front of them, holding it with both hands. One by one, each is asked to present her horse, stating, "This is my horse, and it represents me." After presenting the horse, group members are asked to share their experience and feelings. The experience can be mined for themes around achievement and performance: who I am versus what I do, perfectionism, shame, fears of sharing self, and fears of not being "good enough" in the eyes of others.

Externalization of self is often a significant expression of anorexia and bulimia. The sense of having to do everything perfect for God and others to be acceptable is an emotional and spiritual issue that is shared in the group processing. The idea that God and others can still love and accept them in their less than perfect performance and that achievement is only a small expression of who they really are has helped some patients to begin releasing some of the internal pressures and expectations of perfection.

A Sculpture of the Group Around Commitment

A person well on the road to recovery and with some leadership responsibilities and abilities in the group is asked to do a sculpture of the group around a center focal point in the room, and that client sculpts each member of the group in proximity to the central focal point based on their perception of each person's commitment to "change" and to giving up her eating disorder and related self-destructive behaviors and beliefs. It is a great structural and experiential way to give feedback and to allow for self-exploration and "looking in the emotional mirror." Each group member is invited to respond, sharing feelings and reactions about where she was placed in the sculpture and having the opportunity to put herself in the place she feels is true and accurate for her commitment to change.

Being preoccupied about how other people view them is a big issue for patients with eating disorders. Feeling misunderstood or judged by someone else can trigger old, painful feelings. At an emotional level it takes courage and openness to give and receive honest feedback about any important area and to "stick up" for oneself, if necessary, in a direct and assertive fashion. The key is to remember that no one can really hide where they are in important matters. Once in a while, negative images of God or feelings of shame and unworthiness come up for participants in this activity. We try to help them understand that courage and openness are needed to receive and give honest feedback to others and to God and to speak up for themselves at times when necessary rather than give up and be quiet.

Feedback on Paper

Group members are all given a piece of paper and a pen. They are asked to put their name at the top of the paper. Each person then passes her paper to the left; every person in the group writes some positive and negative feedback on each group member's paper. After the paper passing and writing is complete, the paper is returned to the owner, and each member processes her feelings and reactions to the feedback. It is helpful to have the group clarify and further explain the feedback given. It can help if the facilitator starts by giving a message about perceptions versus reality, giving gifts to others through feedback, "if the shoe fits wear it, if not let it go," the importance of good intentions when giving feedback to others, and also how both receiving and giving can be a gift.

Listening to and receiving positive feedback and messages is a crucial aspect for emotional and spiritual recovery from an eating disorder. Learning how to use helpful negative feedback and to let go of someone else's perceptions that do not really apply can help in letting go of negative self-feedback and messages that get in the way of a spiritual relationship with God. The questions "What seems accurate and what doesn't?" and "What do I keep and let in and what do I let go of?" can help with this process. Receiving affirming as well as correcting spiritual and relational messages leads to healing, self-correction, and change.

Shame Secrets Take a Step Out of the Closet

The group leader initially discusses shame, its sources, and the role of others in healing from it. He or she may also discuss the damage of keeping secrets versus sharing them and give patients permission not to share any specific secrets. The difference between openness and honesty can be explained, and the value of giving others a chance to have their own feelings toward us rather than us "reading feelings and thoughts into their minds" as if our "mind reads" of their thoughts is their truth. The group leader asks all participants to write a secret about which they feel some shame on a piece of paper and place it in a hat. The therapist then informs all members that during the process of the group, members may identify themselves and "own" their secret, or they may remain anonymous. Then a volunteer reads each secret, giving time between each secret for anyone to share her thoughts, feelings, reactions, or similar experiences. Following the reading and discussion of all secrets on paper, the group members are given time to own and talk about their secret and to share feelings, if anyone chooses to do so. The importance of confidentiality, the sacredness of sharing of oneself, and respect should be emphasized as a part of this activity.

Hidden secrets are part of the painful energy that feeds a person's shame about herself. As long as she feels too ashamed to tell or share her hidden secrets to God or others, she remains trapped in the lies of the shame. Often patients learn from this activity that other people are compassionate and loving toward them as they tell their secrets, and this emotional experience increases their hope that God will be accepting of them even with their secrets. Taking ownership for hidden acts is the necessary step before someone is able to let go of the shame of it.

Let Us See What Is Most Important to You

The group members are asked to bring to group several items from their homes or rooms that represent or symbolize what is most important in their lives. Each member places those items in front of them as the group members sit in a circle on the floor. Each member tells the group about the items she chose, their symbolic meaning, and what they represent, and each shares feelings related to each object. Following this sharing, participants are asked to turn their back on these precious things and turn around and face the outside of the group, away from the inner circle where those important things are placed. The group members are asked to process their feelings of loss, hurt, anger, sadness, and fear related to the loss of these important things in their lives and to talk about how their eating disorders are something that turns them away or takes them away from that which is most important to them. The activity can also address issues of commitment, congruence or incongruence between their stated messages of "what's important" and their behaviors. Therapy discussions can also address the need to grieve losses and make hopeful plans for the future. Group members then turn and face again that which is most important and are invited to share feelings, desires, and commitments to make needed changes.

For many women suffering with eating disorders, the symbolic objects of importance in this activity include spiritually based objects. The objects often symbolize their faith in God, love, family, religion, hope, truth, friendship, education or learning, peace, future dreams, spiritual influences, family legacies and traditions, and so on. To turn their backs symbolically on what means the most to them to pursue an eating disorder reminds them all of how much they have given up emotionally and spiritually over the course of the illness.

Dyads for Awareness of the Eating Disorder Impact

In pairs, the group members sit facing each other as dyads in two chairs. The dyads are given sentence stems to complete and discuss with each other. Taking turns, directed according to time limits by the prompts of the therapist, they are asked to say whatever comes to their minds in completing each sentence. They continue responding to each sentence stem until the group leader asks them to stop. The sentence stems might include the following: "One way my eating disorder has hurt me is . . . ," "One way my eating disorder has hurt my loved ones is . . . ," "One way my eating disorder has betrayed me is . . . ," "One way my eating disorder has affected my spirituality in a negative way is . . ." These sentence stems can be modified to meet the pressing needs of the group. Participants frequently trade chairs and work with new partners to increase interaction and to allow participants to get to know more individuals in the group. Afterward, the group members can process what they learned and felt.

A patient has difficulty listening to her heart again if she has to be too careful about what she says to others. This exercise encourages the women to trust what comes to them as they respond to the sentence stems and to listen and learn from themselves as truths, insights, and information emerge with each question. When we ask a patient to pray from her heart to God, she undergoes a similar experience. She can simply say what comes to her, hold nothing back, and tell God what is true in her heart and mind. In addition, as she listens with her heart to the answers, insights, and truths that come to her heart in response to those prayers, she can also learn new questions to ask God and enlarge her spiritual understandings.

Love and Tissues

If one individual in the group has extreme difficulty accepting or noticing love from others, a group activity can be arranged. The patient is asked to sit in the center of the group circle, and the other group members are given boxes or piles of white tissues. Each member is invited to approach the person in the center who is to be "the recipient of loving messages," and kneel or sit in front of her to share loving observations or positive feelings. With each statement of love, the speaker places a white tissue in the recipient's hands or lap. As each person expresses love and places a tissue, the distressed woman holds a visual manifestation of the love and support offered to her. After the activity, the woman with the tissues and all group members can process and describe their feelings. The facilitator may suggest that the recipient keep the tissues as a reminder of the love others have for her. If the group is small, every group member may have an opportunity to be the recipient of loving messages.

Many patients with eating disorders have lost the ability to feel love, or, because of their fears, they have refused to receive the love given or expressed to them. This exercise gives the recipient a concrete way to see the love and open her heart to the feelings of love in the room and in her life. Receiving love from God and the other significant people in her life is a significant healing experience.

Giving Permission

Many patients with eating disorders lack trust and confidence in themselves, and they may want others to tell them what to do; they may wait for others to take care of them. This "waiting" is often in place of listening to and supporting themselves or of giving themselves permission to feel, think, desire, or seek whatever they choose. This group activity helps make explicit the process of giving oneself permission. A group member picks another person in the group to represent her, taking a seat in front of the representative. By talking to the "representative of self," the individual symbolically gives herself permission, for example, to feel, believe, act, care for herself, and take risks in any way that she truly desires but has lacked the self-confidence to do in the past. The therapist can prompt and help deepen the support and "permissions" the client needs to give to herself.

Other members of the group can repeat this procedure for themselves, and then process the experiences of the activity.

Sometimes patients are waiting for God or other people to give them permission for what they already know or desire in their hearts. This waiting for permission "to be," "to act," "to feel," and "to change," is really a way to avoid the emotional or spiritual vulnerability and discomfort of being in new or unfamiliar territory. Some patients need to give God permission in their hearts and minds to speak to them, to help them, to love them, and to empower them after they have given themselves permission for the same things.

What Does the Line Mean for You?

The therapist uses masking tape to make a 10-foot line in the middle of the floor. Each member of the group is asked to stand up to the line, one at a time, and tell what the line means to them. Because the line can have many meanings, this activity can open up discussions on topics such as crossing emotional boundaries, taking risks, taking a stand, holding themselves back, taking a leap of faith, and opening up to others. Having the therapist and group members give reactions and feedback to individual members at the line can open up therapeutic interactions and lead to further actions and interpretations in relation to the line.

A spiritual dilemma for some religious patients in the course and development of the eating disorder is that they have fallen away from or wandered from many of the moral and spiritual values. If the line represents the "straight and narrow path" or an extreme standard of perfection in spiritual matters, then being far away from the line can be evidence, proof, or punishment for being weak, sinful, or bad. The woman can then feel unworthy and hopeless of ever being able to come back and live in harmony with the spiritual line. This activity can be used to broaden their images of forgiveness, self-forgiveness, and self-correction as they undertake the process of getting back to where they want to be in religious life without the self-sabotage or self-punishment.

FAMILY THERAPY INTERVENTIONS FOR PATIENTS WITH EATING DISORDERS

When working with families, therapists must be sensitive to individual differences in the degree of comfort with theistic therapy. Not all family members may be receptive to such approaches. Deep differences in religious belief and practice may exist, and spirituality may be an intensely emotional issue. In addition, some family members may use religion as a weapon or means of control during conflicts (Richards & Bergin, 2005). Spiritual interventions may be appropriate for some family members, but not for all. With sensitivity to such possibilities, we have found that the interventions described in this section can be used in family therapy without compromising treatment efforts with the patient or family.

Father–Daughter Dance

At the conclusion of a family group session or a multiple family therapy group session stressing love, trust, support, and positive intentions in family relationships, music is played, and the patients and their fathers are invited to stand in "slow-dance position" and dance together. They are gently urged to allow feelings to emerge, considering the dance to symbolize their future relationship including their commitment to continuing to build and improve their relationship into the future. The therapist may furnish prompts for expressing feelings and making commitments, and the dance can symbolize a healing or renewing relationship, either current or future.

Sometimes issues of a negative image of God or feelings of being neglected or abandoned by God can emerge in individual therapy after this activity. Typically the father–daughter dance feels powerful and healing for the patients, providing hope for resolving dissonance or conflicts with their own father, if needed, as well as with God.

Blind Walk Through the Mine Field

A large room is prepared with an obstacle course of books, chairs, and other items strewn randomly yet tightly throughout the room. The client is led into the room blindfolded, and the family is brought into the room. The family is asked to take chosen positions around the outside edges of the room. The client is placed on one end of the room with instructions to find her way to the other side of the room without touching any object on the floor with any part of her body. She is further informed that touching any object will mean she must start over at the original spot and that the activity may take as long as needed, up to 4 hours. The family is instructed to help the patient across but only with words, and they must stay in their places outside of the obstacle course. As the patient and family journey through this experience, issues arise, including frustration, anger, helplessness, control, coping styles, helping styles, leadership, and family roles. The patient can be guided to discuss what it is like to navigate through recovery, and the family members can talk about their desires to help, their feelings of powerlessness, and their style or approaches to support—whether they are helpful or nonhelpful.

Life can often feel like a frightening and hazardous place for women with eating disorders. Giving up control and relying on others for direction and safety is a big trust challenge. Relying on spiritual influences and guidance requires them to relinquish control and surrender spiritually—forms of progress that can be discussed in therapy sessions in relation to this activity.

What Has It Been Like, What Is It Like

The family participates in a therapy session during which each member discusses what it has been like to have a loved one with an eating disorder and describes the impact of that disorder on their lives, feelings, and relationship with the patient. The patient is then asked to discuss her eating disorder—what it is like, what it has done to her life, and how she feels about it. In the early stages of treatment, this session increases the patient's awareness of the impact of her eating disorder on others, and it can also help to increase understanding across the family. Empathy and compassion within the family can become stronger as members get past frustration and into more tender emotions of hurt, fear, and love.

The impact of an eating disorder is significant for everyone whose life touches the sufferer. As patients and their families talk about the costs and consequences of anorexia or bulimia on relationships, many talk about spiritual losses, fears, and complications.

Truth, Ownership, and Forgiveness

In a family session, the patient has prepared herself to tell the truth about her eating disorder and to be thorough in doing so; she includes secrets, dishonest acts, manipulations, and deceptions, and she explains the impact of her actions on each family member. Each family member is asked to identify any hurtful acts he or she has done or negative feelings felt toward the patient related or unrelated to the eating disorder. All are encouraged to tell the truth without minimization. Each family member is then asked to approach the other family members, express feelings, and ask for forgiveness. If a patient or family members tend to minimize their hurtful behavior and its impact, the experience can be enhanced by having those asking forgiveness kneel in front of the person who is being asked to forgive.

Telling the whole truth and pursuing forgiveness instead of deception, manipulation, or self-defense can be an important healing intervention in the context of family therapy. Humility and genuineness enable honest relationship communication and forgiveness; these family interactions and processes can be extended for matters of the heart and for spiritual renewal.

Stacking the Books: Ownership, Responsibility, and Barriers

When issues arise in family therapy concerning personal responsibility over the eating disorder, other issues and feelings, such as marital happiness, individual happiness, or choices about health and wellness, may also arise. For this intervention, the family sits around a table that holds a stack of books that is at least five feet tall. The therapist or the family members can divide up the books proportionate to the responsibility each family member carries. Stacks of books can also be used as symbols of barriers in relationships, symbolizing how family members cannot see each other because of barriers. Feelings and reactions about barriers and responsibility can be shared and understandings solidified when members see the burden of responsibility or the barriers to each other in a visual form and experience those things physically as well as emotionally.

This family activity can be followed by a therapeutic discussion examining the barriers or obstacles that prevent spiritually minded patients from seeing the hand of God or providence in their daily lives. Exploring the effects of false guilt, shame, or overresponsibility on the patient or her family members and helping them understand new concepts of responsibility, accountability, and choices in relationships can be a turning point for lightening the heavy loads of false beliefs.

Family Eating Disorder Sculpture

The purpose of this intervention is for each family member to create "pictures," visually and spatially, of the patient's family, representing personal perceptions of the family and the place of the eating disorder within it. As the patient and each family member process aloud their emotional reactions to these sculptures, they become more aware of and open about the impact of the disorder on the family. This activity and period of sharing can lead to an open discussion on how the family could live together without the eating disorder as an unwanted "extra" family member. It is important to stress that although the illness is unwanted, the patient is very much wanted and loved in the family. One message of this activity is the importance of getting new or more accurate perspectives on old images and views to make spiritual shifts, strengthen faith, and create positive energy and progress.

CONCLUSION

The spiritual interventions that we encourage and emphasize during treatment depend on the client's own beliefs. We always permit clients to take the lead in their own spiritual journey and recovery. When incorporating a spiritual perspective into recovery from eating disorders, therapists must respect each client's perspective and simply encourage her to open the door to spiritual influences within the context of her beliefs (Lewis, 2001; Richards & Bergin, 1997, 2000). We have found that important spiritual needs, issues, and themes can and do emerge in response to individual, group, and family therapy interventions. Therapeutic acceptance and encouragement of spiritual or religious connections and discussion within the therapy process has been helpful for many patients and their families.

8

A SPIRITUALITY GROUP FOR PATIENTS WITH EATING DISORDERS

In this chapter, we describe a structured spirituality group and workbook that we have been using for several years in our treatment center. We describe the findings of an experimental outcome study that evaluated the effectiveness of the group in an inpatient treatment setting. We provide information to assist practitioners who are interested in using the spirituality group and workbook in inpatient or outpatient settings.

OVERVIEW OF THE SPIRITUALITY GROUP

When patients are admitted to our treatment center, they are invited to attend a spirituality group and to read *Spiritual Renewal: A Journey of Faith and Healing* (Richards, Hardman, & Berrett, 2000), a self-help workbook that we wrote for our patients with eating disorders, which includes scriptural and other spiritual readings and educational materials about topics such as faith in God, adversity, spiritual identity, life purpose and meaning, responsibility, forgiveness, congruence, balance, love, belonging, gratitude, and spiritual harmony. Patients in the inpatient and residential treatment programs attend the spirituality group once a week for 60 minutes. A senior psychologist on the treatment staff leads the group.

The spirituality group is optional in our treatment program. Although patients are given permission to skip this group, less than 1% of patients have chosen not to participate. We find that almost all patients enjoy and benefit from the spirituality group, although the nature of patients' participation and the benefits they receive seems to change depending on the stage they have reached in their treatment and recovery. For example, although the spirituality group helps to instill hope and encourages patients to begin looking at their faith and spirituality as potential resources in their recovery, many patients are so depressed, physically malnourished, and shameful during the first few weeks of inpatient treatment that they are unable to participate fully in or benefit from the spirituality class. Later during inpatient and residential treatment, patients are usually in a healthier place physically and emotionally and can participate and benefit more fully from the group and workbook readings. They are also more capable of taking advantage of quiet, solo times during their schedules to ponder, pray, feel, and reflect on spiritual issues. Patients in the residential treatment program also assume some leadership in the spirituality group by preparing and presenting materials from the workbook readings, as well as supplemental material about spirituality that they think may be helpful to other patients.

During the weekly group meetings, the group leader encourages the patients to discuss spiritual thoughts and feelings they have experienced during the past week—both uplifting experiences and thoughts as well as spiritual challenges and struggles they may have experienced. The group leader also asks the patients to share what they learned that week from the workbook readings and exercises. With inpatients, the group leader also makes a brief presentation about the most critical points of content and principles of the next assigned chapter in the workbook to help patients understand the material and to pique their interest in it. With residential patients, who are further advanced in treatment, the group leader invites patients on a voluntary basis to prepare and present information about the theme and topic of the next week's spirituality group. Workbook readings and any supplemental materials of the discussion leader's choosing are used. At the conclusion of each group, the leader asks the patients to choose at least one experiential activity from the workbook that they will do that week in an effort to further their personal work in spirituality and to link the spirituality group sessions.

An important initial overall goal of the spirituality group and its workbook readings and assignments is to help patients with eating disorders begin to place their faith in God and in the resources of their personal spirituality rather than viewing their disorder as the solution to their problems. These patients have too often put their faith in the illness. They believe the eating disorder will bring them happiness and help them find what they are really looking for in life. In the spirituality group when the possibility of putting faith in God is discussed, some patients react with astonishment or resistance at the group leader's proposal of such an idea. The leader challenges such patients by asking, "You've been putting your faith in an illness for many years—how well has that worked?" The leader invites the patients to think about the possibility of putting their faith into something else, such as the possibility that God and other people care about them, as well as faith in the possibility that they are good, capable, and beautiful. If patients quit putting their faith in the illness, this gives them the opportunity to nurture faith in many good things, including God, members of the treatment staff, family and friends who care about them, and in their own goodness, lovability, capability, and the potential of a bright future.

An important part of using faith and spirituality with patients with eating disorders is to help them acquire a longer term view of things. During the spirituality group, we often tell our patients that we are going to "slow down." We seek to take away the expectation that recovery is going to happen immediately or "on demand." Part of the longer term perspective is to help patients trust that with God's help the details will be worked out and necessary changes will eventually occur. We do not have to know in advance how and when all the details and challenges of recovery will be worked out. Patients can begin the treatment and recovery process with the hope that with faith and hard work they will succeed.

We teach our patients that part of having faith is accepting that God may not make everything turn out exactly the way we want it to or the way we think it should. We can, however, have faith that God will give us strength, support, and guidance even if everything doesn't turn out the way we want. Even if bad things happen, there can be comfort in believing and having faith that we will receive the strength and support we need to deal with what life "brings to our table" and to find a sense of peace amid the storms.

We try to help our patients understand that even when things do not turn out exactly the way that we want them to, God's will and providence will be better than what we thought things should have been like. When things don't turn out the way we hope, if we give it enough time, we will eventually be able to see that God has a better plan for us.

Another important overall goal of the spirituality group and workbook readings is to help patients grow in spiritual harmony with God. We share our understanding with patients that spiritual harmony is about finding peace in one's heart. This is the peace of mind that comes when we are living in harmony with our own heart and when we are living according to God's will. There is a sense of rejoicing in the experience of life's good moments and comfort in the face of hard things. There is also a feeling of closeness to God and an assurance that God loves us and will help us in times of need.

During the spirituality group, we share our view that spiritual harmony is a blessing that comes from how we live. For example, if we are responsible, if we are congruent, if we love others, if we accept love from others into our lives, if we live by faith, if we honor and live congruent with our spiritual beliefs, if we forgive others and ourselves, then we can begin to "enjoy the fruit" that comes from living in harmony with spiritual truths, God's will, and our own hearts. Within this context, and during the 10-week course of the group, we explore a variety of spiritual topics and truths with patients, including adversity, spiritual identity, life purpose and meaning, responsibility, forgiveness, congruence, balance, love, belonging, and gratitude.

We also discuss with patients how eating disorders and other unhealthy behaviors may serve as counterfeits to true spiritual peace and harmony. We invite patients to share what they think spiritual harmony is and what that would mean in their life if they had it. We ask patients to talk about moments when they have felt spiritual harmony and affirm that it may feel somewhat different or unique for everyone. We also invite patients to share what they think they can do to increase the spiritual harmony they feel in their life and to make commitments to do those things and live those ways that will bring it more fully into their life.

We emphasize that spiritual harmony is an ongoing process, not a state we permanently achieve. We do not want our patients to feel guilty, ashamed, inadequate, or incompetent when they are not experiencing feelings of spiritual harmony. We try to teach our patients to seek it, to notice it, and to enjoy it when it is there. We try to teach them to pay attention to their recent past and to their experiences today and tomorrow so they can notice those moments when they feel in harmony with spiritual influences and so they can start feeling more confident in their abilities to gain harmony and to enjoy it more frequently. We try to help them see that not only is it possible to have spiritual harmony but also that they have already felt it earlier in their lives. We seek to help them understand that experiencing spiritual harmony is not a rare or strange experience. It is a common, everyday experience for people who are seeking to live in harmony with their spiritual beliefs and values.

During their participation in the spirituality group, many of our patients express a personal realization that God does not want them to have an eating disorder, and they know that part of achieving increased spiritual harmony is to remove the eating disorder from their lives one step at a time. It is a powerfully motivating experience when patients come to know in a deep spiritual way that God does not want them to suffer with the eating disorder and that He will help them overcome it. This realization strongly motivates patients to work harder to overcome their eating disorders.

Description of the Spirituality Workbook

The purpose of the *Spiritual Renewal* workbook is to help patients in their own personal quest for spiritual, emotional, and relational healing and growth. It is based on the premise that as people grow spiritually, they will find increased strength and power to help them cope with and overcome the problems and challenges in their life, whether those challenges are physical, emotional, interpersonal, or spiritual in nature.

The workbook is based on the theistic worldview which assumes that there is a God, that all human beings are God's creations, and that there is a spiritual purpose and meaning to our lives. Furthermore, it describes spiritual realities and influences in the universe that can help people in their efforts to cope, heal, and grow. Such beliefs are in harmony with all of the major theistic world religions, including Judaism, Christianity, Islam, Sikhism, and Zoroastrianism.

The theoretical basis for the workbook is set forth in *A Spiritual Strategy for Counseling and Psychotherapy* (Richards & Bergin, 1997). The workbook builds on this scholarly foundation and provides patients with eating disorders with an applied, self-help guide for pursuing spiritual renewal and growth from a theistic perspective.

Throughout the workbook, we seek to help readers understand how they can heal, change, and progress toward a more balanced, spiritual, and peaceful way of living. We begin each chapter by discussing a spiritual truth that, once understood and experienced, has the power to heal and transform. We seek to help readers understand this truth through our own explanations and experiences, as well as from quotes and ideas of great thinkers.

The spiritual truths discussed in the workbook are not new in the sense that they have been taught by many of the great religious and spiritual leaders of the world. Nonetheless, the insights about how these spiritual truths can help people cope, heal, and grow spiritually and psychologically are based on our many years of providing psychotherapy, as we have walked with clients in their journeys of pain, healing, and growth. The workbook's table of contents is shown in Exhibit 8.1.

Part I of the workbook, "Vision, Faith, and Promise," affirms that there is great healing power in people's spiritual convictions. In chapter 1, research providing evidence that faith in God and spiritual involvement is associated with better physical and mental health is briefly discussed. The importance of faith in God in healing and therapeutic change is also affirmed. Readers are invited to engage in a journey of emotional and spiritual exploration, healing, and growth.

Chapter 2 discusses the universal human predicament—that is, life is difficult! It also affirms the belief that with God's help, humans can cope

EXHIBIT 8.1
Contents of the *Spiritual Renewal* Workbook

Part I.	VISION, FAITH, AND PROMISE
	Chapter 1. The Healing Power of Faith and Spirituality
	Chapter 2. Understanding and Accepting the Human Predicament
	Chapter 3. Affirming Your Divine Worth
	Chapter 4. Discovering Your Personal Life Purpose and Mission
Part II.	SELF-EVALUATION, RESPONSIBILITY, AND CHANGE
	Chapter 5. Accepting Responsibility
	Chapter 6. Forgiveness and Saying Good-Bye to the Old
Part III.	RENEWAL, BALANCE, AND HARMONY
	Chapter 7. Embracing Congruence and Balance
	Chapter 8. Understanding and Growing in Divine Love
	Chapter 9. Belonging and Gratitude
	Chapter 10. Embracing Spiritual Harmony

Note. From *Spiritual Renewal: A Journey of Faith and Healing* (p. 2), by P. S. Richards, R. K. Hardman, and M. E. Berrett, 2000, Orem, UT: Center for Change. Copyright 2000 by P. S. Richards, R. K. Hardman, and M. E. Berrett. Reprinted with permission.

with, heal, and transcend all of life's challenges. Chapter 3 discusses one crucial reason why humans have the capacity to transcend life's difficulties—namely, they are creations of God with transcendent worth, capability and potential. Chapter 4 discusses how humans can gain an understanding of the meaning and purpose of their existence and a vision of their own personal mission of life. The importance and power of commitments and promises in fulfilling one's life vision and mission is discussed.

In Part II of the workbook, "Self-Evaluation, Responsibility, and Change," we share our conviction that to fulfill our life's personal vision and mission, we must begin the process of healing and change by saying good-bye to past trauma, pain, mistakes, and unhealthy ways of thinking and behaving. In chapter 5, we discuss the process of honestly recognizing and accepting responsibility for painful mistakes and experiences of the past, as well as current unhealthy ways of thinking and behaving. We also emphasize the importance of affirming our strengths and potential when engaging in the self-evaluation process. In chapter 6, we discuss how people can face and work through our pain, grief, and anger and why doing so is important for our healing and growth. We discuss the importance of forgiveness in the healing process, including forgiveness of God, others, and self. We also discuss how we can say good-bye to old mistakes and pain and move on to a new phase of our life.

In Part III of the workbook, "Renewal, Balance, and Harmony," we share our conviction that as we let go of the past, we can be emotionally and spiritually renewed to a way of living that is more balanced, congruent, loving, and in harmony with God's will. In chapter 7, we discuss why it is essential that we live congruently with our values and achieve balance in our lives. In chapter 8, we discuss the importance of love and how we can grow in love of God, others, and self. We also discuss the importance of service and giving good gifts and how reaching outside of ourselves to lift others can contribute to a life of growth and harmony. In chapter 9, we discuss the importance of gratitude and belonging. In chapter 10, we further discuss the concept of spiritual renewal and harmony and how we can embrace and continue in it.

Also included in each chapter is a brief description of a spiritual practice that is endorsed by the world's major religious traditions, such as prayer, meditation and contemplation, worship and ceremony, reading sacred writings, values education and clarification, fellowship and service, repentance and forgiveness, and seeking spiritual direction from spiritual leaders. We included these "spiritual practice highlights" because we believe that such practices can potentially help our readers in their efforts to cope, heal, and grow (Miller, 1999; Richards & Bergin, 1997). Examples of spiritual practice highlights are provided in Exhibits 8.2 and 8.3.

The second part of each chapter invites readers to engage in a self-assessment to determine to what extent the spiritual truth is currently being realized in their lives. The last part of each chapter contains suggestions, guidance, activities, and self-help experiences that readers can participate in to help them more fully internalize and experience the spiritual truth in their lives. Examples of self-assessments and self-help activities are provided in Exhibits 8.4 through 8.7. Patients are invited to choose one or two self-help activities from the workbook chapter at the end of each group session. They are asked to choose one that they relate to the most or that they feel will be the most helpful to them.

Facilitating Safety in the Spirituality Group

One of the most important aspects of facilitating our spirituality group—any spirituality group—is safety. Patients need to feel psychologically, emotionally, and spiritually safe. They need to know that staff and other patients will listen attentively and respectfully to their ideas and beliefs. They need to know that they will receive compassion, kindness, and help with their spiritual struggles and that they will be loved and accepted for who they are, no matter what their beliefs, thoughts, and feelings about spirituality are.

One day, after spirituality group, a 19-year-old woman approached the group leader and said, "I don't feel like I am very spiritual, and that makes me uncomfortable in this group." The group leader asked her to tell him more. She talked about how she heard others speak of experience with prayer and answers to prayers. She said, "I don't pray—I don't even believe

EXHIBIT 8.2
Spiritual Practices Spotlight From the *Spiritual Renewal* Workbook

Prayer

> Prayer is a force as real as terrestrial gravity. As a physician, I have seen men, after all other therapy had failed, lifted out of disease and melancholy by the serene effort of prayer. Only in prayer do we achieve that complete and harmonious assembly of body, mind, and spirit which gives the frail human reed its unshakable strength. (Dr. Alexis Carrol)

Prayer has been defined as an inward communication or conversation with God or a higher power. Prayers can be offered verbally or silently. All of the Western world religions (Judaism, Christianity, Islam, Sikhism, and Zoroastrianism) advocate prayer. There are prayers of *petition* (asking something for oneself), *intercession* (asking something for others), *confession* (acknowledging wrongdoing and asking for forgiveness), *lamentation* (expressing distress and asking for support), *adoration* (expressing honor and praise to God), *invocation* (asking for the presence of the Almighty), and *thanksgiving* (offering gratitude). Although the specific manner in which prayers are offered differs from religion to religion, there is general agreement that prayer may include (1) addressing God by His name (e.g., "Heavenly Father . . ." or "Dear God, or Dear Lord . . ."); (2) thanking God for His goodness and blessings; (3) asking God for his assistance and blessings; and (4) closing the prayer in some manner (e.g., "Amen."). We encourage you to pray in the manner and using the language that is consistent with your own religious tradition or spiritual beliefs. If you have questions or concerns about prayer, we encourage you to discuss them with your spiritual leader, family members, and/or therapist.

There is evidence that people who pray feel that it helps them both physically and psychologically (Benson, 1996; Dossey, 1993). There is also some fascinating evidence that praying for other people benefits them, perhaps even when they do not know we are praying for them (Dossey, 1993). If you believe in prayer, we encourage you to consider how prayer could help you as you seek to cope with and overcome your problems and challenges.

Note. From *Spiritual Renewal: A Journey of Faith and Healing* (p. 17), by P. S. Richards, R. K. Hardman, and M. E. Berrett, 2000, Orem, UT: Center for Change. Copyright 2000 by P. S. Richards, R. K. Hardman, and M. E. Berrett. Reprinted with permission.

in God, so I must not be spiritual." The group leader spoke to her briefly about the differences between spiritually and religiosity, and then asked her if she would be willing to lead the discussion in group the next week. He asked her to begin by sharing the concerns she had expressed to him with the group and to share with the group her beliefs about what spiritually is. The following week, she shared her feelings, which the group received with love, acceptance, and respect. She taught the group about service, love, kindness, and integrity—her personal model of what spirituality is—a model she not only spoke about but lived by example. All group members were inspired that day, and the group became more cohesive.

We do many things to create and nurture a safe environment in the spirituality group. The following are a few examples:

EXHIBIT 8.3
Spiritual Practices Spotlight From the *Spiritual Renewal* Workbook

Meditation and Contemplation

> Meditation is the language of the soul. It is defined as a form of private devotion or spiritual exercise, consisting in deep, continued reflection on some religious theme. . . .
>
> Meditation is one of the most secret, most sacred doors through which we pass into the presence of the Lord. (David O. McKay)

The word *contemplate* is defined in the dictionary as "to consider carefully and at length; meditate on or ponder" (American Heritage Dictionary, 1992, p. 406). Meditation is a form of contemplation that involves concentrated practice (Miller, 1994, p. 3). Smith (1975) defined meditation as a "family of mental exercises that generally involve calmly limiting thought and attention. Such exercises vary widely and can involve sitting still and counting breaths, attending to a repeated thought, or focusing on virtually [anything]" (p. 558). Both Western and Eastern religions encourage their followers to engage in various forms of contemplation and meditation—although the specific forms recommended may differ from tradition to tradition.

There is much research evidence that meditation and contemplation, as well as spiritual imagery, can have significant healing effects on the mind and body (Benson, 1996). It also appears that such practices are more powerful when they draw on people's deepest religious and spiritual convictions (Benson, 1996). There is evidence that contemplation, meditation, and spiritual imagery promote coping and healing in people with a variety of problems, including depression, anxiety, posttraumatic stress disorder, hypertension, cardiovascular problems, cancer, and weakened immune systems (Benson, 1996; Martin & Carlson, 1988).

Note. From *Spiritual Renewal: A Journey of Faith and Healing* (p. 37), by P. S. Richards, R. K. Hardman, and M. E. Berrett, 2000, Orem, UT: Center for Change. Copyright 2000 by P. S. Richards, R. K. Hardman, and M. E. Berrett. Reprinted with permission.

1. We ask patients to avoid proselytizing to each other in any way, understanding that pressure to explore any specific religious denomination is never appropriate, but especially when patients are in a vulnerable place as they are when in need of inpatient care.
2. We own our religious beliefs as theistic while actively asking each patient to own, express, share, and uphold her personal spiritual framework.
3. We broaden the definition of spirituality to include the spiritual framework that each patient brings, whether it places emphasis on theism, nature, mindfulness, treatment of others, character building or character congruence, yoga and mediation, and so on.
4. We go out of our way to have anyone who is a "spiritual minority" within the group take time to teach the group about her spiritual beliefs and increase each group member's understanding.

EXHIBIT 8.4
Self-Help Activity From the *Spiritual Renewal* Workbook

Family and Childhood Religious Experiences Worksheet

1. What is your earliest childhood memory about religion? What kind of feelings do you have as you recall this memory?

2. Were your parents involved in a religious community when you were growing up? Did they make you participate in religious activities when you were a child and adolescent? How did you feel about the way your parents handled religion in your family and home?

3. Please describe briefly how you felt about religion as a child and then later as an adolescent? Did you like it? Dislike it? Was religion a source of enjoyment, meaning, and peace? Or was it a source of guilt, conflict, and resentment? Or both?

4. What were some meaningful spiritual experiences you had as a child or adolescent?

5. How do you currently feel about religion, spirituality, and God, and in what way are your current feelings similar to or different from your feelings as a child and adolescent?

6. Do you have any other thoughts or feelings about religion and spirituality you would like to share with your spiritual leader and/or therapist?

Note. From *Spiritual Renewal: A Journey of Faith and Healing* (pp. 15–16), by P. S. Richards, R. K. Hardman, and M. E. Berrett, 2000, Orem, UT: Center for Change. Copyright 2000 by P. S. Richards, R. K. Hardman, and M. E. Berrett. Reprinted with permission.

5. Rather than focusing on differences, we believe in a practice of acceptance and inclusion and of finding spiritual commonalities that unite the human family.

An Outline of Our 10-Week Spirituality Group

We now briefly describe some of the themes we explore and activities we suggest during each week of the spirituality group. Week 1 of the group corresponds to chapter 1 of the workbook readings, Week 2 of the group to chapter 2 of the workbook readings, and so on.

Week 1: The Healing Power of Faith and Spirituality

One way we ask patients to look at the power of faith in their lives is to confront them about their misplaced faith. We point out that in attempts to deal with feelings, concerns, and life stresses and in attempts to gain fulfillment, they have put their faith in eating disorders, drugs and alcohol, or other addictions or problematic behaviors. We challenge them to put their faith in something else—anything else besides an illness. For example, we invite them to put their faith in themselves, in their heart, in trustworthy loved ones, in God, in a higher power, in the goodness of humans, in their future. We ask them to take a step in faith and then return and share their experience in the next group.

Week 2: Understanding and Accepting the Human Predicament

In helping patients look at the truth that life is difficult, we attempt to change their belief that life should be easy. We tell stories and give examples of how people have been and can be heroic in moments of adversity; we remind them that they personally have been, and can be, heroic. In the workbook assignments, patients are given an opportunity to take inventory and ownership of their own life adversity and to look both at healthy ways they have coped and at ways that have created additional, self-induced problems. We ask them to clarify for themselves what works and what does not, to contemplate the future "beginning today," and to make commitments about how to view, approach, and face the adversities of life. Patients can learn much from each other by sharing their failures and successes in dealing with adversity.

Week 3: Affirming Your Divine Worth

During Week 3, the leader explains that everyone has the opportunity to recognize their inherent spiritual worth. They may not be able to learn everything about their spirituality, but they can at least realize this spiritual worth, which transcends human understanding. The leader explains that in mainstream American culture today, self-worth is often equated with appearance, achievement, and what other people think of us. The leader teaches instead that inherent self-worth comes from spiritual beliefs and from the belief that we are creations of God. Self-worth has more to do with what is going on inside than outside; it has more to do with one's intentions, heart, capacity, and capabilities, regardless of how well-developed these are at present.

One way we try to help people recognize their inherent spiritual self-worth is to look at things that get in the way of it, including shame. We talk about love and acceptance in nurturing and maintaining one's feelings

EXHIBIT 8.5
Example of Self-Assessment From the *Spiritual Renewal* Workbook

Feelings About God and Self Questionnaire

Directions: Please indicate how strongly you agree or disagree with each statement below by circling the response that best describes how you feel. Remember that there are no right or wrong answers. Just do your best to share how you personally feel at this time of your life.

(1 = *strongly disagree*; 2 = *disagree*; 3 = *somewhat agree*; 4 = *agree*; 5 = *strongly agree*)

1. I feel worthless.	1	2	3	4	5
2. Sometimes I feel like a weak little child.	1	2	3	4	5
3. I am not a lovable person.	1	2	3	4	5
4. God is displeased with me.	1	2	3	4	5
5. I feel ashamed of myself.	1	2	3	4	5
6. I feel unworthy before God.	1	2	3	4	5
7. I feel defective.	1	2	3	4	5
8. God does not love me.	1	2	3	4	5
9. I feel incompetent around others.	1	2	3	4	5
10. I don't like myself much.	1	2	3	4	5
11. I believe that God loves me.	1	2	3	4	5
12. God comforts me in times of trial.	1	2	3	4	5
13. God is concerned with my well-being.	1	2	3	4	5
14. I feel that I have a meaningful relationship with God.	1	2	3	4	5
15. God will help me grow spiritually.	1	2	3	4	5
16. I believe that God forgives me of my mistakes.	1	2	3	4	5
17. God has a purpose for my life.	1	2	3	4	5
18. I believe that God hears my prayers.	1	2	3	4	5
19. I am a lovable person.	1	2	3	4	5
20. I am a creation of God.	1	2	3	4	5
21. I believe I am of great worth.	1	2	3	4	5
22. I believe I have great potential.	1	2	3	4	5
23. I am comfortable with myself.	1	2	3	4	5
24. I like myself even with my imperfections.	1	2	3	4	5
25. I feel comfortable disclosing who I really am.	1	2	3	4	5
26. My spiritual identity is eternal.	1	2	3	4	5

(continued)

EXHIBIT 8.5 *(Continued)*

Scoring and Interpretation Instructions for "Feelings About God and Self Questionnaire"

Add up items 1–10 to obtain your *Feeling of Shame* score. If your score was above 33, you have strong feelings of shame. You may often feel unlovable, unlikable, incompetent, flawed, defective, and unworthy. If you scored between 23 and 33, it appears that you have some feelings of shame, but they are not that intense or frequent. If you scored below 23, it appears that you are for the most part free of feelings of shame and worthlessness. If you scored above 33, feelings of shame may be a significant problem in your life, and you may benefit from visiting with your therapist or spiritual leader about this issue.

Add items 11–18 to obtain your *Relationship with God* score. If your score was above 30, you have a positive image of God and believe that He loves you and helps you in your life. If you scored between 22 and 29, you have some positive images of God, but your perceptions of him are not that positive and your faith that He is concerned about you is not that strong. If you scored below 22, it appears that your image of God is negative and that you believe that God does not love you or help you in your life. If you scored low on your Image of God score, your feelings of alienation from God may be a significant problem in your life, and you may benefit from visiting with your therapist or spiritual leader about this issue.

Add items 19–26 to obtain your *Positive Self-Identity* score. If your score was above 30, you have a positive image of yourself and believe that you are lovable and of great worth. If you scored between 22 and 29, you have some positive images of yourself, but you don't feel completely lovable or worthwhile. If you scored below 22, it appears that your image of yourself is negative and that you believe you are unlovable and not of worth. If you have scored low on your Image of Self score, shame may be a significant problem in your life, and you may benefit from visiting with your therapist or spiritual leader about this issue.

Note. From *Spiritual Renewal: A Journey of Faith and Healing* (pp. 54–55), by P. S. Richards, R. K. Hardman, and M. E. Berrett, 2000, Orem, UT: Center for Change. Copyright 2000 by P. S. Richards, R. K. Hardman, and M. E. Berrett. Reprinted with permission.

of self-worth. We challenge patients to work with their therapist on issues that make them feel degraded, shameful, and not "good enough," issues that detract from their feelings of spiritual worth. The group leader invites patients to describe times in their life when they felt they were of great worth as well as times when they have felt worthless; patients then are asked to reflect on what was going on in their lives at those times.

We also talk about the difference between love and approval and how approval does not maintain inner feelings of self-worth whereas love can. We talk about the value of having our own and God's approval as opposed to seeking approval for external things, such as body shape. One of the invitations that we give patients is to suggest that they read and study the sacred writings of their religious tradition or the writings of great thinkers and philosophers, to learn what their thoughts and feelings are about the worth of a human being.

EXHIBIT 8.6
Example of Self-Help Exercise From the *Spiritual Renewal* Workbook

Perceptions I Have of My Father, Mother, and God

Instructions: Think carefully about the qualities and characteristics of your father and mother. Then do your best to honestly describe what you believe are their positive, as well as negative, qualities and characteristics (e.g., intelligent, loving, judgmental, harsh, cold, distant, playful, etc.). After you have done this, think carefully about how you view God. What positive and negative qualities and characteristics do you believe He has? Do your best to honestly write these down. Then compare your descriptions of your father and mother with your description of God. Do you see much similarity? Are there any important differences in the way you view your parents and the way you view God? We encourage you to discuss what you learned with your therapist, spiritual leaders, or a trusted friend.

My Perceptions of My Mother	My Perceptions of My Father	My Perceptions of God

Note. From *Spiritual Renewal: A Journey of Faith and Healing* (p. 56), by P. S. Richards, R. K. Hardman, and M. E. Berrett, 2000, Orem, UT: Center for Change. Copyright 2000 by P. S. Richards, R. K. Hardman, and M. E. Berrett. Reprinted with permission.

Week 4: Discovering Your Personal Life Purpose and Mission

One of the most important things we discuss during Week 4 is that there is a meaning and purpose in life. We share our view that patients can learn about the meaning of their lives; it does not have to be unknown or beyond reach. In the workbook and in group discussions, patients are taught about great and heroic people who found purpose and meaning in life. We discuss Victor Frankl's (1959) book *Man's Search for Meaning* and share insights from it.

We discuss with patients the connection between having purpose and meaning in life and allowing that purpose and meaning to guide or be the catalyst for creating a vision for life. We discuss how a vision for life can help keep them focused and guide them in keeping their priorities straight so that they can focus their energy toward those things that are most important to them. We also teach that their vision should come out of their deepest desires. Once patients have a vision about who they are, where they are headed, and what is important in life, they can begin to make a plan to make their vision come to pass. They can make commitments to their vision, and they can begin to make all of the sacrifices necessary to live that commitment.

One group activity that we do in Week 4 is to have the patients form dyads and talk to each other about what they really want in life. Sometimes sharing what they want with others helps patients begin to feel excited

EXHIBIT 8.7
Example of Self-Help Activity From the *Spiritual Renewal* Workbook

Gratitude List

Instructions: See if you can write down at least 100 things that you feel grateful for in your life. There may be some "big things" that you feel grateful for, such as your health, children, and so on. But do not overlook the many "little things" that you may feel grateful for, such as the smell of flowers, the warmth of sunshine, the fresh cool fall breeze, the taste of good food, and so on. Be as specific as possible. Please use additional pages when you run out of room on this page.

I feel grateful for . . . .
I feel grateful for . . . .
I feel grateful for . . . .
I feel grateful for . . . .
I feel grateful for . . . .
I feel grateful for . . . .
I feel grateful for . . . .
I feel grateful for . . . .
I feel grateful for . . . .
I feel grateful for . . . .
I feel grateful for . . . .

Note. From *Spiritual Renewal: A Journey of Faith and Healing* (p. 141), by P. S. Richards, R. K. Hardman, and M. E. Berrett, 2000, Orem, UT: Center for Change. Copyright 2000 by P. S. Richards, R. K. Hardman, and M. E. Berrett. Reprinted with permission.

about hoping, dreaming, and living again. Patients are often scared to say what they want because of their feelings of chronic failure or their fear that after every good thing, something bad will happen. Many patients with eating disorders have learned to quit hoping, dreaming, and making commitments in their lives. So part of the focus of the group is to move patients to dream and hope again, to declare publicly the things that they want, and to begin to make promises and commitments in their lives so that they can have these things.

One workbook assignment for Week 4 asks patients to think about a person they have met and respect who has a purpose and meaning in life and to reflect on what they have learned from that person. We also invite patients to spend private quiet time in prayer and meditation to ponder about their purpose, mission, and meaning in life. We encourage patients to write in their journal any impressions or insights that come to them during those quiet moments, and we invite them to share some of those insights in the following week's group.

Week 5: Accepting Responsibility

During Week 5, we discuss the process of honestly recognizing and accepting responsibility for painful mistakes and experiences of the past, as well as current unhealthy ways of thinking and behaving. We also emphasize with patients the importance of affirming their strengths and potential when engaging in the self-evaluation process. We discuss the importance of telling the truth, in microscopic detail, about things that they have done and have not done, both positive and negative. We discuss descriptive versus evaluative truth. We try to help patients understand that if they describe the truth of what happened without judgment, they do not have to feel shame or put themselves down but simply learn from their experiences and move on.

We help patients understand roadblocks to taking responsibility. One of the biggest roadblocks is perfectionism—the belief that they have to be perfect. Patients with eating disorders are often afraid to take responsibility for things, fearing that if they do they will experience self-condemnation, shame, and self-disgust. We discuss how accepting responsibility for their lives can give them power to make choices again. If their illness is their responsibility, then so, too, is the cure; this gives patients hope that they can have some control in their recovery. To blame others or to wait for others to "fix" them is a way to remain a victim throughout life, and it takes away from their personal power.

We talk about *overresponsibility*—that is, being responsible for things they cannot control versus being responsible for things that they can control. We teach the concept of *spiritual responsibility*, or *stewardship*, which means being responsible for and taking care of what they have—their bodies, their talents, their lives, their relationships. We encourage patients to talk to the group members about weaknesses they have and mistakes that they have made and to tell the truth and be honest about such things. We ask patients to take responsibility for their successes and progress and for good things that they accomplish and do in their lives.

Week 6: Forgiveness and Saying Goodbye to the Old

During Week 6, we discuss how patients can face and work through their pain, grief, and anger and why doing so is important for their healing and growth. We discuss the importance of forgiveness in the healing process, including forgiveness of God, others, and self. We discuss how they can say good-bye to old mistakes and pain and move on to a new phase of life. We ask patients to share and discuss their beliefs about forgiveness. We invite them to discuss questions such as, "What do you believe are the steps of forgiveness?" "If you want to forgive someone, what steps do you need to take?" "If you want to forgive yourself for things you've done or mistakes you have made, what steps do you need to take?" We discuss the idea that forgiveness is a process, it is not a place that can be arrived at immediately. Forgiveness can take time—sometimes years. But we affirm that patients can learn to be forgiving and that they can take gradual steps toward this goal.

We invite patients to talk about times when they have been forgiven and what it was like to be on the receiving end of forgiveness. We invite them to share experiences where they have forgiven someone, and we ask them to share how they did it. We also ask patients to share how they may feel stuck with forgiveness and to discuss what help they feel they need. We invite patients to think about where they need to forgive themselves, and we help them explore how they might succeed in doing so.

We talk about roadblocks to forgiveness, such as the fear of being hurt or abused again. We talk about the roadblock of anger. We suggest that people may need anger to protect them if they do not believe their boundaries and rights will be respected. We affirm patients' right to establish boundaries and to insist that people respect their boundaries. We talk about the roadblock of taking on the role of God in punishment. We invite patients to give the task of judgment to God instead of attempting to be the prosecutor, judge, and jury themselves.

Week 7: Embracing Congruence and Balance

During Week 7, we discuss why it is essential that patients live congruently with their values and achieve balance in their lives. The main theme we emphasize is that if patients' actions are incongruent with their own values and beliefs, it is difficult to find happiness or peace in their hearts, minds, and lives. We discuss the concept of balance, emphasizing that when people have an addiction, life cannot be balanced. We suggest that one of the blessings of overcoming eating disorders, alcoholism, drug addiction, or any other addiction is the opportunity to once again have a balanced life.

We suggest that in life there needs to be a balance between process and outcome. Women with eating disorders most often look at outcome as the only evidence of success—and usually that outcome has to be perfection. They do not look at the process, their effort, their hard work, and their good intentions. They do not look at their progress along the way.

We discuss the importance of living in the present. Balance comes from living in the present more than in the past or the future, and we talk about the consequences of living too much in the past or in the future. We talk about congruence, or having one's intentions, thoughts, and behaviors line up or match. We talk about the importance of being willing to declare one's beliefs publicly, rather than hiding them, as a first step in congruence. We suggest that declaring beliefs publicly can strengthen one's commitment to live congruently with those beliefs.

We invite patients to clarify their values and what is most important to them. An exercise in the workbook asks them to rank their most important values according to different areas of life such as career, children, religious or spiritual activities, spouse, relationships, spirituality, physical fitness, and so on. They are asked to examine where they spend their energy and their time. We ask them to look at whether what they say is important to them is congruent with how they are spending their time and living their lives.

Week 8: Understanding and Growing in Divine Love

During Week 8, we discuss the importance of love and how patients can grow in love of God, others, and self. We also discuss the importance of service and giving good gifts and how reaching outside of ourselves to lift others can contribute to a life of growth and harmony. We talk about what love is not and what love is, and the false notions of love that we are sometimes taught in the media, by the fashion world, and by Hollywood. We ask patients to talk about what they have learned about love in their families, what love meant to them growing up as a child, how love was expressed and shown in their family, and how they knew or felt love. We teach basic concepts of true love, which includes care, responsibility, respect, good intention, and loving behaviors and loving actions.

We ask patients to talk about and do activities with each other in which they express love in ways that have previously frightened them. We suggest that one of the blessings of recovery is to be able to notice love, to feel love, and to express one's love again. We suggest that if they feel like they are not worth very much, they may not express much love because they are afraid that they "have a crappy gift to give." We talk about concepts such as "you love those whom you serve." One of the activities that we do is to ask patients to pick one person in the group with whom they have had a more difficult time feeling comfortable with or one for whom they have had feelings of fondness, care, or love. We ask them to notice that person during the week and to be kind to her and serve her in some way. Almost without fail, patients report that their feelings of love, kindness, compassion, and respect for the person grew out of their willingness to notice and extend a hand of kindness toward her during the week.

We talk about the possibility that making God a partner in love helps create and intensify our love. Finally, for patients who are confused about what love is and whether they have love to give, we try to point out even their smallest acts of love, kindness, graciousness, and service. We also try to affirm their feelings of love. When patients are loving, kind, or gracious or when they feel, express, and show love, even in the smallest way, we try to point it out and affirm their acts of service and love.

Week 9: Belonging and Gratitude

During Week 9, we discuss the importance of gratitude and belonging. We discuss the concept of *belonging* as a deep, spiritual recognition that we are connected to God and to other people. We show how loneliness and feelings of aloneness, even when you are with other people, can be the antitheses of a sense of belonging. Women with eating disorders tend to feel strongly that they do not belong. They do not feel like they are good enough to belong. They believe they need to make up for deficits or be more perfect so that they can be worthy of belonging with others or with God.

We seek to help patients understand that they do belong. We invite the group members to express their happiness about having a relationship with other group members, including their happiness that the other patients came to group and that they can go through treatment with other women who are courageously facing an eating disorder. We teach patients about "belonging with self" through congruence and integrity. We talk about the possibility of feeling a sense of belonging by developing a relationship with God. We discuss how when people feel like they belong, it is easier for them to feel grateful. We speak of gratitude as a spiritual experience, which may include oneness with God and other people and a connection with those who brought good things into their lives.

We invite patients to share what they are grateful for in this moment of their life, whether it is the smallest thing they notice waking up or something big and powerful. We teach that gratitude is something that can grow and develop. We affirm that patients need not feel ashamed if they feel that they do not have as much gratitude as they would like. We talk about roadblocks to gratitude and how it is harder to feel it and notice it when you are depressed and having a difficult time.

One of the workbook assignments we invite patients to do is to make a gratitude list. They are invited to list 100 things that they feel grateful for, including small and big things. Sometimes we also ask patients to write letters of gratitude to family members, close friends, or even to God.

Week 10: Embracing Spiritual Harmony

During Week 10, we further discuss with patients the concept of spiritual renewal and harmony and how they can embrace it. We talk about harmony as something that many people throughout the ages have sought in life. We talk about the concepts of nirvana, inner peace, peace of mind and heart, and fulfillment. We ask patients to talk about what they believe spiritual harmony is and to share with each other definitions, ideas, and beliefs about spiritual harmony. We ask patients to share with each other times when they have felt that they were in spiritual harmony and times when they have felt they were not. We ask them to share experiences when they have met people whom they thought were in spiritual harmony, what it was like being around those people, and what they can learn about those people.

We talk about how the possibilities of congruence with self and with God's will, if one believes in God, have much to do with spiritual harmony. We suggest that the qualities of a little child have much to do with spiritual harmony—love, trust, acceptance, truth, vulnerability, gratitude, and honesty. We talk about the opportunity they have to experience more spiritual harmony early in life instead of waiting for the fall or autumn of their lives to recognize what is important and to experience and enjoy those things that are the most important. We suggest that listening to, following, and being in tune with one's heart, as well as expressing one's heart to others, are keys to living in spiritual harmony.

We suggest that spiritual harmony is something that is not handed to people but that it takes effort and work. It requires being congruent. It requires taking risks. It requires being vulnerable. It requires having integrity. It requires sacrifice. Harmony, change, repentance, honesty, risk taking, and relationships all take work and effort.

We encourage patients who believe in God to ask for God's help to enjoy a greater spiritual harmony. We ask patients to continue to work on self-correction without self-punishment and judgment. We ask patients to continue to look for things they are grateful for and to express gratitude to others. We ask patients not only to reach out to others to help them but also to be willing to ask for help.

We ask patients to decide what they need to do to nurture their spirituality and to keep it as a part of their lives. We ask them to consider questions such as, "In which spiritual practices will you involve yourself?" "Are there any worship ceremonies, rites, or practices that you will follow, such as reading scriptures, saying prayers, meditating, doing yoga, or spending time in nature?" "Are their other things you need to do to keep nurturing your spirituality?" We ask patients to write up to five things that they need to do to keep themselves in their best place of spiritual harmony.

EMPIRICAL EVALUATION OF THE SPIRITUALITY GROUP

Because little empirical evidence exists to support the effectiveness of using spiritual interventions in the treatment of women with eating disorders, after we wrote the *Spiritual Renewal* workbook and added the spirituality group to our treatment program, we felt it was important to evaluate its effects. We therefore conducted a controlled experimental outcome study to evaluate the effectiveness of the spirituality group and to compare its effectiveness with a cognitive therapy and an emotional support group. We hypothesized that the adoption of the spirituality group into our eating disorder inpatient treatment program would positively affect treatment outcomes. The complete findings of this study have been reported elsewhere (Richards, Berrett, Hardman, & Eggett, in press).

Participants

Participants for this study were 122 women living with anorexia nervosa, bulimia nervosa, or eating disorder not otherwise specified (NOS). Of these patients, 42 (34.4%) were diagnosed with anorexia nervosa, 47 (38.5%) with bulimia nervosa, and 33 (27.0%) with eating disorder NOS. The average length of patients' stay in the inpatient treatment program was 68 days.

The ages of the participants ranged from 13 to 52 years (M = 21.2; *SD* = 6.6); 80% of participants were in the 16 to 26 age range. Most participants were Caucasian (*n* = 119; 97.5%). The majority of participants were Latter-Day Saints (N = 84; 68.9%), 6.5% were Protestant (*n* = 8), 5.7% were Catholic (*n* = 7), 1.6% were Jewish (*n* = 2), 7.4% said they were affiliated with some other religious denomination but did not specify which one (*n* = 9), and 7.4% of the participants were not affiliated with a religious affiliation but viewed themselves are having their own spiritual beliefs (*n* = 9).

Participants came from 19 states. The largest number of participants was from Utah (*n* = 62; 50.8%). Smaller numbers of participants were from California (*n* = 14; 11.5%), Idaho (*n* = 7; 5.7%), and Colorado (*n* = 6; 4.9%). The majority of participants were single (*n* = 105; 86.1%), a smaller number were married (*n* = 14; 11.5%), and a few were divorced or separated (*n* = 2; 1.6%). A high percentage of participants (77%; *n* = 94) suffered from a comorbid psychiatric diagnosis.

Study Procedures

Treatment and data collection for the study began on October 1, 1999, and ended on January 31, 2001. When participants were admitted to the inpatient program, they were informed about the purpose and possible benefits and risks of the study. In accordance with ethical guidelines of the American Psychological Association (APA), they were also informed that they had the right not to participate in the study or to withdraw at any time. After consenting to participate, they were randomly assigned to one of three treatment groups, each led by a doctoral-level psychologist.

Treatment Conditions

Patients who were assigned to the spirituality group read *Spiritual Renewal: A Journey of Faith and Healing* (Richards et al., 2000). Patients also attended a weekly 60-minute spirituality group in which the group leader highlighted some of the most important concepts from the workbook readings and encouraged patients to share what they had learned that week about their personal spirituality from the workbook readings and exercises and from their life experiences during the week.

Patients who were assigned to the cognitive group read *Mind Over Mood: Change How You Feel by Changing the Way You Think* (Greenberger & Padesky, 1995), a self-help workbook that describes a variety of cognitive and behavioral techniques. They also attended a weekly 60-minute group during which the group leader highlighted some of the most important concepts from the cognitive workbook readings and encouraged the patients to share what they had learned about the influence of their thoughts on their emotions and behavior from the workbook readings and exercises and their related life experiences during the week.

Patients who were assigned to the emotional support control group attended a weekly 60-minute "open-topic" support group each week. They were encouraged to bring up topics for discussion in the group that were specifically related to the treatment facility's education class offerings for the week (e.g., self-esteem, nutrition, assertiveness). The group leader was instructed to steer the patients away from discussions about religion, spirituality, and cognitive therapy.

Group Leaders

The three group leaders were all Caucasian men in their late 40s. The leaders of the spirituality and cognitive groups had doctoral degrees in counseling psychology and the leader of the Emotional Support group had a doctoral degree in instructional psychology and was receiving supervision as he pursued respecialization in counseling psychology. The two counseling psychologists alternated every 3 months between leading the spirituality group and the cognitive group. Because of scheduling problems, it was not possible to rotate the leader of the emotional support group with the other two group leaders.

Research Design

The study used a randomized, pretest–posttest control group design (Kazdin, 1994). Patients who participated in the emotional support group received the regular inpatient treatment program, with the addition of 1-hour per week of group discussion and emotional support about issues and topics that were already part of the regular inpatient program. This group was not a "no-treatment control group" and was expected to have some treatment effects. In addition to 1-hour per week of group support and discussion, participants in the spirituality and cognitive groups also received spirituality or cognitive therapy readings and self-help exercises. All of the patients in the three treatment groups received the regular and full intensive treatment program at the treatment center. The randomized, pretest–posttest control group design helped control for the variety of possible confounding variables that can jeopardize research designs in clinical settings, such as length of treatment, nature of a patient's individual therapy, effectiveness of patients' individual therapists, and a variety of patient variables (e.g., patient's commitment to therapy, age of patient, severity of eating disorder, eating disorder diagnosis, religious affiliation, etc.).

Treatment Fidelity Checks

During the course of the study, the principal investigator (Richards) met bimonthly with the treatment condition group leaders to discuss whether they were adhering to the treatment protocols for each of the treatment conditions and to resolve any procedural questions that arose. The group leaders verified that they closely adhered to the content of their respective self-help manuals in their treatment conditions and that patients participated in the readings and group discussions.

Outcome Measures

Several outcome measures were administered at admission and discharge (posttreatment), including the Eating Attitudes Test (EAT; Garner & Garfinkel, 1979), Body Shape Questionnaire (BSQ; Cooper, Taylor, Cooper, & Fairburn, 1987), Outcome Questionnaire (OQ-45; Lambert & Burlingame, 1996), Multidimensional Self-Esteem Inventory (MSEI; Epstein & O'Brien, 1983), and Spiritual Well-Being Scale (SWBS; Ellison & Smith, 1991). As noted in chapter 6, the EAT is a 40-item self-report measure that assesses symptoms associated with anorexia nervosa and bulimia nervosa (e.g., restricting, bingeing, purging). The BSQ is a 34-item measure that assesses concerns about body shape and feelings of self-consciousness and shame about one's body. The OQ-45 is a 45-item outcome measure that assesses patients' functioning on three subscales: Symptom Distress (i.e., anxiety, depression, and substance abuse), Interpersonal Relations (i.e., relationship conflict), and Social Role (problems in work and school). The MSEI is a 116-item measure that assesses patients' global self-esteem, eight subcomponents of self-esteem (i.e., competence, likeability, self-control, personal power, body functioning, body appearance, moral self-approval, lovability), as well as identity integration and defensive self-enhancement. The SWBS is a 20-item measure that assesses patients' feelings of spiritual well-being on two subscales: Religious Well-Being, which measures whether patients feel that God cares about them and helps them with their problems and Existential Well-Being, which measures whether patients feel a sense of life purpose, satisfaction, and direction. Evidence supporting the reliability and validity of these instruments is reported in the sources cited here.

Outcome measures that were administered weekly during the course of treatment included the Symptom Distress subscale of the OQ-45, Eating Disorder Self-Monitoring Scale (EDSMS; Richards, 1996), and Theistic Spiritual Outcome Survey (TSOS; Richards et al., 2005). The EDSMS is a weekly self-monitoring scale that asks patients to indicate the frequency and intensity of their thoughts about bingeing, purging, and restricting during the past week on a 5-point Likert scale (0 = *never*, 1 = *rarely*, 2 = *occasionally*, 3 = *often*, 4 = *very often*). Age of eating disorder onset, history of childhood sexual abuse, comorbid diagnosis (Axis II diagnoses), and religious affiliation were obtained from patient files. The TSOS is a 17-item measure of patients' spiritual health and well-being from a theistic perspective and contains items that assess clients' feelings of love toward God, others, and self (Richards et al., 2005).

Results

Preliminary Analyses

Preliminary analyses were conducted to determine whether patients' eating disorder diagnosis (anorexia nervosa, bulimia nervosa, or eating disorder—not otherwise specified) or religious affiliation (Latter-Day Saints versus non–Latter-Day Saints) were associated with treatment outcomes. Analyses of variance revealed that the study participants with different eating disorder diagnoses did not differ from one another on the dependent measures, nor were there any significant interactions between eating disorder diagnoses and treatment condition. Analyses of variance also revealed that the study participants with different religious affiliations did not differ from one another on the dependent measures, nor were there any significant interactions between religious affiliation and treatment condition. On the basis of these findings, we proceeded with the analyses described in the following sections.

Pretest to Posttest Outcome Measures

Paired *t* tests on the mean scores of pre- to posttreatment outcomes measures for all three treatment groups combined revealed that the 122 patients reported statistically significant improvements on all of the outcome measures as presented in Table 8.1. Cohen's *d* effect sizes revealed that the pre- to posttreatment changes on most of the outcome measures were large: *d* (EAT) = 2.81, *d* (BSQ) = 1.58, *d* (OQ-45 symptom distress) = 1.92, *d* (OQ-45 relationship distress) = .91, *d* (OQ-45 social role conflict) = 1.39,

TABLE 8.1

Eating Disorder Patients Scores on the Pre- to Posttreatment Outcome Measures and Analysis of Covariance Results

Measure	Treatment group	Pretreatment		Posttreatment		Gain score[a]	*F* and *p* values[b]	LSD[c]
		Mean	*SD*	Mean	*SD*			
Eating Attitudes Test (EAT)	1. Spirituality	64.8	20.4	12.3	9.1	49.7	$F = 4.56$	1 > 2
	2. Cognitive	61.0	20.6	19.5	15.7	42.0	$p = .013$	1 = 3
	3. Support	57.1	23.0	13.8	8.7	47.5		2 < 3
Body Shape Questionnaire (BSQ)	1. Spirituality	151.8	35.1	90.2	28.3	61.2	$F = 1.70$	
	2. Cognitive	156.7	26.2	104.4	40.3	48.9	$p = .187$	
	3. Support	143.8	40.1	96.3	31.4	52.3		
Religious Well-Being (RWB)	1. Spirituality	48.5	10.0	54.9	5.8	7.7	$F = 3.74$	1 > 2
	2. Cognitive	45.0	14.1	50.2	9.6	4.2	$p = .027$	1 > 3
	3. Support	42.2	15.8	47.7	13.7	4.0		
Existential Well-Being (EWB)	1. Spirituality	41.4	11.6	52.4	5.8	12.6	$F = 3.07$	1 > 2
	2. Cognitive	37.5	8.7	47.9	8.7	8.9	$p = .050$	
	3. Support	39.4	12.3	48.9	7.6	10.1		
Global Self-Esteem (MSEI)	1. Spirituality	28.0	11.5	47.1	13.3	18.8	$F = 1.11$	
	2. Cognitive	27.6	10.8	43.0	14.2	15.1	$p = .332$	
	3. Support	29.5	11.4	43.1	12.1	15.0		
Symptom Distress (OQ-45)	1. Spirituality	52.7	12.8	24.7	11.2	28.3	$F = 3.78$	1 > 2
	2. Cognitive	55.5	15.2	31.2	13.9	22.7	$p = .026$	1 > 3
	3. Support	50.6	12.7	29.4	10.2	22.6		
Relationship Distress (OQ-45)	1. Spirituality	16.3	6.9	9.4	4.4	7.6	$F = 5.37$	1 > 2
	2. Cognitive	18.2	6.6	12.8	6.0	4.6	$p = .006$	1 > 3
	3. Support	16.8	6.2	12.7	5.8	4.2		
Social Role Conflict (OQ-45)	1. Spirituality	15.1	4.5	7.8	3.0	7.6	$F = 5.91$	1 > 2
	2. Cognitive	17.2	5.6	11.3	5.2	4.7	$p = .004$	
	3. Support	14.3	4.6	8.9	3.2	6.4		

Note. Sample sizes: spirituality group, $n = 43$; cognitive group, $n = 35$; emotional support group = 44. From Richards, Berrett, Hardman, and Eggett, in press.

[a]Gain score = adjusted mean gain scores from analysis of covariance.

[b]*F* and *p* values = between groups *F* test.

[c]LSD = least significant difference pairwise comparisons on gain scores.

d (global self-esteem) = 1.36, *d* (religious well-being) = .47, and *d* (existential well-being) = 1.15.

Analysis of covariance (ANCOVA) comparisons on gain scores between patients in the three treatment conditions using pretest scores as the covariates revealed that patients in the three groups significantly differed at the conclusion of treatment on the EAT, $F(2, 111) = 4.56$, $p < .05$ (see Table 8.1).[1] Post hoc least significant difference (LSD) pairwise comparisons revealed that patients in the spirituality group scored significantly lower on the EAT than did patients in the cognitive group, but they did not significantly differ on this measure from patients in the emotional support group (ESG). Cohen's *d* effect sizes revealed that the differences among the three treatment groups on their EAT gain scores ranged from moderately large to small: *d* (spirituality vs. cognitive) = .68, *d* (Spirituality vs. Emotional Support) = .19, and *d* (Cognitive vs. Emotional Support) = .49.

ANCOVAs also revealed that there were significant differences between the treatment groups on the OQ-45 Symptom Distress, $F(2, 113) = 3.78$, $p < .05$; Relationship Distress $F(2, 113) = 5.37$, $p < .01$; and Social Role Conflict $F(2, 113) = 5.91$, $p < .01$ subscales (see Table 8.1). Post hoc LSD comparisons revealed that patients in the spirituality group scored significantly lower on symptom distress and relationship distress than did patients in the cognitive and emotional support groups. They scored significantly lower on social role conflict than did patients in the cognitive group, but they did not significantly differ on this measure from patients in the emotional support group. Cohen's *d* effect sizes revealed that the differences among the three treatment groups on these measures ranged from moderately large to very small: *d* (OQ-45 Symptom Distress: Spirituality vs. Cognitive) = .53, *d* (OQ-45 Symptom Distress: Spirituality vs. Emotional Support) = .54; *d* (OQ-45 Symptom Distress: Cognitive vs. Emotional Support) = .01, *d* (OQ-45 Relationship Distress: Spirituality vs. Cognitive) = .59, *d* (OQ-45 Relationship Distress: Spirituality vs. Emotional Support) = .67; *d* (OQ-45 Relationship Distress: Cognitive vs. Emotional Support) = .08, *d* (OQ-45 Social Role Conflict: Spirituality vs. Cognitive) = .79, *d* (OQ-45 Social Role Conflict: Spirituality vs. Emotional Support) = .34; *d* (OQ-45 Social Role Conflict: Cognitive vs. Emotional Support) = .45.

[1]We set our critical value for rejection of the null hypothesis (no differences between the treatment groups) at alpha < .05. Given that we conducted eight separate ANCOVAs, there is a 40% chance that one of the significant findings reported here occurred by chance. Performing a Bonferroni correction would mean setting the critical value at an alpha of .00625, which would have led to the conclusion that the only statistically significant differences in Table 8.1 were on the OQ-45 Relationship Distress and Social Role Conflict subscales. Given that research is in an early stage in this domain, the relatively small sample sizes in our treatment groups, and the relatively low statistical power of the ANCOVAs, we felt that a critical value of .00625 was overly conservative. We preferred the possibility of making a Type I error rather than a Type II error in this situation.

ANCOVAs also revealed that there were significant differences among the treatment groups on the Religious Well-Being subscale, $F(2, 108) = 3.74, p < .05$, and Existential Well-Being subscale, $F(2, 109) = 3.07, p < .05$, of the SWBS (Table 8.1). Post hoc LSD comparisons revealed that patients in the spirituality group scored significantly higher on religious well-being than did patients in the cognitive and emotional support groups. Patients in the spirituality group also scored significantly higher on existential well-being than did patients in the cognitive group, but they did not significantly differ on this measure from patients in the emotional support group. Cohen's *d* effect sizes revealed that the differences among the three treatment groups on the religious well-being subscale were moderate to small: *d* (Spirituality vs. Cognitive) = .40, *d* (Spirituality vs. Emotional Support) = .29, *d* (Cognitive vs. Emotional Support) = .11. Cohen's *d* effect sizes revealed that the differences among the three treatment groups on the Existential Well-Being subscale were also moderate to small: *d* (Spirituality vs. Cognitive) = .56, *d* (Spirituality vs. Emotional Support) = .38, *d* (Cognitive vs. Emotional Support) = .18.

Patients in the spirituality group also had slightly lower mean scores on the BSQ and slightly higher mean scores on the Global Self-Esteem Scale of the MSEI compared with patients in the cognitive and emotional support groups. ANCOVAs revealed that these differences were not statistically significant, however: BSQ, $F(2, 112) = 1.70, p > .05$; Global Self-Esteem, $F(2, 105) = 1.11, p > .05$. Cohen's *d* effect sizes revealed that the differences among the three treatment groups on the BSQ were moderate to small; *d* (Spirituality vs. Cognitive) = .40, *d* (Spirituality vs. Emotional Support) = .29, and *d* (Cognitive vs. Emotional Support) = .11. Cohen's *d* effect sizes revealed that the differences among the three treatment groups on the global self-esteem scale were small; *d* (Spirituality vs. Cognitive) = .29, *d* (Spirituality vs. Emotional Support) = .30, and *d* (Cognitive vs. Emotional Support) = .01.

Relative Rates of Improvement on the Weekly Outcome Measures

A hierarchical linear modeling (HLM; Bryk & Raudenbush, 1992) analysis for all 8 weeks of TSOS, OQ-45 Symptom Distress, and EDSMS data revealed that the main effect for Week was statistically significant on all of these variables: TSOS, $F(1, 88) = 45.4, p < .0001$; OQ-45 Symptom Distress, $F(1, 88) = 139.3, p < .0001$, EDSMS—Bingeing, $F(1, 99) = 48.6, p < .0001$, EDSMS—Purging, $F(1, 99) = 32.9, p < .0001$; EDSMS—Restricting, $F(1, 99) = 72.7, p < .0001$. These findings indicate that, collectively, the patients improved at a significant rate on all outcome measures during the first 8 weeks of treatment. The Week by Group interaction effects on the outcome measures for Weeks 1 through 8 were not statistically significant, which indicates that the relative rates of improvement did not differ on the measures among the treatment groups across all 8 weeks of treatment.

The Week by Group interaction effect on the TSOS and OQ-45 Symptom Distress for weeks 1 through 4 was statistically significant: TSOS, $F(2, 88) = 3.12, p < .05$; OQ-45 Symptom Distress, $F(2, 88) = 3.12, p < .05$). These findings indicate that the relative rates of improvement on Spirituality and Symptom Distress (depression and anxiety) among the treatment groups during the first 4 weeks of treatment differed. The HLM slopes for each treatment group on the TSOS (Spirituality = 2.30, Cognitive = 0.43, Emotional Support = 1.09) and OQ-45 Symptom Distress (spirituality = −3.78, Cognitive = −1.60, Emotional Support = −2.60) indicate that the Spirituality and Symptom Distress scores of patients in the spirituality group improved more rapidly during the first 4 weeks of treatment compared with patients in the other treatment groups. On the EDSMS, the Week by Group interaction effect for Weeks 1 through 4 on the bingeing, purging, and restricting items were statistically nonsignificant.

Discussion

A number of important findings emerged in this study. First, the findings indicate that the spirituality group did enhance the overall effectiveness of the eating disorder inpatient program, somewhat more so than did the cognitive and emotional support groups. There was a consistent pattern of findings, many of them statistically significant, that favored the spirituality group. Although the magnitude of these differences were often not large as reflected in the relatively small to moderate effect size differences among the treatment groups, they appear theoretically and clinically meaningful given that these treatment effects were observed in the context of an intensive and effective inpatient treatment program.

Second, the finding that the spirituality group enhanced treatment outcomes overall somewhat more strongly than did the cognitive group is of interest because cognitive therapy is widely regarded as the most effective treatment for women with bulimia nervosa (Richards et al., 2000). However, it needs to be kept in mind that the *Mind Over Mood* workbook used in the cognitive group was not designed specifically for patients with eating disorders. We considered using a cognitive therapy workbook that was specifically written with these patients in mind (Apple & Agras, 1997) but abandoned the idea because it was not designed for patients with anorexia nervosa. The relative lack of effectiveness of the cognitive group compared with the spirituality group in this study may have been due in part to our decision not to use a better validated cognitive–behavioral therapy intervention.

Third, the finding that patients in the spirituality group experienced somewhat larger decreases in depressive and anxiety symptoms as measured by the OQ-45 Symptom Distress subscale is consistent with and extends the findings of previous studies that have found spiritual therapy approaches to be effective for the treatment of depression (McCullough, 1999; Propst, Ostrom, Watkins, Dean, & Mashburn, 1992). The findings that patients in the spirituality group tended to report somewhat larger reductions in their relationship distress compared with patients in the other groups and somewhat larger reductions in social role conflict compared with the cognitive group were also of interest given that relationships and social roles are both recognized as important recovery issues for women with eating disorders (APA, 2000b).

Fourth, the finding that patients in the spirituality group tended to feel somewhat more positive about their relationship with God (religious well-being) compared with patients in the other groups and better about their life purpose and direction (existential well-being) compared with patients in the cognitive group was of interest. This finding is consistent with Hawkins, Tan, and Turk's (1999) finding that clinically depressed inpatients who received spiritually oriented Christian cognitive–behavioral therapy reported larger improvements in their religious and existential well-being than did patients who received standard secular cognitive–behavioral therapy. Perhaps it is common sense that spiritual treatment approaches should promote better spiritual treatment outcomes compared with secular approaches that ignore spiritual issues, but this has rarely been documented. The findings of both the Hawkins et al. (1999) study and our own suggest that clients and therapists who wish to include growth in spirituality as a treatment goal might be more likely to achieve it if they engage in a spiritually oriented treatment approach.

Finally, and perhaps most important, this study provided evidence that helping patients with eating disorders with their spiritual growth and well-being exerts a causal influence on reductions in depression and anxiety, relationship distress, social role conflict, and eating disorder symptoms. Although a number of studies have provided evidence that positive associations exist between spiritual exploration and spiritual growth and recovery from eating disorders (Garrett, 1996; Hall & Cohn, 1992; Hsu, Crisp, & Callender, 1992; Mitchell, Erlander, Pyle, & Fletcher, 1990; Rorty, Yager, & Rossotto, 1993; Smith et al., 2003), our study is important because it used an experimental design and is the first to demonstrate that these relationships may be causal in nature. The finding that the spirituality group enhanced treatment outcomes somewhat more strongly than did the cognitive group is particularly important in light of the fact that cognitive therapy is widely regarded as the most effective treatment for women with bulimia nervosa (Richards et al., 2000; Striegel-Moore & Smolak, 2001).

Several limitations of this study should be kept in mind. The sample sizes in the three treatment groups were relatively small, although they were larger than those in previous studies of spiritually oriented therapy approaches (McCullough, 1999). The magnitudes of the treatment effects favoring the spirituality group were small even though many of them were statistically significant. We cannot generalize our findings with any degree of confidence beyond this treatment setting, especially considering that there was a higher proportion of Latter-Day Saints than in the general population among both the treatment staff and the patients. In addition, efforts to control for therapist effects and treatment fidelity were limited, given that we were unable to rotate therapists across all three treatment groups and relied only on therapists' self-reports that treatment conditions were being implemented properly.

It also needs to be kept in mind that patients in all three treatment groups showed large improvements on the pre- and posttreatment outcomes measures and that the gains favoring patients in the spirituality group compared with patients in the other two groups were small by comparison. The treatment dosage for all three treatment conditions was relatively small in that we added only 1-hour groups and some readings to an already intensive inpatient treatment program. Increasing the treatment dosage by having patients spend more time in the groups and integrating the workbook readings more fully into the inpatient treatment program could potentially lead to stronger treatment effects in all treatment conditions. Finally, although the therapists in this study helped patients adapt the content of the cognitive therapy workbook so that it was relevant to their eating disorder issues, the fact that we did not use a workbook specially designed for this purpose may have limited the effectiveness of our cognitive therapy intervention.

Our outcome study is consistent with previous research in that we found a spiritually oriented therapy intervention to be as effective, and perhaps slightly more effective, than standard (secular) therapy approaches (e.g., Hawkins et al., 1999; McCullough, 1999; Propst, 1980; Propst et al., 1992). Our study extends the findings of previous research to the domain of eating disorders and gives incentive for additional outcome studies in this clinical area. We hope that researchers and practitioners at many eating disorder treatment centers will assist with this effort.

In addition to outcome studies that investigate whether spiritual treatment approaches promote symptom reduction, studies that investigate whether religiously devout patients with eating disorders prefer such approaches to secular ones are also needed. Evidence suggests that religiously devout clients may prefer spiritually oriented therapies because they perceive them as more culturally sensitive to their religious values (McCullough,

1999; Richards & Bergin, 1997, 2000; Worthington, Kurusu, McCullough, & Sanders, 1996). Studies are needed to investigate this possibility in the eating disorders field.

CONCLUSION

The large pretreatment to posttreatment improvements reported for all three groups in the study reported in this chapter provides some empirical evidence that a multidimensional theistic inpatient treatment program is effective for treating women with eating disorders. It also provides initial empirical evidence concerning the effectiveness of a structured spirituality group for women with eating disorders. Professionals who would like to implement a similar spirituality group in their treatment settings can contact us to obtain copies of the *Spiritual Renewal* workbook. We hope that structured spirituality groups will be implemented and empirically evaluated in a wide variety of eating disorder treatment settings.

9

TWELVE-STEP GROUPS FOR PATIENTS WITH EATING DISORDERS

In this chapter, we describe how 12-step groups can be tailored for use with patients with eating disorders. We provide some brief background information about the 12-step philosophy of Alcoholics Anonymous (AA). We also describe how we adapt the 12-step philosophy for the treatment of eating disorders in our inpatient and residential programs. On the basis of our clinical experience and the writings of other professionals, we discuss potential concerns and benefits of 12-step groups and offer some general recommendations for implementing such groups in an ethical and effective manner.

THE 12-STEP APPROACH

The 12-step approach of AA is the largest and most influential self-help group in contemporary society (McCrady & Delaney, 1995). AA estimates that it has approximately 87,000 groups in 150 countries and more than 1.7 million members worldwide (Alcoholics Anonymous World

We thank Bobbi L. Carter who wrote the first draft of this chapter and who, in doing so, provided valuable insight into how 12-step groups can be used in the treatment of women with eating disorders. The authors of this chapter were Bobbi L. Carter, P. Scott Richards, Randy K. Hardman, and Michael E. Berrett.

EXHIBIT 9.1
The 12 Steps of Eating Disorders Anonymous

1. We admitted we were powerless over our eating disorder—that our lives had become unmanageable.
2. We came to believe that a Power greater than ourselves could restore us to sanity.
3. We made a decision to turn our will and our lives over to the care of God as we understood God.
4. We made a searching and fearless moral inventory of ourselves.
5. We admitted to God, to ourselves, and to another human being the exact nature of our wrongs.
6. We were entirely ready to have God remove all these defects of character.
7. We humbly asked God to remove our shortcomings.
8. We made a list of all persons we had harmed and became willing to make amends to them all.
9. We made direct amends to such people wherever possible, except when to do so would injure them or others.
10. We continued to take personal inventory and when we were wrong, promptly admitted it.
11. We sought through prayer and meditation to improve our conscious contact with God *as* we understood God, praying only for knowledge of God's will for us and the power to carry that out.
12. Having had a spiritual awakening as the result of these steps, we tried to carry this message to others, and to practice these principles in all our affairs.

Note. Adapted from *A.A. Big Book* (pp. 59–60), by Alcoholics Anonymous World Services, 2001, New York: Alcoholics Anonymous World Services. Copyright 2001 by Alcoholics Anonymous World Services. The 12 Steps of Eating Disorders Anonymous, as adapted by Eating Disorders Anonymous with permission of Alcoholics Anonymous World Services, Inc. (AAWS), are reprinted with permission of Eating Disorders Anonymous and AAWS. Permission to reprint AAWS' 12 Steps does not mean that AAWS has reviewed or approved the contents of this publication, or that AAWS necessarily agrees with the views expressed therein. Alcoholics Anonymous (A.A.) is a program of recovery for alcoholism only—use or permissible adaptation of A.A.'s 12 Steps in connection with programs and activities which are patterned after A.A., but which address other problems, or in any other non-A.A. context, does not imply otherwise.

Services, 1990). Numerous other fellowships that subscribe to the AA 12-step model of recovery have been created, such as Narcotics Anonymous, Gamblers Anonymous, Overeaters Anonymous, and Sex and Love Addictions Anonymous. Several professionals have also adapted the 12-step approach for patients with eating disorders, referring to it as Overeaters Anonymous or Eating Disorders Anonymous (e.g., C. L. Johnson & Sansone, 1993; Wormer & Davis, 2003; Yeary, 1987).

It is well known that the 12-step approach is based on a spiritual worldview (Hopson, 1996). The 12-step program assumes that to recover from alcoholism or other addictions, people must humble themselves before God or their higher power and acknowledge that they need the assistance of that power. As can be seen in Exhibit 9.1, the entire 12-step process is a spiritual model of healing and recovery.

Religious and spiritual interventions that may be used to facilitate the recovery process in 12-step programs include confession, making restitution, seeking forgiveness from God and others, prayers of petition and invocation, meditation, and service to others. Some 12-step groups also use scriptural interventions that make explicit connections between the Bible and the 12-steps (Friends in Recovery, 1994; McCrady & Delaney, 1995). Secular 12-step programs have been developed for clients and therapists who have less interest in a theistic, spiritual approach (Dupont & McGovern, 1994).

Although empirical evidence supporting the effectiveness of 12-step programs is relatively sparse (Hopson, 1996; McCrady & Delaney, 1995), 12-step programs do enjoy acceptance among some helping professionals. Many therapists look to 12-step groups as a source of assistance and support for their clients and as an important supplement to professional treatment (Castaneda & Galanter, 1987; Hopson, 1996; McCrady & Delaney, 1995). However, many other mental health professionals have not received training in the 12-step approach and may have concerns and questions about the advisability or logistics of implementing a 12-step group with patients in treatment for eating disorders (C. L. Johnson & Sansone, 1993; Yeary, 1987).

We appreciate C. L. Johnson and Sansone's (1993) honesty when they described how they came to incorporate the 12-step approach into their eating disorder treatment:

> The development of our interest in the 12-step approach was quite simple. After an unsuccessful course of long-term multimodal treatment within our program, several eating disorder patients became involved with Alcoholics Anonymous or Overeaters Anonymous and made remarkable recoveries. This was a rather humbling and somewhat irritating experience for us, largely because the simplistic and spiritual nature of the 12-step philosophy threatened some of our conventional notions of psychiatric treatment. In the spirit of continuing to search for effective treatments for our patients, however, we attempted to set aside our prejudices and explore the potential usefulness of this intervention. (p. 122)

We hope that many other mental health professionals who may have concerns about the 12-step approach will be willing to explore its potential usefulness for their patients. We have found that the 12-step approach has been a valuable addition to our multimodal treatment program. In the next section we describe how we use this approach in our inpatient and residential treatment settings.

DESCRIPTION OF A 12-STEP GROUP FOR PATIENTS WITH EATING DISORDERS

Patients in our inpatient and residential treatment programs attend a 1-hour 12-step group once a week. A full-time psychotherapist leads the group. Most women come to our 12-step group with one thing in common—fear: fear of failure; fear of relapse; fear of living a life free of their eating disorder; fear that they are unacceptable, damaged, crazy, or worthless. No two women come to a 12-step group in the same place emotionally or spiritually.

In our 12-step group, we work on acknowledging this fear and build the courage to begin a personal, spiritual journey toward recovery. The women are asked to keep an open mind in allowing their fear to be replaced by the light of their higher power, to meditate or pray on what they need to get out of each step, and to know that they are not alone in their journey.

During the first group meeting, we introduce the concept of "looking for miracles." We talk to the women about how often in treatment they are focusing on what is not working; hence, looking for miracles is a way of changing the way they are looking at things with evidence that a higher power is helping them in their lives through a difficult time. Miracles can be anything from a productive therapy session to how things fell into place to get a woman into treatment. We tell the women, "If you set out to write down three miracles, twenty more will come to mind and you'll see 23 miracles."

We encourage the women to use miracles as a way to get in touch with their spirituality. Often women with eating disorders have been "numbing out" for so long that they are detached from body sensations; miracles are another way to get a woman back in touch with her spirit and body. Thereafter, at the beginning of each meeting, patients are invited to share one or two miracles that they have experienced during the week. This often seems to be the highlight of group, when the women can understand and experience how God acts in the group, their own life, and in their peers' lives.

Working the 12 Steps

Step 1

The women begin working on Step 1 by describing their "rock bottom" story. As they relay that they were out of control and unable to manage their lives, these stories often include a failed suicide attempt. For example, a 29-year-old patient said,

> I had been using laxatives and over-the-counter diet pills to try to lose weight since I was 15 years old. I thought that my marriage would solve everything and my eating disorder would just disappear. However, the stresses of a new marriage, coupled with difficulty getting along with my husband, only exacerbated the eating disorder symptoms. I started starving myself and then bingeing and purging. My mother was bulimic for 35 years, and if I ate too much, she would make negative comments. Both of my children were born prematurely. After each pregnancy I

would starve myself to the point of not even being able to enjoy my children. I would also take so many laxatives that I would get sick and vomit. It got to the point that I was overwhelmed, tired, and not enjoying anything about my life. I tried to overdose on sleeping pills three times, which only put me into a state of seizures. My husband thought I had a seizure disorder. I let him know what I was doing and this is when he told me that if I didn't get help with my eating disorder, he would divorce me and take the kids.

Step 1 is a "confrontation step" for patients and their families. The patients are confronting themselves and looking at the many ways their lives are not working. Step 1 also gives permission to get off of the "emotional roller-coaster," knowing that there is a better way, providing a willingness to give up their illusion of control. During Step 1, patients begin to ask questions about their pain. "What are the emotions that I act out with my eating disorders?" Women start to ask themselves how they have been living in "survival mode" versus "joy." What excuses are they using for their eating disorder behavior? How have they tried to manipulate external conditions in an attempt to create internal changes?

Finally, in Step 1 patients examine the myths about giving up control and acknowledge that the only control they have is how they react to their life circumstances. Women with eating disorders often have many perfectionistic traits, and when they cannot live up to their own high expectations, they react with shame and anger. Women are encouraged to explore their own reactions to their life circumstances. Do they react with shame, peace, anger, or perfectionism? How do they want to react? What would give them more joy? What would give them more peace? How could they act differently or more effectively with their emotions?

Step 2

Usually after Step 1, the patients experience a sense of confusion, frustration, and often emptiness. Women can acknowledge that "Of course I want to react differently to my life circumstances, but I don't know how." Step 2 is about faith. It is about "moving over" and allowing something bigger than oneself to take charge. In Step 2, patients also begin the process of exploring their beliefs about God and themselves. They start to question their childhood belief systems.

A 25-year-old patient wrote,

> Growing up, we did not separate church and our spirituality. Church was something we had to do. By the time I was a teenager, I was rebelling against everything, and rebelling against going to church was one way I knew I could really get to my parents. So I stopped going. It's really hard for me to get into this spiritual stuff without thinking I'm giving in to what my parents want me to do. So, I guess, when I

> think about my spirituality, I go back to the 8-year-old who was afraid to tell my parents "no" and thought that God was angry at me all the time for not living up to His expectations.

In Step 2, patients work on a "Spiritual Credo." They look at the ways that childhood beliefs about a punishing, judgmental God are not working and what we need to do to remedy the problem. In Step 2, patients continue to write down daily miracles. They look at the rock-bottom stories as divine intervention. In Step 2, the women explore what faith means to them. Are they living in faith or in fear? In facilitating Step 2, we really try to get the women to understand how they might be projecting their own ego onto their higher power. We ask them to look at these projections, pick them apart, and throw away what does not work. The women are encouraged to get to know their higher power as something that is working in their lives on a daily basis and that they can use their higher power in their recovery process. We teach them that they do not have to meet some perfectionistic high expectation to receive their higher power's love.

An important idea we teach during Step 2 is the understanding that their higher power may be something different from what they grew up believing in their religious traditions. Step 2 requires that the women become aware of their surroundings. Something or someone bigger than them exists. It requires the women to identify their faith and begin to exercise trust. By writing a Spiritual Credo, the women are asked to look at their own spiritual development. Finally, the women are asked to examine what current events in their lives interfere with their relationship with God.

For women with eating disorders, Step 2 seems to be a breaking away from the spiritual ambivalence that they have been living with while practicing their eating disorder. Often we will hear women say, "Well, I want to believe in a higher power, but. . . ." A lot of conditional beliefs surface in Step 2. They often raise difficult questions such as, "Why was I given an eating disorder?" "Why did I suffer childhood abuse if there is a God?" "I want to believe that there is something bigger than me, but I just can't because of how hellish my life has been. A loving God wouldn't let me go through that." Such questions lead to discussions about trust.

Women with eating disorders talk about how they have been able to trust a number on a scale to tell them if they are going to have a good day. They have trusted a clothing size to tell them if they are a good person or not. They have measured their own self-worth on a daily basis on whether they add up to the latest style or a model whom they see in magazines. They have trusted an illness—their eating disorder—to solve the internal and external struggles of their lives. They begin in Step 2 to consider that perhaps they have placed their trust in the wrong place. Step 2 is not the "feel good" step. It is blatantly and honestly looking at the irrational belief that has kept patients stuck in a pattern of destructive behavior. It begins the process of transcending these beliefs to a spiritual awakening.

Step 3

Step 3 is about surrender. Step 3 is really the cornerstone in working the 12 Steps. Steps 1 and 2 are the foundation that help patients to understand why surrender is necessary. In Step 3, we begin to ask the women to explore what events in their lives have occurred that enable them to understand that they must turn their will over to and trust in a higher power. The women begin to ask themselves if they have turned certain parts of their lives over to their higher power, or if they still feel they are in control or that they need to be in control. They are asked if they are bargaining with their higher power or if they feel like they have done enough by surrendering their eating disorder in treatment.

One assignment given in Step 3 is that the patients are asked to note stressful situations during the following 24 hours and to turn the situation over immediately to their higher power. After the 24-hour experience, they are to journal what happened during that time and bring it back to discuss in group. Often the women develop remarkable insight into how turning things over to their higher power for 24 hours reduced their stress. Before the experience, the women truly believed that if they turned things over to their higher power, it would increase their stress because it would mean that they were no longer in control. Again we encourage the women to get in touch with their bodies, to see what it feels like not to be in control, and to know that they are taken care of and that they are not alone.

A 42-year-old former patient wrote,

> All my life I have felt that I have had to be the one in control. I was the oldest child in a family of four. I literally felt that I had to keep my family together. When I married in my 20s and began having children, I again took over full responsibility of the house, parenting, and held a full-time job. After all, if I didn't hold the family together, it would fall apart. I guess you could say I was my higher power and I honestly believed that relying on something bigger than myself was a cop-out. I didn't realize that most of my life my relationships were damaged by my "I have to get things done" attitude. I liken it to the story in the Bible of Mary and Martha. Like Martha, I was constantly busy getting everything done and didn't realize how angry I was that people just didn't do their fair share. Of course, I never talked about this anger, because that would be selfish. I took my anger out on myself by using my eating disorder, I'm 42-years-old and I've had a more intense relationship with food than I've had with my children or with my husband. Working Step 3 and learning how to turn things over made me look at these relationships and at the damage I've done to myself.

> I felt stressed. I couldn't believe that instead of increasing my stress, turning things over to my higher power actually helped me feel calm and peaceful. I decided to do it for another 24 hours. By the end of the week, I was able to see how things really did fall into place without my own miraculous interventions. I then made a commitment to myself and to my higher power that I would literally take this 1 day at a time, because if I think about living my life this way in years to come, I will instantly go into control mode. But I can think of turning things over to my higher power for 24 hours.

In Step 3, we tell patients, "Don't try to figure out or analyze the process, but only to believe in the process of letting go." We start to look at our issues and problems symbolically and at how to transcend them. Another exercise to do in Step 3 is to take a nature walk and ask each woman to identify with something that she knows she will have to give up for her recovery. Often many of the women return with rocks symbolizing rigid thinking. Some bring back other pieces of nature that they can symbolically associate with unhealthy relationships, believing in things that are not real, or coaddictions such as alcohol, cigarettes, and relationships. Then we have a ceremony during which we throw these things away and chant to each other to "give it up and turn it over." After this ritual, we talk about how it feels to give up these things. The women are asked to write down when they have been successful in letting something go and when they have not been successful. They are asked how both of these experiences manifest in their bodies and how they are feeling at the time.

In Step 3, we use guided meditation as a tool and encourage the women to have dialogue with their higher power. We encourage the women to ask their higher power in prayer and meditation for answers and then to become aware of what is going on around them. In Step 3, we also begin to talk about humility. The women are asked to look at and learn from situations that illustrate their ability to be humble and also situations that illustrate their lack of humility. A willingness to surrender and to give up a false sense of control is the doorway into an ability to be more honest with oneself.

Step 4

Facilitating Step 4 is a two-part process. First, the women look at their use of denial. We talk extensively about denial and how it is often incredibly difficult to recognize our denial because it is usually an unconscious effort to keep us safe. The women are asked to look at how their denial is manifested. Some ways may be blaming, making excuses, attacking, "awfulizing," or overgeneralizing. We let the women know that when their "buttons are pushed," it can be a gift that can enable them to look at something about which they may be in denial.

The women are also asked to look at themselves and examine areas of their lives where they use denial. We talk about how difficult doing a moral inventory of our weaknesses and strengths can be. It is a rigorous step, but in the end, we offer these character defects or shortcomings up to our higher power. The women are asked to take a journey into the shadow side of their personality and to cast light on those aspects of their character that they have been masking for years. They are asked to tell the truth about themselves—both their weaknesses and their strengths.

Before working each step, the women are asked to pray or meditate to their higher power and asked what they need to work on or what they need to get out of each step. To bring some humor into Step 4, we tell the women to "hold on because you're about to get your buttons pushed on a daily basis, and you need to look at this as a blessing in disguise." This is a process of letting go. We start to look at the issues and problems symbolically and how to transcend our problems.

The second part of Step 4 is that the women are asked to work through a packet from their workbook, *The Twelve Steps—A Way Out* (Friends of Recovery, 1995). This packet takes certain negative character traits and asks questions in a way that the women can go through each one and then rate themselves on a self-evaluation of where they are on a scale from 1 to 10. One example is resentment. The packet describes how resentment feels and asks the women to give instances of when they feel resentful. Then they are to rate themselves on a resentment scale. Other character traits that women are asked to look at are fear, anger, approval seeking, care taking, control, abandonment, fear of authority figures, frozen feelings, irresponsibility, isolation, low self-esteem, inappropriately expressed sexuality, and any additional weaknesses or strengths that can be evaluated.

After the women complete this packet, we then do an experiential exercise of letting things go and turning all of these negative character traits over to a higher power. In the balloon exercise, the women write on a helium-filled balloon all of the negative character traits they want to turn over to their higher power. Before the balloons are let go, we process with the women how it is going to feel not to have certain character traits in their lives. We then go outside and form a circle. There is silence when the women can ask their higher power to take these character traits from them and replace them with something more positive. Together the women then let their balloons go and watch them disappear. The visualization is an important part of this exercise. The patients are asked to take this into their daily lives by being aware of when they do feel a character trait that they have let go, such as jealousy or hatred, and remember that they have turned that particular character trait over to their higher power. They are asked to say a prayer for peace at that moment. This reinforces the notion of letting go, trusting, and not "picking it up again." A 33-year-old former patient wrote,

> The balloon experience was an amazing "letting go" for me. I'll never forget how difficult it was for me to even admit that I had a shadow or a side of myself that I was not proud of. But then, to have to write it down and verbalize it, the only thing that helped me through it was knowing that I was going to turn this over to my higher power. I continued to practice the visualization when those feelings of resentment or anger would come up, and after a year, I decided to do the balloon exercise on my own. That's when I realized how I had grown. My first balloon was covered with character traits that I wanted to let go of. A year later, I struggle to think of five. I would say that of all the experiences I had in the 12-step program, that one was the most profound.

Step 5

In Step 5, the women begin to work on their shame. We usually start off Step 5 by asking the women to write something on a piece of paper that they have never told anyone and that they are extremely embarrassed about. Patients then fold up the paper and throw it in the middle of the room. Patients start asking many questions such as, "Who is going to read this," "Are you going to tell this to my therapist?" "Do I have to do this exercise?" Again the women are told to concentrate on their feelings and body.

We then talk about the difference between shame and guilt. We ask the women to identify exactly what it is that they are feeling shame about (e.g., "I'm a bad person" or "I've done something that I don't like"). This leads into a discussion about unresolved shame and how this often will lead them back to their addiction unless they get some type of closure or start to forgive themselves. We go around the room and ask each woman to talk about the feelings that she is having with what she wrote on a piece of paper.

Some common reactions are the following: "I feel like if people know what I've done, they will hate me." "I hate myself for what I put on the paper." "I'm so embarrassed." "I feel like everyone will hate me if they know that I've done something so horrific." "I feel like an awful person." Before the exercise has ended, we ask the women to take a vote on whether they want us to read what is written on the pieces of paper. We have never had a group where they have not wanted us to read the papers.

After reading the papers, the women's response is generally positive. They realize that they are not judging anybody else for what they have done, so possibly no one is judging them for what they have done. Often in a group of 16, 2 or 3 women have had the same experience. Comments after we leave may include, "I feel like weights have been lifted off my chest." "I feel like now I can do Step 5." I didn't realize that other people share the same pain that I have." "I don't feel so alone."

The women are encouraged to pick someone that they trust to whom they can tell everything, someone such as a therapist, a trusted friend, a religious leader, or a member of the 12-step group. We encourage the women to choose someone whom they believe will provide unconditional acceptance.

Women with eating disorders constantly judge themselves in a negative way. Working with Step 5 allows women to reveal everything about themselves that they have not told another person and to not be judged. In doing so, self-acceptance is a possibility. The patients are encouraged to come to group with their shameful feelings and experiences, learn from them, and move on.

Before we move on to Step 6, the women complete an assignment called the Spiritual Hierarchy of Needs (see Figure 9.1). At the bottom of the pyramid is "survival." In survival mode, we talk about how the women are living in addiction. They are usually judgmental of others and of themselves because of unresolved pain. There is a lack of trust, no joy, and delayed gratification is not practiced. Their eating disorder gives them instant—although pseudo—"happiness."

The next level is passion or meaning in life. We ask the women, "What is your joy or passion?" "Are you living or surviving?" The next level on the pyramid is "power and control over your life." This is when we talk about taking responsibility for personal choices. We discuss consequences and cause and effect.

The next level is acceptance of self and others. With acceptance, there is absolutely no need for gossip because not only are you learning how to accept yourself but also accepting others as they are. Even though you may not agree with someone, you can validate that person and still remain centered and keep your sense of self. You seek to empower others rather than have power over them.

The next level of the pyramid is "compassion." The compassion level is where there is no judging of others. You are able to do volunteer work with an open heart. Instead of judging others, you have empathy and understand the hardships that they have gone through.

At the top of the pyramid is "unity." Examples of those at the unity level would be Christians who say, "We are all one in Christ" or Buddhists who would say we have reached "nirvana." In 12-step group, we talk about living connected to a higher power or being "one with all."

When we work the pyramid, the women give examples in their own lives where they have been living in survival versus living in passion. They are beginning to understand the sensations of their body and remember back to when they were in survival mode versus joy and discovering meaning

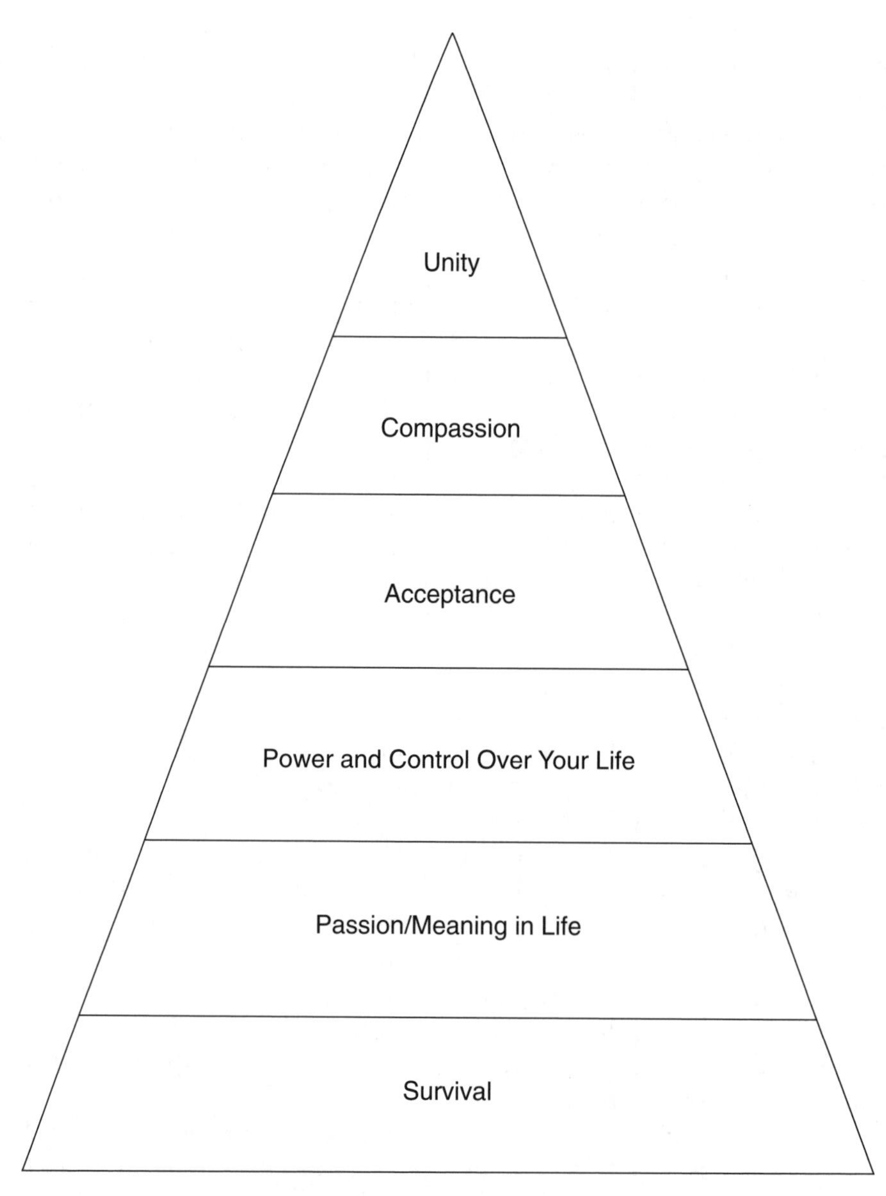

Figure 9.1. The spiritual hierarchy of needs.

in their life. Women also understand that often they can have glimmers of unity, and that this can be a place where they can live. Women are asked to think of someone who they know who lives in unity and what it feels like to be around that person. They are shown that they can surround themselves with people living in unity. Completing the Spiritual Hierarchy of Needs is a nice transition into Step 6.

Step 6

In Step 6, the women are encouraged to look at the phrase "entirely ready" and ask themselves questions as to where their current level of trust in a higher power is for each of them. Are they allowing their higher power to work in their lives, or are they continuing to try to control their lives with their own willpower? In Step 6, the women are encouraged to continue to develop spiritual tools to bridge their relationship with their higher power and to pray and meditate on a daily basis to nurture that relationship. Often in Step 6, we use guided meditation.

One experiential assignment we do in Step 6 is to help patients draw a picture of where they see themselves 5 years later and how God's help will assist them in reaching their goals. In Step 6, we often talk about how we create our own realities, and how in the past our judgments of ourselves have been projected on others. We talk to the women about how, just as their eating disorder is not going to go away overnight, some of the character traits that are not helpful also will not subside without effort. Another assignment is asking patients to become aware when negative character traits, such as jealousy or being judgmental, surface and to determine what is going on underneath, what they are not letting go of, what they are not allowing God to change or help them to change.

Women suffering with eating disorders often feel so guilty and ashamed for what they have done and are doing that in Step 6 we seek to help them understand that they are a "work in progress" and that these negative character traits will come and go. Once they stop beating themselves up for feelings such as greed and pride, they can accept the feeling, ask their higher power for help in letting them go, and then let them go without self-judgment.

Step 7

In Step 7, we talk about the humbling experience of needing others and being able to ask for help. Often women with eating disorders state that they feel they need to fight their eating disorder on their own, that they have messed up their life to the point that they feel unworthy to go to God and to others, and that they do not deserve help. A common statement is, "I messed up my life. I should be able to get myself out of it." Asking for help seems shaming and demeaning, and so to them it becomes evidence of perceived weakness or "not being good enough."

While working Step 7, an experiential exercise we use is to have the women join with a partner and talk about one experience that they have had during the past week that shows their ability to be humble. We also ask them to share an experience that showed their lack of humility. We talk about the distance between humility and vanity and about "the bridge that one can walk" to go to the side of humility. We discuss how often the great spiritual leaders had a time in their life when they needed to ask for help. We try to encourage the women to think of this time in recovery as their time of needing to ask for help. In the future, they will be giving back.

Step 8

In Step 8, the patients are asked to slow down, ponder, and reflect on themselves and their past behaviors and to become aware and willing to make amends. An exercise to start off this group is for the women to sit and reflect on all those they may have harmed, including themselves, when they were involved in their eating disorder. They write a list of these names and then go back over them and reflect on each person, the relationship they have with that person, and how they may have harmed them. They talk about the feelings that may have come up when doing this exercise, such as resentment, guilt, shame, and often low self-worth. We remind the women that as they are working this step, it is important to stay in touch with how they are feeling, even if they are having uncomfortable feelings, and ask their higher power to remove these feelings of shame, resentment, and low self-worth. We are reminding the women that in facing difficult feelings, they are choosing to live with integrity and self-awareness.

Patients in our treatment program create a mask at some point during their art therapy. In Step 8, we have the women bring their masks to group and present how they are continuing to put a mask on to face the world. The women are then encouraged to look at what is stopping them from taking off their mask and how they might be able to work through these uncomfortable feelings. Often the women report that when they find themselves getting defensive or blaming others while working Step 8, the culprit is low self-worth.

In Step 8, the women are asked to think about when they were at Step 4 and were able to list major character defects. We bring that awareness into Step 8 as we explore how these defects caused injury to themselves or others. Women are reminded that Step 8 is a continuation of working through these character traits with which we no longer want to live. This also allows the women to see the personal growth that they have made since working Step 4, and it allows them to have empathy and take a kinder and gentler approach to themselves as they move forward. In Step 8, the women make direct amends to such people whenever possible, except when to do so would injure themselves or others.

Steps 9 Through 12

By the time patients get to Steps 9 through 12, they are usually in an outpatient setting and involved in an Eating Disorders Anonymous group.

We think of Steps 9 through 12 as the "maintenance steps," and we encourage the women to work these steps with a sponsor. We often encourage the women to use the Spiritual Hierarchy of Needs as a gauge of where they are in their progress as they work through these the final four steps.

In Step 9, women are asked to admit fault and regret without blame and to take responsibility for their actions. In Step 10, they are asked to follow the 24-hour rule, which is if they engage in any eating disorder behavior, they promptly tell someone within 24 hours. In Step 11, women are encouraged to continue to listen to their hearts and to validate themselves, understanding that they are not perfect, but giving themselves credit for their efforts. In Step 12, women are encouraged to share what they have learned during their recovery to help others who may be struggling with eating disorders.

General Process Guidelines and Suggestions for Using 12-Step Groups

We have found that 12-step groups are beneficial for most patients in treatment for eating disorders, whether they are receiving treatment in an inpatient, residential, or outpatient therapy setting. Although such groups may be contraindicated for patients who do not believe in a higher power, 12-step groups for nonreligious people are available and may be considered. Patients with severe eating disorders in the early stages of treatment may not be ready to benefit from 12-step groups until they have been stabilized medically. Twelve-step groups may also be contraindicated for women with eating disorders who are still in denial about the illness, think the eating disorder is a viable solution for their problems, and are not yet committed to giving up their eating disorder.

Twelve-step groups can be an especially significant resource for clients with eating disorders who are receiving outpatient psychotherapy because they can provide a powerful source of connection, community, and support for women who withdrew into social isolation as their eating disorder worsened. It gives an opportunity for clients not only to receive support from others but also to give something to others and to affirm that they truly do have something worthwhile to offer. Outpatient therapists can provide clients with contact information about 12-step groups in their community for those who suffer from eating disorders and encourage them to attend these meetings. When clients choose to attend, we encourage therapists to invite them to report on their 12-step group experiences during their individual therapy sessions. We also encourage therapists to become familiar with the 12 steps as they apply to clients with eating disorders and to spend some time in their sessions discussing the step their clients are working on. Therapists can support clients in their efforts to work the steps by giving them therapeutic assignments that are in harmony with the steps.

Potential Concerns About 12-Step Groups for Patients With Eating Disorders

Mental health professionals have raised a variety of concerns over the years about 12-step groups in general and, more recently, about 12-step groups for those with eating disorders (e.g., C. L. Johnson & Sansone, 1993; Yeary, 1987). For example, some professionals feel concerned that the spiritual emphasis of the 12-step approach may exclude patients who are agnostic or atheistic. Others worry that participants will feel pressured to accept a specific definition of God or a higher power. We agree that such dangers may exist in some 12-step groups. In our treatment setting, we are careful to work within the belief and value systems of our patients and to encourage the patients to show respect for those whose beliefs differ from their own. We encourage the patients to define their higher power consistently with their beliefs.

Some professionals object to the 12-step notion that individuals are "powerless over their eating disorder" on the grounds that such a message may reinforce feelings of powerlessness that women with eating disorders may already have. We agree with C. L. Johnson and Sansone's (1993) perspective that the 12-step concept

> does not suggest that one acknowledge powerlessness over all aspects of life. Instead, it targets one area with which the individual is usually obsessively concerned. For our eating-disordered patients this obsessive concern is often focused on weight, body size, and shape. (p. 125)

"Handing it over" does not mean abdication of responsibility. It is our belief that help from God and others is more likely to come to those who work hard and help themselves to the best of their human abilities. The 12-step approach encourages women to give up to their higher power things they cannot control but also to take responsibility for things they can control. We view this as a healthy perspective and coping strategy.

A third important objection that some professionals have raised about the use of 12-step groups with patients with eating disorders is that some people involved in the 12-step program assume that it is the only pathway to recovery and that medical and psychological treatment is not needed (C. L. Johnson & Sansone, 1993). Related concerns are that the 12-step program is one-dimensional or superficial in its treatment approach. We agree with professionals who raise such concerns in that we do not view the 12-step approach as sufficient by itself for treating those with eating disorders; medical and in-depth psychological treatment is also needed. Although the 12-step approach is valuable for helping patients explore spiritual issues that are relevant to their recovery, as we have discussed earlier in this book, we believe a multidimensional, multidisciplinary clinical treatment approach is needed for the successful treatment of eating disorders.

Potential Benefits of 12-Step Groups for Patients With Eating Disorders

We have found that there are many potential benefits of including a 12-step group in a multidimensional eating disorders treatment program. First and foremost, a 12-step group provides a tried and tested method for including spirituality in treatment. The 12-step approach is ecumenical and thus allows patients from diverse religious and spiritual backgrounds to come together in an accepting atmosphere where they can support each other in their spiritual exploration and growth. The 12-step approach also offers a number of other potential benefits, including (a) instilling hope and faith for recovery, (b) giving women a common language for discussing spirituality, (c) providing a concrete action plan for using one's faith in recovery, and (d) offering a support network that can help prevent relapse, particularly after professional treatment has ended (C. L. Johnson & Sansone, 1993). We have found that the 12-step group in our treatment program also provides learning experiences that patients can take to individual, group, and family therapy where they can do more focused, in-depth work on their spiritual issues.

CONCLUSION

We hope this chapter has given some useful and practical examples of how a 12-step group can be used in multidimensional treatment and how some experiential activities can deepen the potential of 12-step groups beyond the benefits of simply talking and sharing. We also hope that it has addressed some of the concerns and questions mental health professionals may have about the use of the 12-step approach with patients in treatment for eating disorders. In addition to this chapter, we refer professionals to additional helpful resources about the 12-step approach and its application to those with eating disorders, including C. L. Johnson and Sansone (1993), Yeary (1987), Wormer and Davis (2003), and the Eating Disorders Anonymous Web site (http://www.EatingDisorders Anonymous.org).

IV

RESEARCH DIRECTIONS

10

RECOMMENDATIONS FOR RESEARCH ON SPIRITUALITY AND EATING DISORDERS

In this chapter, we propose a research agenda for theistic treatment, spirituality, and eating disorders. We offer some recommendations about how scholars and practitioners can contribute to research on spirituality and eating disorders. We conclude with some thoughts about the role of faith and spirituality in science and practice.

RESEARCH DIRECTIONS RECOMMENDED BY THE AMERICAN PSYCHIATRIC ASSOCIATION

Exhibit 10.1 presents the American Psychiatric Association's (2000b) recommended directions for research on eating disorders. Here it can be seen that a broad range of research questions need investigation, including studies about (a) biological and psychosocial risk factors for eating disorders, (b) developmental issues in eating disorders, (c) influence of comorbid conditions on eating disorders, (d) effects of exercise and food restriction on the onset of eating disorders, (e) women's athletics and eating disorders, (f) family influences on the onset and maintenance of eating disorders, (g) primary prevention of eating disorders, and (h) outcome studies of various treatment approaches for eating disorders. It is clear that much research is

EXHIBIT 10.1
Research Directions on Eating Disorders Recommended by the American Psychiatric Association

Further studies of eating disorders are needed that address issues surrounding the epidemiology, causes, and course of illness. Areas of specific concern include the following:

1. Genetic and other biological, gender-related, psychological, familial, social, and cultural risk factors that contribute to the development of specific eating disorders, greater morbidity and higher mortality, treatment resistance, and risk of relapse.
2. Structure–function relationships associated with predisposing vulnerabilities, nutritional changes associated with the disorders, and changes in recovery examined through imaging studies.
3. The differential presentation of eating disorders across various developmental periods from early childhood through late adulthood.
4. Linkages between physiological and psychological processes of puberty and the onset of typical eating disorders.
5. The impact of various co-morbid conditions (including mood, anxiety, substance abuse, obsessive–compulsive symptoms, personality disorders, PTSD [posttraumatic stress disorder], cognitive impairments, and other commonly encountered concurrent disorders) on course and treatment response.
6. The effect of exercise, including the role of extreme exercise, and food restriction in precipitating and maintaining eating disorders. Conversely, the possible protective effect of contemporary women's athletics on girls' eating and weight attitudes.
7. Further delineation and definition of eating disorder not otherwise specified and binge-eating disorder, with clarification of risk factors, morbidity, treatments, and prognosis.
8. Family studies on factors associated with onset and maintenance of eating disorders, as well as concerning the impact of eating disorders on other family members.
9. Culturally flexible diagnostic criteria to allow for the identification and treatment of the many "atypical" cases, which may represent a large number of eating disorders patients in non-Western societies.

(continued)

needed in the years ahead to help professionals better understand the etiology and treatment of eating disorders. It is also evident in Exhibit 10.1 that little attention was given in the American Psychiatric Association's research recommendations regarding religious and spiritual issues in the etiology and treatment of eating disorders.

PROPOSED RESEARCH QUESTIONS ABOUT SPIRITUALITY AND EATING DISORDERS

In chapter 2, we reviewed research and scholarship concerning eating disorders, religion, and spirituality. We drew several tentative conclusions from our review: (a) religious teachings about asceticism and fasting may

EXHIBIT 10.1 *(Continued)*

Additional studies and assessments of new interventions are also needed, specifically with regard to the following:

1. Primary prevention programs in schools and through the media.
2. Targeted prevention through screenings and risk-factor early intervention programs.
3. Improved guidelines for choice of treatment setting and selection of specific treatments on the basis of more refined clinical indicators and a better understanding of the stages of these disorders (including follow-up issues for short-term and long-term treatment studies).
4. Development and testing of newer biological agents affecting hunger, satiety, and energy expenditure as well as commonly associated psychiatric symptoms and conditions.
5. Development and testing of various individually administered and "bundled" individual and group psychotherapies including cognitive behavior, interpersonal, psychodynamic, psychoanalytic, and family therapies as well as nutritional therapies and other psychosocial therapies (creative arts, 12-step models, and professional or layperson-led support groups and self-help groups for patients and families).
6. Treatment outcome studies related to various systems or settings of care, including HMO versus fee for service; limitations of hospital or other intensive treatment resources due to managed care and other resource limitations; treatment in eating disorder specialty units versus general psychiatry treatment units; and impact of staff composition, professional background of providers, system or setting characteristics, and roles of primary care versus mental health providers in the treatment of eating disorders.
7. Further development and testing of professionally designed self-administered treatments by manuals and computer-based treatment programs.
8. Modifications of treatment required because of various comorbid conditions.
9. The impact of commonly used "alternative" and "complementary" therapies on the course of illness.
10. New methods for assessing and treating osteopenia, osteoporosis, and other long-term medical sequelae.
11. Further delineation of proper education and training for psychiatrists and other health care providers to deal with patients with eating disorders.

Note. From *Practice Guideline for the Treatment of Patients With Eating Disorders* (2nd ed., pp. 57–58), American Psychiatric Association, 2000b, Arlington, VA: Author. Copyright 2000 by the American Psychiatric Association. Reprinted with permission.

contribute to the development of anorexia nervosa in some women; (b) patriarchal or male-dominated cultures may contribute to women's feelings of powerlessness, and anorexia may represent an attempt by some women to exert control in their lives in such cultures; (c) the development of bulimia nervosa may be associated with a decline in religious devoutness in some women; and (d) many women who have eating disorders believe that their personal faith and spirituality helped in their treatment and recovery.

We concluded that the first three conclusions lack strong empirical support, whereas the fourth conclusion is more strongly supported. We also concluded that research and scholarly literature about the use of spiritual perspectives and interventions in eating disorder treatment is almost non-existent. Our review made it clear that much more empirical and scholarly work is needed if the role of religion and spirituality in etiology, treatment, and recovery is to be more fully understood. Thus, in our view, the American Psychiatric Association's (2000) recommendations concerning future research directions about eating disorders are incomplete because they almost completely ignore the need for more research about religion, spirituality, and eating disorders. In an attempt to help compensate for this deficiency, we propose the following general research questions about religion and spirituality that we hope researchers and scholars will investigate the following:

1. Do women with anorexia nervosa and bulimia nervosa understand, justify, or attempt to maintain their disorder by appealing to religious teachings about asceticism, fasting, or thinness?
2. Do women with anorexia nervosa and bulimia nervosa attach other religious meanings to their disorder (e.g., view it as an attempt to achieve spiritual connection or purity)?
3. Do women with anorexia nervosa and bulimia nervosa report that their disorder undermined their personal faith and spirituality?
4. What is the association between severity of anorexia nervosa and bulimia nervosa symptoms and religious devoutness?
5. As women recover from anorexia nervosa and bulimia nervosa does their level of religious devoutness and spirituality increase?
6. Do women who are recovering from eating disorders view faith and spirituality as helpful in treatment and recovery?
7. Do helping professionals think that patients' faith and spirituality may be helpful in treatment and recovery?
8. In what ways do women who are recovering from eating disorders believe that faith and spirituality are helpful in treatment and recovery?
9. How do helping professionals go about implementing spiritual perspectives and interventions in the treatment of eating disorders?
10. What percentage of patients with eating disorders would prefer to receive treatment from programs, or from helping professionals, who incorporate spirituality into treatment?
11. Does the use of spiritual interventions in the treatment of eating disorders enhance the effectiveness of treatment?
12. Do faith and spirituality help prevent relapse and promote long-term recovery from eating disorders?

13. How can spiritual interventions best be integrated into medical and clinical treatment of eating disorders?
14. Is there a difference in efficacy and outcome between spiritual and clinical treatment in inpatient versus outpatient treatment for patients with eating disorders?
15. Is faith and spirituality important in the etiology and treatment of men who have eating disorders?

We recognize that these 15 proposed questions only scratch the surface in regard to research questions that may be of interest concerning the topics of religion, spirituality, and eating disorders. The previous chapters of this book, as well as those that remain, may help stimulate additional questions that may be of interest to researchers. We hope that scholars and researchers with interests in eating disorders and spirituality will use their creativity and resources to advance scholarship in this neglected domain.

METHODOLOGICAL ISSUES IN RESEARCH ON SPIRITUALITY AND EATING DISORDERS

We now briefly describe some of the major quantitative and qualitative research designs that we think can help advance the scholarly study of spirituality and eating disorders. Tables 10.1 and 10.2, adapted from Richards and Bergin (2005), describe the defining characteristics of the major designs, their main strengths and weaknesses, and the types of research questions regarding spirituality and eating disorders that they are most suitable for investigating.

Quantitative Research Designs

Table 10.1 summarizes four quantitative research designs that we think have potential for furthering the understanding of role of spirituality in the etiology and treatment of eating disorders: survey, correlational, experimental, and single subject. Survey designs could be helpful for learning about patients' and therapists' attitudes and beliefs about the role of faith and spirituality in treatment. Such designs could also find out which types of spiritual practices and interventions patients and therapists believe are helpful in treatment and recovery. Correlational designs could be helpful for exploring the relationships between eating disorder symptoms and various types of religious and spiritual orientation. They could also be used to explore whether various types of religious and spiritual beliefs and practices are predictive of eating disorder onset, severity, and recovery prognosis.

Experimental therapy outcome studies of spiritually oriented treatment approaches for patients with eating disorders are almost nonexistent, and

TABLE 10.1
Comparison of Quantitative Research Designs for Research on Eating Disorders and Spirituality

Design or strategy	Defining characteristic	Types of research questions	Type of measures	Major advantages	Major limitations
Survey	Participants are contacted by phone or mail and asked to describe their beliefs, attitudes, and practices.	What are therapists' and patients' attitudes, beliefs, and behaviors concerning eating disorders, religion, and spirituality?	Relatively brief, researcher-constructed questionnaires	Efficient method for ascertaining the beliefs, attitudes, and practices of large numbers of patients and/or therapists.	Relies only on self-report data with all of its potential distortions; cannot establish causality.
Correlational	The relationship between two or more variables is explored through correlational statistics or causal-comparative methods.	What is the relationship between variables (e.g., what is the relationship between eating disorder symptom severity and level of religious devoutness or spiritual well-being)?	Quantitative, standardized measures	Good for exploring associations among eating disorder and religious and spirituality variables when experimental manipulations of variables is not possible.	Cannot establish causal relationships.
Therapy outcome study (experimental)	Random assignment to treatment conditions and control groups used in actual therapy situations.	Are spiritual approaches and interventions effective for treating eating disorders? Which spiritual treatments are most effective with which types of patients?	Quantitative, standardized outcome measures; ratings from trained judges	Can demonstrate treatment effects and differences between various spiritual therapy approaches and between spiritual and secular approaches for the treatment of eating disorders.	Difficult to conduct in real therapy situations: expensive, time consuming, difficult to control all confounding variables, and ethical concerns with using control groups.

(continued)

TABLE 10.1 *(Continued)*

Design or strategy	Defining characteristic	Types of research questions	Type of measures	Major advantages	Major limitations
Single subject	Study one patient at a time and take repeated outcome and process measurements over the course of treatment.	Did a specific spiritual intervention work for treating eating disorders? What components of a spiritual approach were most effective? What in-session spiritual interventions or processes were associated with what outcomes?	Quantitative, standardized outcome and process measures; ratings from trained judges	High ecological validity; Feasible for therapists to use in clinical settings; can demonstrate treatment effects of spiritual interventions and isolate the effects of specific spiritual components of treatment for eating disorders.	Limited external and internal validity unless the design is repeated many times with many patients and therapists.

Note. Adapted from *A Spiritual Strategy for Counseling and Psychotherapy* (2nd ed., pp. 330–331), by P. S. Richards and A. E. Bergin, 2005, Washington, DC: American Psychological Association. Copyright 2005 by the American Psychological Association.

TABLE 10.2
Comparison of Qualitative Research Designs for Research on Eating Disorders and Spirituality

Design or strategy	Defining characteristic	Types of research questions	Type of data	Major advantages	Major limitations
Phenomenology	Studies the meaning of people's experiences.	Meaning questions (e.g., the meaning of patients' spiritual experiences).	Audiotaped or videotaped conversations; written anecdotes of personal experiences	Can give insight into the meaning that patients give to their religious and spiritual experiences and to how they influenced eating disorder recovery.	Limited generalizability
Ethnography	Studies people's values, beliefs, and cultural practices.	Descriptive questions about the values, beliefs, practices of cultural group (e.g., patients' beliefs, values, and practices about their eating disorder and their faith and spirituality).	Unstructured interviews; participant observation; field notes	Can provide rich, detailed description and insight into the religious and spiritual values, beliefs, and practices of patients, therapists, and eating disorder groups and treatment programs.	Limited generalizability
Grounded theory	Studies people's experiences over time.	Process questions that ask about experiences over time (e.g., how do patients with eating disorders change spiritually during treatment?).	Interviews (audio or video recorded); participant observation; memos, diaries	Can provide rich, detailed description and insight into the emotional, religious and spiritual changes that patients with eating disorders experience during the course of treatment.	Limited generalizability; amount of change is not quantifiable.

(continued)

TABLE 10.2 *(Continued)*

Design or strategy	Defining characteristic	Types of research questions	Type of data	Major advantages	Major limitations
Biographical	Documents the history of a person's life.	What can be learned from this person's life (e.g., about the role of religion and spirituality in the patient's eating disorder, treatment, and/or recovery)?	Letters, journals, memoirs, documents, and interviews	Can provide rich insight into how religious and spiritual beliefs and practices affect the development of eating disorders and/or recovery from eating disorders.	May be difficult to establish the factual status of the materials used; biases of the biographer can distort the truthfulness of the account.
Case study	Studies a person or group.	What can be learned from the treatment of this person or group (e.g., what role did faith, spirituality, and/or spiritual interventions play in their healing from an eating disorder)?	Clinical observations and recollections, case notes, patient history, patient self-reports, and reports of significant others	Can provide rich insight into patient's eating disorder, faith, and spirituality, as well as the process and course of treatment, and the perceived effects of specific spiritual interventions.	Limited generalizability; biases of the therapist can distort the truthfulness of the report; outcomes are not objectively measured and documented.

Note. Adapted from *A Spiritual Strategy for Counseling and Psychotherapy* (2nd ed., pp. 333–334), by P. S. Richards and A. E. Bergin, 2005, Washington, DC: American Psychological Association. Copyright 2005 by the American Psychological Association.

thus there is a great need for more of them. Therapy outcome studies using rigorous experimental designs are time consuming and expensive, but they are essential for investigating outcome questions such as the following: "Are spiritual treatment approaches and interventions effective for treating patients with eating disorders?" "What types of changes do they promote?" "Are spiritual treatment approaches for patients with eating disorders more or less effective than secular ones?" "Is eating disorder treatment more effective when secular and spiritual approaches are integrated?" "With which types of patients with eating disorders are spiritual interventions most effective (e.g., patients with anorexia or bulimia; inpatients or outpatients; etc.)?"

We think that single-subject research designs (Kazdin, 1994) also have great potential for contributing to the understanding of the role of spirituality in eating disorder treatment and recovery. Although these designs are more limited in terms of traditional notions of internal and external validity, they are more feasible to carry out in clinical settings because they are less intrusive, ethically problematic, costly, and time consuming. They are also more clinically relevant in that they allow the exploration of research questions that are more meaningful to psychotherapists (Kazdin, 1994).

Single-subject designs could prove especially useful for evaluating the effectiveness of religious and spiritual interventions with patients with eating disorders. Psychotherapists in clinical settings can use these designs relatively easily to evaluate their own practices. In a single-subject study, the patient serves as her own control. By measuring changes in the patient's symptoms or problems over time, the therapists can see the impact of the treatment (Kazdin, 1994). If therapists who use spiritual interventions in clinical settings are willing to invest the relatively small amount of effort needed to administer repeated outcome measures to their patients during the course of treatment, they could document the effectiveness of their own work and contribute to the establishment of a large database on the outcomes of spiritual interventions with these patients.

Qualitative Research Designs

There are numerous qualitative research designs or strategies and many ways of categorizing them (Denzin & Lincoln, 1994). In Table 10.2, we present five major qualitative research strategies that we think have considerable potential for contributing to the understanding of the role of religion and spirituality in the etiology, treatment, and recovery from eating disorders: phenomenology, ethnography, grounded theory, biographical, and case study research. Qualitative designs hold considerable promise for helping researchers gain richer insight into the religious and spiritual perceptions, experiences, understandings, feelings, beliefs, values, desires, and practices of patients with eating disorders, and similarly into how their religious beliefs or spirituality may intertwine with their eating disorders. These designs could also provide considerable insight into the role of faith and spirituality in healing and recovery from eating disorders, as viewed from the perspectives of patients and therapists. Biographical and case study strategies have been used for a long time in psychology and psychotherapy; they can provide insight into the role religion and spirituality may play in the development of eating disorders and in their treatment and recovery.

MEASURING RELIGION AND SPIRITUALITY IN EATING DISORDER RESEARCH

As mentioned in chapter 6, the handbook *Measures of Religiosity* contains copies and critical reviews of more than 120 measures of various types of religiousness and spirituality (Hill & Hood, 1999). This resource should help make religious and spiritual measures more easily accessible to eating disorder researchers. Because most existing measures of religiousness and spirituality were not specifically designed for use in clinical settings as psychotherapy outcome measures (Hill & Hood, 1999), research is needed with them to see if they will prove useful for this purpose (Richards & Bergin, 1997). In addition, most of them were developed within a Christian theological framework and their suitability for non-Christian clients is unclear.

In our own research about spirituality and eating disorders, we have found measures of intrinsic and extrinsic religious orientation (Gorsuch & McPherson, 1989) and spiritual well-being (Ellison, 1983) useful. These measures assess patients' general levels of religious and spiritual maturity and well-being. Copies of these measures are available in the cited articles as well as in Hill and Hood (1999).

To help meet the need for spirituality treatment outcome measures, we developed the Theistic Spiritual Outcome Survey (TSOS; Richards et al., 2005). The TSOS is theoretically grounded in a theistic view of spirituality, thus in general harmony with the beliefs of many devout Christians, Jews, and Muslims. This perspective of spirituality includes several dimensions or components: (a) faith in God's existence and loving influence; (b) awareness of one's spiritual identity and purpose as a creation of God; (c) love for other people, including a desire to promote their welfare; and (d) feelings of moral congruence, worthiness and self-acceptance.

A 17-item version of the TSOS was found to have adequate reliability and validity in a sample of college students, and the findings overall supported the use of the TSOS as a spiritual outcome scale in psychotherapy research, although additional validation work is needed (Richards et al., 2005). A copy of the TSOS is provided in Exhibit 10.2.

EXHIBIT 10.2
Theistic Spiritual Outcome Survey

Directions: Please help us understand how you have been feeling spiritually this past week, including today. Carefully read each item below and fill in or mark the circle that best describes how you felt.	Name ____________ ID # ____ Age: ________ Gender: F M Religious Preference: ____________				
Session # ________ Date __/__/__	Never	Rarely	Some-times	Frequently	Almost Always
1. I had feelings of love toward others.	0	0	0	0	0
2. I felt there is a spiritual purpose for my life.	0	0	0	0	0
3. I felt good about my moral behavior.	0	0	0	0	0
4. I wanted to make the world a better place.	0	0	0	0	0
5. I felt peaceful.	0	0	0	0	0
6. I felt appreciation for the beauty of nature.	0	0	0	0	0
7. I felt like praying.	0	0	0	0	0
8. I felt spiritually alive.	0	0	0	0	0
9. I felt worthy.	0	0	0	0	0
10. My behavior was congruent with my values.	0	0	0	0	0
11. I felt love for all of humanity.	0	0	0	0	0
12. I had faith in God's will.	0	0	0	0	0
13. I felt like helping others.	0	0	0	0	0
14. I felt God's love.	0	0	0	0	0
15. I praised and worshipped God.	0	0	0	0	0
16. I felt forgiveness toward others.	0	0	0	0	0
17. I loved myself.	0	0	0	0	0

Note. From Richards et al. (2005).

Several other religious and spiritual measures have recently been developed that we think have potential as instruments for research with patients with eating disorders, including the Religious Commitment Inventory (Worthington et al., 2003) and the Spiritual Transcendence Scale (Piedmont, 1999). Copies and brief descriptions of these measures are provided in Chapter 6.

RESEARCH ON SPIRITUALLY ORIENTED TREATMENT APPROACHES

Although empirical research on religious and spiritual issues in mental health and psychotherapy has increased rapidly during the past 2 decades

(Worthington, Kurusu, McCollough, & Sanders, 1996), we are aware of only one outcome study about spiritual treatment approaches for patients with eating disorders, which we conducted (described in chap. 8; Richards et al., in press). Six experimental outcome studies have examined whether religiously accommodative versions of cognitive or rational emotive behavior therapy (REBT) are as effective as standard cognitive or REBT therapy (Hawkins, Tan, & Turk, 1999; McCullough, 1999). Three experimental outcome studies have also investigated the effectiveness of a Muslim-accommodative cognitive therapy approach for anxiety and depression (Azhar & Varma, 1995a, 1995b; Azhar, Varma, & Dharap, 1994).

Several other recent outcome studies of spiritual treatment approaches with other clinical issues and populations have been conducted, including a spiritually integrated reminiscence group for assisted-living facility adults (Emery, 2003), a religiously integrated forgiveness group for college women who had been wronged in a romantic relationship (Rye & Pargament, 2002), a spiritually informed cognitive–behavioral stress management workshop for college students (Nohr, 2001), a spiritually focused therapy group for cancer patients (Cole, 2000), a spiritually focused puppet therapy for adults with chemical dependency (Vizzini, 2003), and psychospiritual manualized individual therapy intervention for female sexual abuse survivors (Murray-Swank & Pargament, 2004). These studies, in general, have found that spiritual interventions are equivalent to and sometimes more effective than standard secular treatment approaches for religious clients. Collectively, they represent a growing body of evidence that spiritual treatment approaches may be effective with a wide variety of clinical issues and populations.

We hope that the number and quality of carefully designed experimental outcome studies on spiritual approaches for patients with eating disorders will increase. We agree with W. B. Johnson (1993), who described a number of important methodological criteria or standards for spirituality outcome research, including (a) treatment manuals, (b) multiple therapists, (c) therapists trained to criteria, (d) evaluation of therapists' competence, (e) establishment of internal validity, (f) consistent verification of treatment integrity, (g) homogeneous subject samples, (h) clinical samples, (i) multiple channels of measurement, (j) evaluation of clinical significance, and (k) follow-up assessment.

SUGGESTIONS FOR COLLABORATION BETWEEN PRACTITIONERS AND RESEARCHERS

We recommend, if possible, that eating disorder practitioners enter into collaborative arrangements with researchers in academic settings. Collaboration between practitioners and academic researchers can bring the best of both worlds together: a treatment site where clinically relevant questions can and need to be investigated and the academic world where time, money, encouragement, and expertise for conducting research is available. We have used this collaboration model in our treatment center, and it has proven productive and rewarding for professionals in both the clinical and academic settings.

We recognize that research is hard work and that it takes time and costs money. It also takes some understanding of basic research design and outcome assessment techniques. Yet although it can be challenging, research on eating disorders, spirituality, and treatment outcomes is more feasible for practitioners today than it has ever been. Computerized and Web-based outcome assessment systems and data analysis software packages make data collection and analysis easier than it has ever been. These technologies also make collaboration between practitioners and researchers more feasible than ever before.

Many years ago, when we opened our inpatient eating disorder treatment program, we made a philosophical and financial commitment to using research to help inform our clinical practice. Although at times we have wondered if the effort and cost were worth it, we are now seeing the major benefits of our decision. First, we have been able to document empirically that our treatment program is effective and that the vast majority of women whom we treat benefit substantially from our program on both immediate and long-term bases. Second, our research program has helped us provide needed documentation about our treatment outcomes to accrediting agencies and insurance companies. We assume the need for such accountability will only increase in the managed care environment of contemporary health care. Third, we have used the information garnered from empirical data to make specific positive changes and improvements in various components of our treatment program. Fourth, we have published articles with the hope of helping other professionals who treat eating disorders. Last, and certainly not the least, we have gained valuable insight into women with eating disorders and how we can more effectively treat them. We feel that we are better practitioners today because of the research we have done.

As practitioners and collaborating researchers plan research studies in clinical settings, they will need to decide which design or designs may be most suitable given the research questions they wish to investigate and the practical constraints they may face in your setting (e.g., time, money). After they have decided on the research questions they wish to investigate and the research design or paradigm they think would be most useful for addressing these questions, it is important to select carefully some assessment and outcome measures.

Several considerations should be kept in mind when selecting measures. First, in clinical settings it is usually important to select measures that are relatively brief. Most patients and clinic directors do not appreciate it if completing the assessment measures consumes large amounts of time. Second, it is crucial to select measures that have good reliability (i.e., there is evidence that they have good consistency of measurement) and validity (i.e., there is evidence that they really do measure the construct or variable they claim to measure). Third, it is important to select measures that are sensitive to change. Fourth, it is important to simplify and standardize the test administration procedures so that patients can complete the measures in a comfortable and consistent manner.

Computerized assessment systems are especially helpful because they enable patients to complete the measures conveniently on a computer, and there is no need to have secretarial or support staff do data entry before the test scores can be computed. This simplifies and speeds up test scoring, data analysis, and report writing. Patients' test scores not only can be available for research purposes, but they can also be provided in a timely fashion to clinicians for treatment planning.

Generally, experts in psychotherapy research recommend that when selecting outcome and other assessment measures, it is desirable to take assessments from the perspective of the patient, of the therapist or other treatment staff, and, if possible, of significant others, such as parents, spouse, and employers (Lambert & Hill, 1994). Selecting measures that allow you to assess various relevant dimensions of the patient's symptoms (e.g., cognitive, affective, and behavioral symptoms of the eating disorder) and functioning (e.g., intrapersonal, interpersonal, and social role) is also desirable (Lambert & Hill, 1994). For those who wish to assess eating disorder-specific symptoms, a variety of assessment and outcome measures are available that have established reliability and validity, including the Eating Attitudes Test, the Eating Disorder Inventory, the Bulimia Test—Revised, and the Body Shape Questionnaire, each of which were briefly described in chapter 6. Kashubeck-West and Saunders (2001) provided a helpful summary of a variety of additional inventories used to assess eating disorder symptoms in clinical settings. We also recommend that researchers consider assessment measures that assess other dimensions of patients' functioning, including their psychological, physical, social, and spiritual status.

CONCLUSION: INCLUDING THEISTIC SPIRITUALITY IN SCIENCE AND PRACTICE

During the 1980s and 1990s, the alienation that had existed between psychology and religion ended, and a more spiritually open zeitgeist arose (Richards & Bergin, 1997). Discoveries in physics, developments in the philosophy of science, a new dialogue between science and religion, research on the brain and human consciousness, research on religion and mental health, the movement toward eclecticism within the psychotherapy profession, the multicultural movement, interest in spirituality in the medical field, the recognition that science and psychotherapy are value-laden enterprises, and renewed societal interest in spirituality—all these have contributed to the rise of this spiritual zeitgeist (Richards & Bergin, 2005). There is a growing belief among scientists that the naturalistic, scientific worldview does not adequately account for the complexities and mysteries of the universe and that spiritual perspectives may enrich scientific and clinical understandings.

A growing number of scholars during the past 2 decades have challenged psychology's historical commitment to naturalistic assumptions and argued that a theistic, spiritual perspective has much to offer the behavioral sciences (e.g., Bergin, 1980; Griffin, 2000; Jones, 1994; Richards & Bergin, 1997, 2005; Slife, 2004). For example, Bergin (1980) argued that mainstream psychological theories and treatment approaches based on naturalistic assumptions "are not sufficient to cover the spectrum of values pertinent to human beings and the frameworks within which they function. Noticeably absent are theistically based values" (p. 98). He further wrote,

> Other alternatives are thus needed. Just as psychotherapy has been enhanced by the adoption of multiple techniques, so also in the values realm our frameworks can be improved by the use of additional perspectives.
>
> The alternative I wish to put forward is a spiritual one. . . . What are the alternative values? The first and most important axiom is that God exists, that human beings are the creations of God, and that there are unseen spiritual processes by which the link between God and humanity is maintained. (p. 99)

Jones (1994) also argued for the inclusion of theistic perspectives in psychological theory and practice:

> [T]here is no compelling reason not to include the existence of God among the fundamental worldview assumptions brought to the scholarly, scientific task. . . . Albert Ellis and B. F. Skinner, among others, have explicitly made naturalism (to the exclusion of belief in God and the transcendent) a part of the fundamental commitments they bring to the scientific task. If disbelief in the supernatural can suitably be among the control beliefs of some scientists, it would seem that belief in God and related beliefs about human persons could be allowable for others as part of their control beliefs. (p. 195)

Jones (1994) encouraged the psychology profession to engage in a more constructive relationship with religion and suggested that religious world-views could contribute "positively to the progress of science by suggesting new modes of thought that transform an area of study by shaping new perceptions of the data and new theories" (p. 194).

We agree with Bergin and Jones that a theistic spiritual perspective has much to offer science, the helping professions, and the clients and patients we serve. Herbert Benson (1996), a physician at Harvard Medical School, concluded that interventions designed to promote the relaxation response are more powerful when they draw on people's deepest religious and spiritual convictions. He referred to this as the "faith factor" and indicated that it appears that people's faith in an "eternal or life-transcending force" enhances "the average effects of the relaxation response" (pp. 151, 155). Consistent with Benson's finding that people's faith in an "eternal or life-transcending force" enhances the healing benefits of meditation techniques, we have found that faith in God and spiritual interventions often enhance treatment outcomes for women with eating disorders. As expressed in the following patient testimonial, faith and spirituality may be the only way that many women can win the battle against their eating disorders.

> A few months ago, I realized that I needed to seek medical help for my eating disorder, bulimia. But the more I thought about it, the more impossible it seemed that anyone could help me. I had no hope and absolutely no faith that I could overcome my eating disorder. After all, I had wasted and ruined the last four years of my life, hadn't I? I'd been so obsessed with myself and trying to escape my problems with a temporary solution that I was so unhappy. I was addicted to my eating disorder and thought that there was no hope in anyone being able to help me. I would be a terrible, miserable, worthless sinner forever.
>
> Then something changed. One night, as I was feeling so depressed and so alone, a dear friend encouraged me to pray and to read my scriptures. I thought to myself, "no way." Like this will really do anything for me. But then I decided that it couldn't hurt me. So I knelt on my knees and cried to God. I told him how worthless and hopeless I felt and that I didn't know what to do with myself. Then I pleaded with him to comfort me. I asked that if there was anyway that I could find someone to help me to please let me find them. I expressed the feelings of doubt and hopelessness I felt about the possibility, but I did know that He knew all things. For the first time, I had a slight ounce of hope and faith that night. I was totally relying on God to save me from my darkness and hopelessness. Before I even ended my prayer, I started to feel a warm and comforting feeling and I strangely knew that there was hope and that everything would turn out okay and that I would find

> help to overcome my bulimia. I thought that maybe there really would be a light at the end of the tunnel; the darkness would soon be gone.
>
> Now that I have been going through therapy and inpatient treatment, I've learned that you have to have hope and faith in yourself and God. It's the only way to win the battle. Without it you can never overcome any kind of obstacle.
>
> It is essential to have hope and faith in order to find true happiness. Believe in yourself. Believe in God. If you do that, you can overcome anything that stands in your way. I've been doing that. And because of that I have found the light at the end of the tunnel. Now I must venture into the light to continue my journey with hope that brings happiness.

We know through our clinical experience that including spiritual interventions and supporting patients in their spiritual convictions and practices can be a powerful therapeutic component in treatment which can add to the helpfulness of well-accepted clinical approaches. We encourage other practitioners to use patients' faith and spirituality in the treatment and recovery process. We hope that both practitioners and scholars will be alert to, and more fully explore and document, how patients' faith in God and spirituality might be used as a resource in eating disorder treatment to facilitate healing and change. We believe that as this is done professionals will advance in their ability to facilitate healing and recovery among women who struggle with eating disorders. We hope that this book will help in this important effort.

V

CASE REPORTS AND PATIENT PERSPECTIVES

11

CASE REPORTS OF THEISTIC SPIRITUALITY IN EATING DISORDER TREATMENT AND RECOVERY

In this chapter we describe in detail several case reports that illustrate the use of spiritual interventions with patients with eating disorders, demonstrating why and how spirituality can serve as a resource in treatment and recovery.

CASE 1: CATHY

Cathy was a 23-year-old Caucasian woman from the eastern United States. Before being admitted to Center for Change (CFC), she had resided with her mother, her sister, and her maternal grandfather in the home of her maternal grandfather, her parents having been separated for 3 years. Just before Cathy's admission, her older sister had married and moved out of the home.

Cathy had graduated from high school with an excellent grade point average (GPA). At the time she entered CFC, she was a senior in college, majoring in liberal studies and preparing for a teaching credential. As a member of the United Methodist Church, Cathy described herself as a very religious person, commenting that God had given her an opportunity for treatment.

Presenting Problems and Concerns

Before Cathy came to CFC, her physician had been concerned about her low heart rate, low blood pressure, and abnormal electrocardiograms, fearing for her safety if she were to expend herself in any way. Cathy had been receiving excellent outpatient care from her dietitian and psychotherapist; however, she continued to decompensate and deteriorate to the point of needing inpatient care. Dr. Michael E. Berrett was assigned to be Cathy's individual psychotherapist during her inpatient stay at CFC.

Client History

Significant Childhood and Family History

Cathy was the younger of three children in her family of origin. She stated that when she was in grade school, she was teased as "fat" and "chubby." She remembered people "oinking" like a pig and calling her "piggy." When Cathy was 7 or 8, her father had asked her, "Don't you think you need to lose a little weight?"

While growing up, Cathy believed that she was socially unacceptable. Although she had a couple of close friends during her early elementary and junior high school years, during most of her childhood and adolescence, she had few friends. Cathy's family moved on a couple of occasions during her childhood, which amplified her feelings of loneliness and detachment and also made her feel frightened that friendships would end, and she would be left lonely and isolated. Cathy's father's chaotic lifestyle—including poverty, unemployment, and failure to provide adequately for the needs of his family—contributed to Cathy's sense of being different, not "good enough," and inferior.

In describing her relationship with her mother, Cathy stated, "She's my best friend. We are very close." Cathy's mother was supportive and loved her daughter very much, but during evaluation Cathy's therapist realized the closeness had become dependency: The mother depended on Cathy to be her ally, confidant, and primary support system.

In describing her relationship with her father, Cathy realized, "My father was emotionally abusive to my mom, and it all hurt me very much." While Cathy was growing up, he made negative comments about her body, which made her very uncomfortable. He also engaged in a type of passive–aggressive behavior that made Cathy feel like she had to prove to him that she really did love him. The marital dynamics were such that Cathy felt that in some ways she had to play the role of the emotional spouse to watch out for and protect her mother from her father.

Cathy described a history of emotional upheaval when her father moved out of the home. Leading up to the marital separation, her father was depressed, unemployed, and impoverished. He was struggling with a drinking problem and had begun a sexual affair. Cathy also reported that just before the separation, her father began "giving me tight hugs, and he wouldn't let go." She also stated that her father would come in to her room when she was going to bed and put his head on her thigh or stomach and make some comments about the sexual parts of her body. There was no overt fondling or molestation, but her father's boundary violations and inappropriate comments were traumatizing to her.

At the time that Cathy's father left the family, he was emotionally demeaning toward Cathy's mother. He left in a way that made Cathy feel sad and abandoned; she reported much ambivalence toward him and questioned whether to continue a relationship with him. She felt that he had extended very little, if any, effort toward the father–daughter relationship and that he had basically disappeared and been unavailable for her since she was a child.

Cathy had no history of criminal activity or arrests. She had no educational concerns or problems. She had been an honor student at her high school and had done well academically in college, with a GPA of 3.97, until her eating disorder symptoms interfered with her work. She had never had a boyfriend, and she claimed that she had gone on no dates. She was harassed in school a couple of times during her senior year; she felt nervous around boys and felt that they were uncomfortable around her.

Eating Disorder History

Cathy first began to diet at age 7 by occasionally restricting meat or cheese. This restriction seemed to fit what others were saying or thinking she needed to do, but she did not like restricting at that time. By the time she was 11 or 12, she was restricting "a lot." With each year that passed, her restriction became more and more intense. Cathy noticed that she had depression at age 17, after she, her parents, and her sister left their house and moved across town. At that time, she lost contact with friends. Her depression deepened severely when her father moved out. She described herself as irritable, numb, very sad, and socially withdrawn.

Cathy first started restricting and overexercising when her father moved away and, because of financial struggles, the remaining family had to move in with her grandfather. She had no prior history of bingeing and purging or of compulsive overexercising. She felt self-conscious, often comparing herself to others. She almost always had a headache, especially when she was nervous.

Two months before Cathy's admission to CFC, her conditions worsened seriously. Her physician ordered her to go on bed rest. Her vital signs were varying so much that she would feel erratic and double beats of her heart.

She became dizzy if she stood up. During her 2 months of bed rest, she lost approximately 15 pounds. She would get most of her calories from a supplemental nutritional drink called Ensure. Solid food might consist of "half a sandwich with no mayonnaise" for the entire day. After her restriction became severe, her outpatient physician recommended inpatient care because of her dangerous medical condition and her inability to profit from outpatient treatment.

Assessment and Diagnosis

When Cathy was admitted to CFC, she underwent a physical examination, nutritional analysis, psychiatric evaluation, and mental status exam. At admission she was 5′6″ and 109 pounds. She stated that the most she had ever weighed was 126 pounds, and the least she had weighed was 93 pounds. She reported thinking about food, weight, body, calories or fat 70% to 80% of her waking time.

Cathy was not happy with her body at her time of admission. She reported her energy level as "low," as a 3 on a scale of 1 to 10. She also reported the following conditions: dry hair, hair falling out, cold body temperature, dry skin, easy bruising, poor wound healing, dry chapped lips, thirst, pounding heart with irregular beating, headaches, and dizziness. Her nutritionist reported that her body weight was below normal and that she was at risk for malnutrition. Through her psychiatric interview and mental status exam with Dr. Berrett, Cathy was given a *Diagnostic and Statistical Manual of Mental Disorders* (4th ed.; *DSM–IV*; American Psychiatric Association, 1994) Axis I diagnosis of major depressive disorder (recurrent, moderate, with suicidal ideation), generalized anxiety disorder (mild), and anorexia nervosa (restrictive type). Her Axis II diagnosis was deferred, with dependent features. Her Axis III diagnoses included orthostatic heart, low blood pressure, fatigue and tiredness, and sleep disturbance. Her Axis IV diagnoses included separation and upcoming divorce of her parents; discomfort living with her grandfather; some dependency in the relationship with her mother; separation from church, school, and work because of the severity of her eating disorder; and her sister's marriage and departure from home. Finally, her Global Assessment of Functioning (GAF) score was 41.

Cathy also completed a comprehensive battery of psychological tests at admission, including the Minnesota Multiphasic Personality Inventory (MMPI–2; Butcher, Dahlstrom, Graham, Tellegen, & Kaemmer, 1989), Eating Attitudes Test (EAT; Garner & Garfinkel, 1979), Body Shape Questionnaire (BSQ; Cooper, Taylor, Cooper, & Fairburn, 1987), Outcome Questionnaire (OQ-45; Lambert & Burlingame, 1996), and the Multidimensional Self-Esteem Inventory (MSEI; O'Brien & Epstein, 1988). At admission, her EAT score was 46, suggesting that she was experiencing clinically significant levels of eating disorder symptoms. Her BSQ score was 160, indicating a clinically significant level of concern and distress about her body shape. Her OQ-45 total score was 95, a clinically elevated score, suggesting that she was experiencing significant levels of overall symptom distress. Her MSEI Global Self-Esteem Subscale score was 23, indicating "very low" self-esteem. On the MMPI–2, Cathy's highest clinical scales were depression (*t* score of 83) and psychoasthenia (*t* score of 84), suggesting a significant amount of depression and anxiety.

Spiritual and Religious Background and Issues

Cathy stated that she believed in God and Jesus Christ. She described herself as a Christian and as a member of the United Methodist church. She said that the church provided her with a community of spiritual support, friendship, and activity. Cathy taught Sunday school in her church to a group of the young people and reported that she was active in church service projects. She also sang in the church choir. Cathy reported that both she and her mother were heavily involved in their church, not only on the "Sabbath day" but also on a regular basis at other times during the week. Religious activities were a major context for relationship connection between Cathy and her mother.

As a child Cathy believed in prayer and had prayed, believing God would answer those prayers. In the latter months of her eating disorder, however, before her admission for inpatient treatment, she had begun to feel unworthy and undeserving of God's love or help, so she withdrew and decreased the amount of time she spent praying and conversing with God. She also decreased her prayers for herself; she prayed for all others, but not for herself. Cathy began to feel that she was a bad person because she had failed to follow through on the promises and commitments that she had made to her mother, doctor, dietitian, and therapist, as well as to God, about what she was going to do to take care of herself.

Because of the severity of Cathy's eating disorder and depression, she began to withdraw more and more socially, with increasing feelings of fear, anxiety, and panic about being in social situations. She also became medically fragile to the point where she needed to have bed rest for 2 months before inpatient treatment. During this time, she was unable to interact with others and carry out her regular roles in her church, which she reported led to feelings of guilt and inadequacy for not being able to serve others in her church community. As a result, Cathy felt like she had lost her spiritual community to some degree. She also began to feel somewhat detached from God, and her sense of self-esteem suffered. Cathy also had feelings of self-disgust and experienced difficulty accepting her body and her sexuality, at least partially because of the inappropriate touching and sexual comments made by her father.

Treatment Process and Outcomes

Psychosocial Issues and Outcomes

Cathy responded well to therapy, especially family therapy. As she worked with her sister, competition between them decreased, along with their fears of sharing feelings and emotions with each other. Thus, they were able to achieve more closeness.

Cathy was also able to make some steps toward resolution in the relationship with her father. She wrote him a letter, which she sent to him by certified mail, confronting him gently about the inappropriate things he had done, including the inappropriate comments he had made about her sexuality and her body. She was also able to confront him about his absence, unavailability, and abandonment in his relationship with her. She expressed an invitation for a relationship if he was willing to "do his part and take responsibility."

Cathy and her mother were able to examine their relationship carefully through multiple family sessions. They were able to look at times when the relationship had become enmeshed, with Cathy becoming her mother's only real confidant. Her mother was able to declare that she no longer needed that relationship from Cathy and that she was feeling better, branching out, and creating more friendships; she encouraged Cathy to do the same. There was much discussion with follow through on being more open, honest, and genuine, and with the kind of mother–daughter relationship in which Cathy felt less responsible for taking care of her mother.

Cathy made important progress socially, developing her own voice, learning to be assertive, and feeling accepted as a part of the group; she felt able to feel loved and to give love to other patients. In her last day at the center, in her good-bye group, she stood on a chair and sang a solo for all the residents, facing many of her social fears and giving that gift of her talent to all the patients. Cathy identified her own challenges and worked hard to meet those challenges; she made life-changing progress.

The Role of Faith and Spirituality in Treatment

Cathy had a strong belief in God and a belief in Christ; she stated, "I desired to be loyal and have allegiance to Jesus Christ and His gospel." Cathy was a strong believer in prayer but felt that she did not deserve God's love, and she would not pray for herself. Early in treatment, Dr. Berrett asked her to begin praying for herself again. He suggested that she pray more specifically, clearly, and honestly by asking for exactly what she wanted from God rather than speaking in generalities. As Cathy began to pray for herself again, she was able to reaffirm that she was not an exception to God's love. She was able to find a place in her heart where she felt connected to God without feelings of self-judgment or selfishness. Because Cathy had expressed respect for her religious leaders, Dr. Berrett suggested that Cathy call her minister on the telephone and talk about her recovery so that she might receive spiritual encouragement from him.

Noticing that Cathy had brought her Bible to the treatment center and expressed a love for scriptural stories, Dr. Berrett encouraged her to read biblical stories and scriptures and to apply them to herself and her circumstances. She chose verses from the New Testament that had themes about self-worth, service, love, and forgiveness. One of the scriptural themes that Dr. Berrett discussed with Cathy during therapy emphasized God's love and kindness. He pointed out that Cathy saw the goodness in everyone else, and considered them deserving of God's love and help, but she could not find this good or this worthiness in herself. Gentle and kind confrontations during therapy sessions concerning Cathy's pattern of making herself the exception to God's love were helpful.

Cathy engaged in a variety of spiritual practices on her own volition. For example, she wrote in her journal about her spiritual experiences, about miracles that had happened in her life that she thought were direct blessings or gifts from God, as well as about indirect blessings that came from God through other people such as friendship, a smile, encouragement, and learning something new in a class or group. She attributed the good things that she had received in life from other people and from herself as gifts that originated from God.

One notable strength that influenced Cathy's spiritual renewal was her gift of gratitude. She had grown up with very little. Cathy's family had lived in meager circumstances with little money, a modest home, and even a shortage of food. Her treatment for her eating disorder was paid for by her church. The treatment center gave a charitable rate so that the cost of the treatment would not exceed the money paid by the church. Many times she expressed her gratitude to the treatment center and to the church. Dr. Berrett drew attention to her grateful attitude on many occasions to help her become aware of and validate her sense of spirituality.

The spirituality group in the treatment center was a comfortable setting where Cathy could talk openly about the spiritual matters relevant to her recovery. She had some strong spiritual beliefs that she was able to express during those group sessions. Cathy took on a leadership role in showing acceptance and finding commonalities—not only celebrating diversity but working hard to find common threads among all members of the group. Her tolerant and accepting attitude was a positive example to the other patients.

Her spirituality helped her talk to others, which was a blessing to her. This talk raised her self-esteem and helped her feel more useful. Providing service to others and sharing her spirituality helped her feel better about herself and remain connected to others throughout her recovery.

Perhaps one of the most poignant moments in therapy that the treatment staff experienced with Cathy occurred just before she left the center. The day before her discharge, Cathy said to Dr. Berrett and several other staff members, "Please come downstairs with me, I've got a gift for you." Cathy led the staff downstairs to the experiential therapy room, where she walked over to a CD player, put on a song, and said, "I want to dance for you." She had given up her interest in dance partly because of medical problems, partly because she felt too fat to dance, and partly because she lacked confidence. At this time, in celebration of her recovery, she performed a ballet dance. Tears were flowing as the staff watched a graceful, beautiful woman express her kind, gentle nature through her dance. Her countenance brightened the room. The gift of herself communicated her inner spirituality. She was fulfilling her belief that the greatest gift one can give is something that comes from deep within oneself.

Medical and Dietary Issues and Outcomes

Cathy's physical and dietary assessment at discharge indicated that Cathy had improved in several areas: (a) a normal metabolic rate; (b) an increase in the variety of foods that she chose; (c) the return of her somatic symptoms to normal, with the exception of nontissue weight shift; (d) an improved food consumption pattern; (e) an improved ability to recognize hunger peaks and respond by eating; (f) the ability to exercise without feelings of compulsion; and (g) the achievement of maintenance weight within a healthy range. Cathy was discharged at a weight of 124 pounds, which was within her estimated healthy weight range. Her body mass index (BMI) was 20 at the time of discharge.

Psychological and Spiritual Outcome Measures

As shown in Table 11.1, Cathy's scores on the various psychological instruments at discharge confirmed that she improved a great deal during her stay at CFC. Her score on the EAT had dropped to 17, which is well below the clinical range. Her score on the BSQ dropped to 117, indicating improved perceptions of her body and acceptance of her body. Her OQ-45 score dropped to 55, which was not clinically significant, indicating that the overall level of distress and symptoms was well within the normal range at discharge. Her global self-esteem score had risen to 35.

TABLE 11.1
Cathy's Scores on the Battery of Psychological Tests Completed Upon Admission and Discharge From Center for Change

Psychological test	Admission score	Discharge score	Normal range
EAT	46	17	< 30
BSQ	160	117	<110
OQ-45 (Total Score)	94	55	< 63
(Symptom Distress)	63	36	< 39
(Relationship Distress)	15	10	< 15
(Social Role Conflict)	14	8	< 13
MSEI (Global Self-Esteem)	24	35	40–59
ROS (Intrinsic)	40	N/A	N/A
ROS (Extrinsic)	23	N/A	N/A
SWBS (Religious Well-Being)	52	55	> 47
SWBS (Existential Well-Being)	30	43	> 43

Note. For the Eating Attitudes Test (EAT), Body Shape Questionnaire (BSQ), Outcome Questionnaire (OQ-45), and Spiritual Well-Being Scale (SWBS), the estimates of what is considered to be in the normal range are based on normative data. The Multidimensional Self-Esteem Scale (MSEI) subscale scores are all *t* scores, and so the normal range is between 40 and 59. N/A = not available.

Cathy's Postdischarge Functioning

Cathy involved herself with her church community again after she was discharged; in fact, as part of her preparation for discharge, Cathy planned some activities within her church community. Cathy enrolled in college and finished her degree. During the first 4 months after discharge, she did not return to her eating disorder, although she continued to struggle at times with food and body image issues. Because she partially relapsed, Cathy returned to residential treatment about 8 months after her initial discharge. She is continuing in her efforts to completely recover from her eating disorder and regards her faith and spirituality as an important resource in that effort.

Commentary on Cathy's Case

Because Cathy felt that true healing comes from God and Christ, her relationship with them was the core of her treatment. All that she did in her life centered on her spiritual relationship with her higher power, and she wanted to talk about this relationship in treatment; she needed to have a therapist and treatment staff who were willing to listen and honor the beliefs, her personality, and be willing to go there as she wanted and to use beliefs she held sacred as part of her recovery.

Ongoing clinical assessment and treatment continued for Cathy in every aspect critical to her progress and recovery. In staff meetings and treatment planning meetings, the emphasis in her case was on the biological, medical, cognitive, emotional, and relational aspects of her treatment and care. The emphasis on spirituality was small in comparison to other clinical and medical modalities of treatment, yet to her the spiritual component was the most important part. Giving her permission to include her faith and spirituality in her recovery efforts was crucial.

The deepest and most important driving force for Cathy in her efforts toward recovery was tied to her spiritual renewal. She had denied herself this most valuable part of her life as her eating disorder had worsened and her feelings of unworthiness had grown over many years. Because of her eating disorder, she believed that somehow she was unacceptable and could no longer reach upward to the spiritual and religious power and influence that had meant so much to her while growing up. As her therapist helped her regain that spiritual resource, she was able to realize that what she had to give spiritually was of merit and value.

In gathering information and history regarding Cathy's religious and spiritual background, those treating her realized that the bond between Cathy and her mother had an important spiritual quality to it, often tied to social, religious, and community activities of their church. For Cathy, this sense of belonging to her religious community, along with positive relationships with her spiritual advisors or leaders, was a great source of encouragement, comfort, and stability in her life. As the eating disorder had intensified and worsened, Cathy had withdrawn herself from that source of comfort. To help Cathy reconnect with her sense of religious community and spiritual belonging, to again interface with her spiritual leaders, became an important treatment goal.

To stop praying for oneself because of a sense of inadequacy is a common false pursuit of eating disorders. In doing this, Cathy had made herself an exception to love or acceptance from God or from other significant people. The reasons for this belief in Cathy's mind were that she had not lived up to the expectations or the standards that she needed to maintain to receive this love and acceptance.

Cathy had a deep sense that she was somehow broken or bad. Viewing herself through this shame, she had developed a sense of spiritual unworthiness. To her it seemed pointless to try to regain her spirituality because the eating disorder prevented her from being what she needed to be to experience God's love, grace, and help again in her life. Her eating disorder became an identity, a way to make up for the deficits she saw in herself by perfecting herself in her anorexia.

In assessing Cathy's strengths in regards to her spirituality and religious traditions, those treating Cathy recognized that her natural tendencies were to be gracious, grateful, and humble in her approach to the good things in her life and the blessings that she believed she received from God. As often happens, false guilt had become intertwined within her desire for humility and meekness; she began to believe that "the only way I can ever be humble enough" is to feel a deep sense of imperfection and unworthiness. This false humility was a no-win situation for Cathy because, in her attempt to be humble, she became more self-critical, deprecating, and devaluing of herself in hopes of becoming "humble enough" to merit God's help. One focus of intervention was to help her separate personal humility from this false sense of unworthiness, so that true humility could again become a positive and self-enhancing pursuit in her life. This new willingness and ability to see providence and the hand of God in her life every day and to see these good gifts as affirming and positive supports in her life for which she could express gratitude to God without negative self-repercussions was critical in her recovery.

Important to Cathy's recovery was the need to address her reduced capacity to love and serve others. She had, because of her false beliefs about herself and her relationship with God prevented herself from serving and loving the people around her. Permission to allow the resurgence of service activity and to look for opportunities for her to serve or to give to other patients and other people in and out of the social community of the treatment center was a helpful addition to treatment. Giving service felt good to her; she wanted to share the love and good will that she felt. She wanted to lift up other people, to help them resolve or improve their own situations. So in that healing process, she went from painfully narrow, self-absorbed beliefs about her own unworthiness to a broader belief that "because I am grateful for the good gifts of God, I want to give good gifts to others" as the focus in her life. Cathy was able to differentiate between caretaking and loving service.

Another important spiritual goal for Cathy was her desire to repair damage to her family, to improve the loving connections between herself, her mother, and father. Her personal pursuit of forgiveness and healing increased her desire to resolve old and difficult family dilemmas by praying for help, acting in faith, taking necessary risks, and reaching out in a loving and forgiving manner. As she made these attempts, she felt empowered in both self- and spiritually affirming ways, avoiding the feeling that she was victimized either by the past or by present conditions over which she had no control. Cathy still had to do the difficult emotional and relational work necessary to change and improve these situations, but approaching relationship work from a position of love and forgiveness enabled her to intervene powerfully in the affairs of her family.

In conclusion, Cathy's case illustrates the importance of assessing and utilizing the spiritual strengths of a patient during treatment and of helping her repair some of the spiritual losses or impasses that resulted from the eating disorder. In addition, the therapists must give ongoing encouraging messages to the patient to develop her spiritual resources. As they encourage patients to use their spiritual and religious resources in treatment, therapists may notice that many patients will go beyond what they encourage during sessions. Cathy accomplished much more progress in her spiritual recovery than Dr. Berrett had planned for in their therapy together. He introduced and taught spiritual concepts and ideas, and he gave assignments in response to the spiritual beliefs Cathy revealed; but in her own private moments, Cathy took these discussions far beyond what he expected. We think that Cathy's response and recovery demonstrate the broad and powerful effects of taking seriously the spiritual and religious aspects of treatment of a patient with an eating disorder.

When Cathy completed her treatment, she showed a self-assurance that was strengthened and amplified by her renewed spiritual connection with God and with her religious community. She was excited and had confidence that she had good things to offer to others. Her confidence reflected a dramatic change in self-perception from the condition when she began treatment. The lessons, insights, inspirations, and understandings that came to her through a spiritual emphasis and through her own private, spiritual experiences brought her a sense of peace. Happiness and inner peace had been lost to her in the eating disorder, and now she had them back in her life.

CASE 2: ANDREA

Andrea was an 18-year-old Caucasian woman from the western United States. She was a member of the Church of Jesus Christ of Latter-Day Saints (Ulrich, Richards, & Bergin, 2000). She completed the requirements for and graduated from high school while she was receiving inpatient treatment.

Presenting Problem and Concerns

Andrea's eating disorder started when she was 14 years old. She reported recurring suicidal thoughts along with wishes to escape from life, but said she had made no suicidal attempts. She was admitted to inpatient treatment after passing out at school. She was taken in an ambulance to the hospital dehydrated and orthostatic. Andrea agreed to enter inpatient treatment because her parents were afraid for her life, and Andrea admitted that "maybe I have a problem." Her parents drove her to the facility directly from the medical hospital.

Client History

Significant Childhood and Family History

Andrea was the oldest of five children. She described her father as "hardworking, fun, and logical." Andrea said she did not have much of a relationship with him because she "always had to do what he wanted me to do." She remembered a time when her 10-year-old sister did not want to go to church, and he picked her up and carried her there. On another occasion, one of Andrea's teachers told her father that Andrea was not eating. She said he held her and tried to push food down her throat. There were also times when Andrea did not clean the house and her father had held her arms and forced her to clean.

Andrea said that her mother was overweight and always depressed. She described her mother as "sweet, sad, loves people, is smart, fat, and likes to be involved in things." She said that her relationship with her mother was OK as long as they did not talk about Andrea's problems, which included her not eating, not wanting to attend church, and not attending classes at school. Andrea also said, "My mom gets really depressed, and I'm her sounding board. She gets depressed sometimes because she thinks that my brother and I are throwing our lives away." She also said, "My mom's been depressed forever." She's "unhappy, hurt, or sad, and the stuff in the present doesn't seem that big, but I feel responsible to try to make her feel different or make her life better." During the initial interview, Andrea said that her mother cried often and that she felt guilty and responsible. Andrea felt that her mother's life was falling apart because Andrea was not the daughter she wanted her to be. Andrea said that her mother wanted her to have straight As, go to college, and be more involved with the family.

Eating Disorder History

Andrea's eating disorder began when she was in ninth grade, at age 14. At this time, her family moved three blocks away, but her church congregation and familiar associations were changed with the move. Andrea also said that around this time, her brother was in the hospital after a physical altercation with her father. While on a trip with her family, Andrea quit eating. She said, "I was proud of it" [and thought] "look at what I can do!"

Andrea reported that she lost 10 to 15 pounds that year. From that time on, she began restricting more and more until she could stop eating for several days in a row. On admission to the center, Andrea stated that she would go 4 to 5 days without eating any food, and that when she did eat, it was usually just a piece of bread or fruit. Even on "a good eating day," she usually consumed fewer than 300 calories.

Andrea had not been menstruating for approximately 8 months before her inpatient admission. She said that she had been taking one or two diet pills a day for 9 months, as well as four pills of Excedrin a day. She also walked a minimum of 1 to 2 hours per day until 2 months before admittance when she cut back because she was physically weak and afraid that she would fall.

Andrea's restrictive pattern of eating in the month before her admission to inpatient treatment allowed for only a bowl of cereal, some apple juice, and a piece of bread per week. Andrea reported a lot of anxiety related to food, her body, and the reaction of peers. Starting 10 months before her admittance, she met with three separate counselors but discontinued with each of them. One of the therapists focused a great deal on family issues and problems but not on her eating disorder. Andrea stated her reason for continuing her eating disorder: "I don't like food; it's hard to give up [the eating disorder] because of the attention." She continued, "I like the attention, even though I hate to admit it. It's my identity." She admitted that the only attention she received or relationship she had with others centered around her being sick.

Assessment and Diagnosis

Andrea was 5′7″ and weighed 101 pounds when she was admitted to CFC. According to the physician who conducted her medical exam, Andrea was "cachectic appearing." Her vital signs were stable. Her cardiac exam revealed a regular rate and rhythm without any obvious murmurs or gallops. Her abdomen was soft, very cachectic, with little, if any, peripheral fat stores noted—just "bone on bone." Her extremities were without edema. Her neurologic exam was normal.

Andrea's MMPI–2 profile suggested that she had clinically significant levels of psychiatric symptoms. Her *D* scale was 101, *Hs* scale was 95, *Sc* scale was 87, *Pt* scale was 84, and *Hy* scale was 82. Her *L* scale was 71, *F* scale was 75, and *K* scale was 46, indicating that her profile was most likely valid. She partially admitted to having serious problems related to anorexia, school failures, and family issues but denied problems in other aspects of her life by repeatedly saying that "everything was fine." Andrea refused to complete any other psychological and spiritual assessment measures at the time of admission.

Andrea was not physically able to walk into the office of Dr. Randy Hardman, her individual therapist, without assistance from two people. Dr. Hardman reported that she was shaking and curled up into a ball during the initial session. She reported feeling dizzy and tired, and she had no sense of control over physical functioning. It took her a great deal of effort to answer the questions during the interview. She reported feeling very frustrated, scared, and sad, but said, "I'm almost excited about maybe getting help."

During initial interviews and sessions with Dr. Hardman, Andrea had periods of crying, sadness, and depression. At other times, she became emotionally detached. She met diagnostic criteria for a major depressive disorder, with severity during the previous 6 months including sleep and appetite disturbance, lethargy, fatigue, feelings of despair, dysphoria, sadness, and irritability, accompanied by extreme feelings of guilt, and inadequacy, low self-esteem, and extreme concentration and memory problems. Her depression seemed to be exacerbated by the malnourishment to her brain resulting from the severity of her eating disorder. She was overwhelmed with "just being home and trying to cope with life." She was not functioning at school, at home, or in her interpersonal relationships.

Dr. Hardman diagnosed Andrea with a *DSM–IV* Axis I diagnosis of major depressive disorder (single episode, severe, with suicidal ideation), dysthymic disorder, and anorexia nervosa (restricting type). Her Axis II diagnosis was deferred. Her Axis III diagnosis was described earlier. Her Axis IV stressors included dysfunction at home and school, debilitating complications of the eating disorder, chronic and long-standing family problems, mother's severe depression, failure at school, and failure of outpatient therapy. Andrea's Axis V GAF score was 40, and her highest GAF level the past year was 45.

Treatment Process and Outcomes

Medical Issues and Outcomes

When Andrea first arrived at the center, she was unable to eat sufficiently on her own, and she needed the assistance of an nasogastric tube for feeding for a couple of weeks. She ate 100% of her food after that time. Her physician prescribed 20 mg of Prozac daily to aid her in overcoming depression.

Psychosocial Issues and Outcomes

Andrea participated in daily individual therapy and daily group therapy, as well as the educational and experiential aspects of the program. Her therapy emphasized the false pursuits and patterns of eating disorders. Andrea's thoughts and behaviors during her first few weeks at the center were completely focused on her anorexia. She was extremely depressed with recurrent withdrawal and had bouts of crying, hopelessness, and despair, at times interspersed with agitation, irritability, and anger.

Andrea resented her parents and her family situation. As the oldest child, she had felt like she had disappointed her parents, failing to live up to their expectations. Hiding many of her true feelings, she was emotionally and verbally dishonest. In the early weeks of treatment, Dr. Hardman challenged her to start honestly addressing the issues that had contributed to her eating disorder. He also asked her to make a commitment to recovery by no longer playing the "undecided game" of recovery and of just going through the motions in treatment.

Approximately 3 weeks into treatment, Dr. Hardman gave an assignment to tell him all of the emotional and personal secrets she had hidden from others, including all her fears and doubts, negative spiritual beliefs, poor decisions, and lies. Her tendency had been to shut herself off—become numb and emotionally disengaged—and to use her "inside" secrets to internally punish herself. These confrontational but encouraging sessions were a beginning point for her positive turn for recovery. These sessions helped her realize that Dr. Hardman's motives were good and that instead of judging her, he had a desire to help and support her. She told Dr. Hardman that these sessions helped her believe that he would accept her, even with her "deep and dark" secrets. By knowing she was accepted in her emotional and relational secrets, Andrea also learned that she could be honest with Dr. Hardman about her painful spiritual beliefs concerning her relationship with God, which, being unresolved, impeded her progress toward self-acceptance.

As Dr. Hardman continued to work with Andrea, he learned about some of the things she had done in her life for which she felt great emotional and spiritual regret, and he saw that she used these regrets as evidence that she was unacceptable and bad. Dr. Hardman also learned of her private fears about being healthy and of the ways that these fears affected her life and her relationships with others. Andrea started to be honest about her lack of true friends or true emotional connections. Her only remaining relationships were based on her role as a victim of her eating disorder.

Andrea also began to be more honest about why she wasn't willing to commit to recovery. In an effort to protect or defend herself from failure, Andrea would often make half-hearted commitments, then change her mind or sabotage herself. She felt like she couldn't succeed or win, so she was going to be in charge of losing. She had an all-or-nothing approach to performance. If she could not anticipate doing something exceptionally well, she would do nothing at all. Thus, the need for being responsible for herself and for making and keeping commitments became a major therapeutic theme.

Andrea's eating disorder had become the indirect expression of her emotional needs, and she felt that her illness was her only way of getting attention, love, and kindness. One of the difficult challenges for her during recovery was to give up her need to be sick. She didn't know how to have a connection or relationship with other people without being sick, being taken care of, and being noticed for her illness.

During family therapy, Dr. Hardman helped Andrea be more perceptually and emotionally honest with herself and with her parents. Some breakthroughs occurred for Andrea when she recognized that her parents' perceptions of her were very different from the negative conclusions she believed they had made about her. In family therapy, Andrea's parents were sometimes astounded by some of her beliefs about them and her projections of their feelings toward her. They also found out that underneath Andrea's oppositional defenses were loving and tender feelings toward them, as well as a desire to have a relationship with each of them. Issues involving anger and conflict, particularly the need to resolve intense verbal and physical encounters that had occurred between Andrea's father and her brother and between Andrea and her father were addressed during the family sessions. Andrea's mother's depression and intense guilt were also discussed, and work was done to establish clear emotional boundaries between Andrea and her mother. Dr. Hardman addressed Andrea's false belief that she was to blame for her mother's depression and lack of self-care. Andrea learned that to love her mother did not mean that she had to take care of or fix her mother's depression, but that she could be emotionally separate and still love her mother very deeply.

Other issues that were important for Andrea to work out in relation to her parents included incongruence between what she believed and how she behaved. Her parents had taught her religious values, which she resisted and rebelled against because she did not want to please them, in part because of her father's angry and hurtful outbursts. Andrea had been inclined to take her father's outbursts as a personal devaluation and as evidence that she was the cause or at least a contributing factor in some of his harmful behaviors. It was helpful in these family sessions for the father to acknowledge that his choices and reactions were inappropriate and wrong and for him to begin taking responsibility for correcting them.

Andrea also began to open up and work through her feelings of sadness, regret, and sorrow for things she had done wrong in the past. She worked hard at trying to uncover the roots and false pursuits of her eating disorder. As she continued to get secrets out in the open rather than using them to punish or sabotage herself, she began to see herself in a new light. She learned how good and powerful her heart truly was, and she told Dr. Hardman that she had always believed her heart was good. Her heartfelt desires were to become congruent with her true self. As she came to trust her inner impressions more often, her self-confidence increased, her communication became more clear and direct, and her behaviors were more positive and self-enhancing.

As Andrea neared the end of inpatient treatment, she became quite fearful again, but these fears were tied to her old expectation that she had to be perfect or she would fail in her recovery. Even though she had made significant progress in her treatment, there was a period of time, just before discharge, in which she partially reverted to old negative coping strategies. After about a week and a half of self-sabotage, she was able to work through her fears and give up her false notions. She recognized that she did not need to be perfect to continue in her recovery but that she needed to be honest in her efforts to keep her commitments to take care of her spiritual, emotional, and relationship needs.

The Role of Faith and Spirituality

Before admission to CFC, Andrea had stopped praying and had avoided participating in her religious activities for several years because she felt she was unworthy and unacceptable to God. She believed that God had abandoned her and that she would only disappoint Him if she tried to regain His favor. She thought that God was displeased with her because she could not live up to God's expectations or her parents' expectations. In essence, she felt like she couldn't succeed or win with God or others, so she wanted to be in charge of losing; she wanted to control her spiritual and relationship failures.

One of the spiritual issues that Andrea needed to resolve was her negative image of God and her assumption that He viewed her as a failure. Her perceptions of God paralleled the beliefs she had had about her father. In addressing Andrea's spiritual questions and impasses, Dr. Hardman used discovery that her father's views of her were very different from what she had believed them to be. Dr. Hardman and Andrea discussed what she could do to understand more accurately how God might perceive her. They also talked about how Andrea could more honestly and positively approach God in prayer. Dr. Hardman and Andrea spent some time talking about how to change her approach to praying and seeking inspiration, so it could be humble, honest, and sincere—and an imperfect process rather than a perfectionistic pursuit.

After Dr. Hardman encouraged Andrea to begin praying again, she did so in private and in her own way. She also searched her scriptures for insights into how God perceives His children. Dr. Hardman encouraged her do some emotional and spiritual writings of the heart, exploring some of what she had felt and discovered in these moments of prayer, scripture, and reflection.

For Andrea to have a more positive and hopeful relationship with God, she had to change her way of approaching Him. Her approach to God had been so negative, despairing, and hopeless that she had refused to feel God's acceptance. The false beliefs of her eating disorder had replaced her efforts to pursue spiritual support. Andrea was also afraid that if she did receive answers to her prayers, she would not be able to do everything she was supposed to be doing and would fail and let God down. For Andrea, not trying was better than trying and disappointing God.

Dr. Hardman repeatedly addressed Andrea's spiritual issue of feeling abandoned by God. In time, Andrea made the connection that part of her isolation and withdrawal from God was due to her hope of being rescued by God from her life and eating disorder. She came to recognize, however, that if God did try to rescue her, she would resist it as a test to determine whether God truly loved her. This realization helped her become aware of her underlying belief that God had repeatedly failed her "litmus test." In shutting herself off completely, she was operating with the subtle belief that "If God truly loved me, He would break through this barrier and rescue me from my problems." In therapy, Dr. Hardman and Andrea discussed how she could open herself to others so that when CFC staff came to support and help her she could accept their efforts, rather than withdrawing and isolating herself. Dr. Hardman applied that principle to Andrea's relationship with God, suggesting she needed to offer her heart to God and open the doors and windows to her soul so that there would be a space for God to support and help her. This new openness became both a relationship and a spiritual breakthrough for Andrea's treatment.

These realizations helped Andrea begin to enjoy more positive interactions with the treatment staff and with other patients. She reported in therapy sessions that she was having more frequent and positive spiritual experiences. She recognized that for too long she had wanted God and others to do her emotional work as part of the test of their love. She talked about the need to "give up the test" so that it would be easier for her to get what she needed from herself, from others, and from God.

Andrea became better at making her own positive self-affirmations so that when she received spiritual affirmations from God, she could hold on to and trust them, rather than chase them away out of fear. Letting in God's will and approbation for her did not have to mean that she would fall short; rather, she could view each spiritual experience as a loving invitation to continue to grow and improve.

Andrea also needed to recognize that God was not responsible or accountable for her choices—she was. She came to realize that if she would make God a part of her choices, He could help her and still love her even if she were to make poor self-care choices. This realization helped Andrea recognize that she was responsible for her positive or negative decisions. She would have to accept the worse consequences of her choices, but God's love for her would remain unchanged. Toward the latter part of her treatment, God's love for her started to feel like a constant reality for Andrea. As she becomes stronger in trusting her own heart and trusting in God's love for her, Andrea's confidence in her abilities grew stronger; she

TABLE 11.2
Andrea's Scores on the Battery of Psychological Tests Completed Upon Admission and Discharge From Center for Change

Psychological test	Admission score	Discharge score	Normal range
EAT	N/A	26	< 30
BSQ	N/A	96	< 110
OQ-45 (Total Score)	N/A	56	< 63
(Symptom Distress)	N/A	33	< 39
(Relationship Distress)	N/A	13	< 15
(Social Role Conflict)	N/A	8	< 13
MSEI (Global Self-Esteem)	N/A	42	40–59
SWBS (Religious Well-Being)	N/A	48	> 47
SWBS (Existential Well-Being)	N/A	45	> 43

Note. For the Eating Attitudes Test (EAT), Body Shape Questionnaire (BSQ), Outcome Questionnaire (OQ-45), and Spiritual Well-Being Scale (SWBS), the estimates of what is considered to be in the normal range are based on normative data. The Multidimensional Self-Esteem Scale (MSEI) subscale scores are all *t* scores, and so the normal range is between 40 and 59. N/A = not available.

had a greater positive influence on the lives of the other patients. When fears came up, she would address them in a way that allowed her to offer them to God. She could admit the truth about these fears to herself and know that she would be able to get through them in a positive fashion.

Psychological and Spiritual Outcome Measures

As shown in Table 11.2, at discharge Andrea's scores on the various psychological instruments fell in the normal ranges. Her score on the EAT was 26, which is well below the clinical range. Her score on the BSQ was 96, indicating perceptions of her body and acceptance of her body comparable to perception of nonclinical populations. Her OQ-45 score was 56, which was not clinically significant, indicating that the overall levels of distress and symptoms were well within the normal range. Her global self-esteem score was 42, which is in the low normal range for women her age. Her religious well-being score was 48, indicating positive feelings she felt about her relationship with God. Her existential well-being score was 45, which reveals that she felt a sense of life purpose, meaning, and direction.

Andrea's Postdischarge Functioning

Dr. Hardman continued to have occasional contact with Andrea for many years after her discharge. She has had both positive and difficult events and experiences in her life, but she has reported that she has never returned to the eating disorder and that anorexia is no longer a part of her life. After discharge, Andrea completed her college education, found good employment, and entered a positive and nurturing marital relationship. The last time Dr. Hardman talked to Andrea, she expressed much hope for her spiritual and relational life and future.

Commentary on Andrea's Case

In Andrea's treatment, the nutritional, medical, family, cognitive–behavioral, assertiveness, and communication skills interventions were as intensive and active as any of the therapeutic work related to the spiritual aspect of Andrea's life. Her treatment was a collaborative team effort of the entire clinical staff. It became apparent early on that underneath Andrea's apathy, defiance, and rebellion was a very sensitive and tender-hearted woman who had experienced a lot of fear, self-doubt, and feelings of unacceptability. She had externalized her focus, and her mechanisms for self-defense included the eating disorder, failures in school, and resistance to her family's religious values.

Recognizing early on that the heart would be most effective means of helping Andrea reconnect with herself, with others, and with God, those planning Andrea's treatment made the importance of listening to her heart become an ongoing theme of her spiritual emphasis. In listening to her own heart, Andrea needed to decrease her excessive overanalyzing, mind-reading, and obsessive circular thinking to hear these quiet impressions. She needed to give up much of her emotional numbness and self-hatred to connect with her loving heart. This inward journey required that she shed her outward defenses and open herself to vulnerability, openness, and genuine honesty in her relationships. Listening to her heart and beginning to trust and act on those impressions and intuitions was a powerful spiritual intervention for Andrea. She came to understand that her heart could be a conduit between herself and other people in her life, even a conduit with God. This knowledge gave her a great deal of hope—hope for healing, hope for love, and hope for real relationships based on honest sharing, not on pretense or on being sick. She came to realize that she could trust the impressions of her heart, even if her choices were not always 100% congruent with what her heart knew. She also learned that she could be kinder to herself in the self-corrections that were a necessary and potentially positive and normal part of life. One reason to use the intervention of Andrea revealing her emotional and relational secrets, and in time her spiritual secrets, was that it was a way to access her heart.

In the process of revealing her heart to Dr. Hardman, Andrea was able to discover that she and her heart would be well received. This relationship included no judgment; Andrea experienced only acceptance, respect, and encouragement. She responded well to the nonjudgmental gentleness, reassurance, and kindness partly because this treatment was so different from the behavior she had experienced with her own father and partly because she came to know that her fear of disapproval and censure from other people would not be realized within the therapeutic relationship.

Many therapeutic discussions and interventions were focused on recognizing various false pursuits and beliefs that supported her eating disorder and prevented her from doing some of the foundational work for necessary change and healing. For example, Andrea's eating disorder gave her a sense of identity, a way to communicate her pain and suffering, and a need to receive support for being ill. It also gave her a reason to feel bad and unworthy and, beyond that, to feel that she had been abandoned by God. Her eating disorder provided a way for her to feel like she could get comfort and safety from the pain, through either numbness or a false sense of control. On another level, the eating disorder was a way to avoid personal responsibility for her life. Her default decision was, "I choose to do nothing rather than to do something and take the risk of having it not go so well." Therefore, the responsibility was on other people or God, to break through her defenses and rescue her from herself and her pain.

During individual therapy, Dr. Hardman made it plain on several occasions that he had no intention of rescuing Andrea from her pain; she would need to resolve that pain herself with God's help. She should be responsible for her commitments, her follow-through, and her growth. Dr. Hardman did promise that he would support her personal responsibility, honesty, and hard work with compassion, encouragement, and acceptance. They could come back to this agreement when there was a temporary lapse into self-sabotage, refusal, or numbing out over the course of Andrea's treatment. Helping her to understand her relationship with her parents more accurately—including their beliefs, perceptions, and feelings toward her—and to express her deep yearnings, love, and tender feelings for them were important in the spiritual aspects of her recovery. She could begin to separate God from her dad, and she could separate her relationship with God from her relationship with her father. She could create her very own relationship with God, a relationship that was not at all like the critical, rejecting relationship she had had with her own father. These insights developed over the course of many weeks in treatment.

Helping Andrea understand that responsibility is not the same as blame, fault, criticism, or judgment was both a psychological and a spiritual intervention. Previously she had considered "responsibility" as proof that whatever she did could not be right, that she would always fail and always be unworthy. This misconception kept her from being proactive in her spiritual life. She came to understand that spiritual responsibility and ownership are her choices, that God had not made these choices for her. Finally, Andrea came to recognize that God's choice for her was to accept her, love her, and help her in the choices she had made, even though they might be imperfect or unwise. God's view of Andrea was not characterized by condemnation, fault, and judgment.

Over the course of treatment, she increased her scriptural studies and doctrinal knowledge of her religion, and her new knowledge increased her prayerfulness. She began to believe that God was on her side and that God's choice was to be with her. She wanted to choose to be true to herself. She expressed a desire to be in harmony with what God wanted for her, and she was willing to have God help her, rather than believing she had to get everything right on her own. This new notion of personal responsibility enabled Andrea to get out of the "all or nothing," or "black or white" thinking that often prevented her from making any choice except the choice of avoidance.

Helping Andrea face her many fears and recognize that her worst fears did not come true required both spiritual and relational interventions. She found that her fears about people inside and outside of the treatment center, her family, and her religious leaders were not true. If she approached these relationships with genuineness, honesty, and openness, people responded positively to her, and they often reciprocated in kind. This discovery motivated her to take more risks in her relationships. In the course of this genuine sharing of self, she found out that people could value her for much more than being sick with an eating disorder. As she re-engaged with her religious leaders and her religious services, she recognized that her false pursuits and beliefs had prevented her from having benefits available in her religious community and through her religious worship. She would often come back from those religious experiences feeling validated, encouraged, hopeful, and more determined to pursue her recovery. Andrea's experiences within her religious community felt good to her, and she no longer feared rejection from this group.

The process of Andrea's recovery represents a powerful shift in personal conviction and energy. Andrea had been committed to her fears, to self-protection, to being right, and to avoiding pain, and she had invested tremendous energy into those defenses. Ultimately she had narrowed her sense of identity to an eating disorder. Over the course of treatment, a therapy approach was developed to shift her negative commitments and energies gradually into new and positive pursuits that required the same amount of hard work, effort, and follow-through as the negative patterns. Emphasis on the spiritual components shifted Andrea's energy into a new direction focusing into the deepest part of herself, allowing her heart to enter actively into new commitments. Because this new direction was self-enhancing and brought positive responses from others, she felt closer to others and to God, and she expanded less energy to sustain improvement over time. Because most people responded to her efforts in positive ways, her feelings of closeness to others and to God improved and the outlay of energy needed to maintain these improvements decreased over time. Andrea felt like she had new spiritual reserves to assist her in her courageous efforts to change. Andrea no longer felt abandoned by God, and she no longer felt alone in her life.

CASE 3: ALEXIS

Alexis was a 21-year-old woman from the eastern United States. Her immediate family consisted of her parents and older brother. Her mother was an employment recruiter; her father was an X-ray technician. Her parents had been married for 35 years. Her older brother had married and was living with his wife and four children.

At the time of her admission to the Center for Change, Alexia was finishing up a 2-year degree at a junior college in general education with plans of transferring to a 4-year university and majoring in art or law. She had been living with a roommate and working for her brother as a freelance artist. Alexis was Jewish, considering herself part of the Reformed tradition within Judaism (Miller & Lovinger, 2000). Dr. Michael Berrett was assigned to be her individual therapist during her inpatient treatment.

Presenting Problem and Concerns

Although she had been in treatment for substance abuse, it had become apparent that Alexis was struggling with a serious eating disorder, and so she was referred for eating disorder inpatient treatment. She presented for her intake interview with flat and guarded affect. Alexis reported on admission that she was thinking about food 100% of the time. Soon after admission, she stated that she wanted to leave treatment because she felt she did not need it but was doing treatment for her parents' sake. She stated, "I have come here to find out if I'm in a better place with my eating disorder and to see if I'm ready to go back out on my own." Nevertheless, she stayed and was cooperative and responsive.

In addition to her eating disorder, Alexis was struggling with a variety of addictive behaviors, including self-mutilation, abuse of prescription pain medications, and abuse of sleeping medications. She reported significant childhood trauma yet resisted talking about it. Recently she had been experiencing a flooding of flashbacks from violent childhood sexual trauma. Alexis was also experiencing paranoid ideation and fear about people from her past trying to kill her. She would hear, see and feel things associated with her past traumas. One of the treatment goals for inpatient care was to help her deal with her childhood sexual abuse so that she would be able to contain and decrease intrusive memories related to that abuse. In addition to the psychological and emotional distress, she was feeling guilt about her parents paying for her treatment.

Client History

Significant Childhood and Family History

Alexis described her father as "generous, stubborn, and sarcastic." She described her current relationship with her father as good, but she stated that when she was growing up this relationship was conflicted. There were also times when her father would give her inconsistent messages such as "you shouldn't throw up or restrict, but you would look better if you lost 10 pounds." Alexis had few positive memories of her childhood (age 6–11). Her memory of age 11 to 13 was of feeling "crazy and chaotic." Her father was "very critical, out of control, and at times physically abusive." Alexis would lock herself in her room to get away from her parents.

When asked to describe her mother, Alexis said she was "critical, oblivious, and strong." She claimed that overall her relationship with her mother was good; however, it was "better over the phone than in person." She stated that after being around her mother for a couple of days, "she gets on my nerves and I feel like I'm going crazy." Alexis described growing up with her mother as "hell" recalling that two were in constant conflict.

Alexis's parents' marital relationship was also conflicted. Alexis said that her parents "should have gotten divorced a long time ago." When Alexis was in sixth grade, her parents' marriage was "on the rocks." At that time, both would go to Alexis for advice. She advised them to divorce. Just before her admission to CFC, Alexis's parents stopped asking her for advice about marital problems. Alexis also felt that her parents treated her like a child during much of her teenage and young adult life by trying to control her life after "not being there for me in childhood."

There was a 14-year age difference between Alexis and her older brother. Alexis said she was never very close to him. When asked how people in her family deal with angry feelings, Alexis said "they all stuff their feelings." Alexis refused to stuff her hurt and angry feelings for the first half of her life. When she realized that her temper outbursts accomplished nothing positive, she joined the rest of the family in stuffing her feelings. When asked what kind of discipline was used in the home, she responded, "Force and control."

Alexis reported experiencing both physical and sexual abuse as a small child over the course of several years. Alexis's report of the abuse revealed that it was "ritualistic, violent, sexual, and involved more than one man." She was forced both to participate and watch others.

Alexis's freshman year at college was chaotic. She described herself as "always in trouble, truant, hyper, and out of control." She was sexually active and reported using sex as a way to manage her emotions and punish herself.

Eating Disorder History

Alexis explained that her eating disorder started when she was 13 years old. At that time she started restricting to one meal a day. After this restrictive pattern, she went on a diet of one glass of milk and one glass of juice per day. During that period of time, she dropped to 89 pounds. Eventually her eating disorder consisted of restricting and purging several times a day. The purging was later reinforced when she realized that through purging she could eat whatever she wanted and maintain a body weight of 100 pounds. Eventually she started to have symptoms of headache, nausea, dehydration, body pains, and fatigue. Shortly after this, a close friend died from an eating disorder. At that point, she told her family she had one. She found an outpatient clinic and started in eating disorder treatment on a regular basis. However, an addiction to pain medication got in the way of her treatment, so the clinic director recommended that she go into a drug rehabilitation program.

After 30 days of inpatient drug rehabilitation, Alexis's eating disorder worsened. Alexis felt that she could get rid of the disorder on her own; however, the hospital disagreed and recommended to Alexis' parents that she be placed in an acute eating disorder treatment program to help her break the cycle of her eating disorder. At admission, Alexis not only had a pattern of abusing pain medications, she also appeared to have a polysubstance abuse pattern; she would take any prescription or over-the-counter drug to change the way she felt inside.

Assessment and Diagnosis

Alexis was 5′5″ and 115 pounds at admission. Her BMI was 19. Her body weight and somatic protein stores were below normal, and she was at risk for malnutrition. Alexis endorsed many symptoms of severe depression and anxiety. She was thin and pale. Her teeth were losing some enamel, particularly in the front incisors. She reported the following: fragile hair and loss of hair, dry skin, frequent bruising, poor wound healing, fluid retention, stomach pain, heart pounding, constipation, diarrhea, cold body temperature, and amenorrhea.

Alexis described feeling confused about everything. She stated that she had suicidal ideation every day, including plans of slicing her wrists, overdosing on pills, hanging herself, and jumping off a building. Alexis's MMPI–2 showed an extremely elevated *F* scale (89) and high clinical scales of *Sc* (85) and *Pt* (84), suggesting that she was experiencing a high degree of chaos and psychic pain, a high degree of emotional and mental disorganization, and a high degree of anxiety. Scores on the EAT and BSQ suggested a significant amount of distress related to her eating disorder symptoms and concerns about her body shape. Her OQ-45 suggested that she was experiencing significant levels of distress in her intrapsychic functioning, interpersonal functioning, and social role performance. Her MSEI score suggested that she viewed herself as "unlikable."

Alexis's Axis I diagnoses were bipolar disorder not otherwise specified; eating disorder not otherwise specified, with both restrictive and binge–purge traits; posttraumatic stress disorder (PTSD), chronic, with delayed onset; generalized anxiety disorder with panic attacks; and alcohol abuse, with early partial remission. Her Axis II diagnosis was deferred initially with the note that she had features of borderline personality disorder. Her Axis IV diagnoses were family of origin issues, past physical and sexual abuse, financial difficulties, chronic and intrusive memories from past sexual and physical abuse, inability to maintain a job, chaotic social interactions, confusion about her sexual life, and fears of being unable to "make it in life." Her intake GAF was 40.

Treatment Process and Outcomes

Psychosocial Issues and Outcomes

In individual therapy, Alexis struggled in her ability to communicate her thoughts and feelings. At the beginning of therapy, she resisted discussing her history of abuse; however, she had some success with art therapy and artwork related to her abuse. As her treatment progressed, Alexis eventually became willing to work on memories, feelings, and beliefs about herself related to her sexual abuse which had occurred when she was between ages 4 and 7. Treatment was difficult and slow, however, because when Alexis would get close to such painful issues, she would act out by using her eating disorder or self-mutilation to cope with her feelings.

Alexis struggled, especially in family therapy. She refused to have family sessions for the first 6 weeks. Eventually, she was willing to do telephone sessions with her parents and live sessions when they came into town. She was able to confront her parents about issues that troubled her; however, she quickly felt guilty after telling them how she felt. Family therapy eventually focused in on the relationship between Alexis and her mother. Issues about boundaries in the relationship, financial stresses, and living arrangement were discussed. Alexis's mother eventually reported that she felt positive about their relationship and about her daughter's progress. Alexis reported increased feelings of being comfortable, being understood, and making connections understood with her mother.

Alexis was ambivalent about experiences in her relationships with her parents; she felt that she had been deeply hurt by them in her growing up years, and she felt that she was a "bad person" who had done nothing but cause them grief. This confusion had not been resolved when she was discharged; however, she had improved her communications with them and was committed to more regular contact with them.

At discharge, Alexis said she did not have any plans for suicide, including any current suicidal ideation. She was not abusing alcohol, bingeing or purging, or engaging in self-mutilation. She expressed commitment to continue to get well and to maintain progress in overcoming her eating disorder.

Medical Issues and Outcomes

At discharge, Alexis's body weight and somatic protein stores were within normal range. Her body weight of 122 pounds was within the lower end of the "healthy normal range," and her discharge BMI was 19.48. Her dietary discharge assessment indicated that she had improved in the following areas: (a) an increase in the variety of foods she was choosing; (b) normal menstruation, better thermal regulation, and better digestive and absorptive functions; (c) ability to accept daily and weekly hydration changes resulting in temporary weight shifts; (d) a regular and helpful pattern of food consumption; (e) the ability to recognize hunger peaks and respond in an appropriate and timely manner; (f) she reduced time spent thinking about food, hunger, and weight (15% of her day); (g) ability to exercise without feeling compulsive; (h) ability to be comfortable eating socially; and (i) ability to eat challenging foods without fear, guilt, or anxiety. Nevertheless, at discharge she still had some areas in which she needed to improve, such as buying food for her home and challenging herself with food intake.

The Role of Faith and Spirituality in Treatment

Initially Alexis discussed little about her religious faith. She referred to her religion only as a cultural and social connection and as part of community life for her family while she was growing up. She expressed extreme self-hatred and felt unworthy even to discuss her beliefs in God. Gradually over time, Alexis responded to a treatment program that provided permission and feelings of safety to explore and discuss spiritual issues; she began to mention God in conversation.

When asked in individual therapy about worship practices, Alexis reported acts of service and support to others of her religion and recalled being involved in activities with the young people in their religious community. These activities gave Alexis others to identify with and relate to. During treatment, she began to desire companionship again with those of her faith. She received permission to go on "therapeutic pass" to attend a synagogue near the treatment center. Associating with others in the Jewish community buoyed her and encouraged both her spirituality and her recovery. She was able to participate with this synagogue in several Jewish holidays and festivals, including some Sabbath activities and the Passover festival (Miller & Lovinger, 2000).

Alexis was able to be open during 12-step group, spirituality group, and individual therapy to challenges to examine spiritual issues because as a Reformed Jew she believed strongly in embracing truth wherever it might be found. This core perspective and practice created an openness that served her well during treatment. Alexis was encouraged to pray to God in a manner consistent with her beliefs. She reported that she prayed for guidance and for increased love toward others and toward God.

With support from Dr. Berrett, Alexis worked on her anger at God for "abandoning" her in her abuse. She was able in her own mind to forgive God by "letting go" of judging God and by embracing a belief in a loving and compassionate God who "was hurt and outraged by my abuse."

Imagery was used to help Alexis forgive herself. She was able to visualize herself in her angry childhood rages, and then go back to the preceding hurt and pain, and back farther to the good intentions and loving, kind nature of herself as a little girl. This helped her experience compassion and self-forgiveness. Alexis was asked during some sessions to see herself as God might see her. In doing so, she was able to realize that the negative way in which she felt that God saw her was a projection of her own self-hatred and self-disgust and that God did not share these feelings.

Alexis had profound faith in God, goodness, and hope for something better. Reminding Alexis of about the importance of her faith and about her knowledge and understanding of spiritual things helped her refocus on what to her was important in life. This perspective enabled her to continue to fight for healing and recovery, even during the most difficult of times.

Psychological and Spiritual Outcome Measures

Posttesting at discharge from the inpatient treatment program indicated that Alexis had made considerable progress in reducing her eating disorder symptoms but that she was still experiencing considerable psychological and relationship distress. As can be seen in Table 11.3, Alexis's EAT score at discharge was 14, which indicates that her eating disorder symptoms (e.g., restricting, bingeing, purging, anxiety about eating, preoccupation with food)

TABLE 11.3
Alexis's Scores on the Battery of Psychological Tests Completed Upon Admission and Discharge From Center for Change

Psychological test	Admission score	Discharge score	Normal range
EAT	43	14	< 30
BSQ	127	119	< 110
OQ-45 (Total Score)	112	104	< 63
(Symptom Distress)	71	63	< 39
(Relationship Distress)	20	21	< 15
(Social Role Conflict)	19	18	< 13
MSEI (Global Self-Esteem)	42	44	40–59
ROS (Intrinsic)	34	N/A	N/A
ROS (Extrinsic)	26	N/A	N/A
SWBS (Religious Well-Being)	51	59	> 47
SWBS (Existential Well-Being)	40	50	> 43

Note. For the Eating Attitudes Test (EAT), Body Shape Questionnaire (BSQ), Outcome Questionnaire (OQ-45), and Spiritual Well-Being Scale (SWBS), the estimates of what is considered to be in the normal range are based on normative data. The Multidimensional Self-Esteem Scale (MSEI) subscale scores are all *t* scores, and so the normal range is between 40 and 59. N/A = not available.

were well within the normal range. Her BSQ score of 119 was still within the clinical range, suggesting that concerns about her body shape were still salient. Alexis's OQ-45 scores were also clinically elevated at discharge, suggesting that she was still experiencing significant levels of depression and anxiety, relationship distress, and social role conflict. Alexis's global self-esteem score was in the normal range. Her religious and existential well-being scores were in the high normal range, indicating that she had positive perceptions about God and was feeling optimistic about her life purpose and direction.

Postdischarge Functioning

Following inpatient treatment, Alexis continued treatment in outpatient and aftercare treatment. She continued to make progress in her eating disorder recovery, as well as with overcoming her depression and her other addictions. Alexis's relationships with her family continued to improve, and her level of functioning was generally good. She did, however, continue to struggle with her PTSD symptoms and the aftereffects of her severe childhood trauma. Alexis is doing well overall. She has yet to feel fully comfortable socially, despite her great social and interpersonal abilities. Nevertheless, she has progressed much and is well on her way toward complete recovery.

Commentary on Alexis's Case

Alexis had an intense feeling of shame and unworthiness as a result of terrible childhood abuse. In many severe abuse situations, entry into the spiritual or religious aspects of recovery begins later in the process. Some of the reasons for that delay are tied to the overwhelming sense of abandonment, betrayal, or mistrust that abused patients carry with them. These feelings, along with the belief that God allowed this to happen to the patient because he or she was such a terrible child, must be faced and worked through. These two aspects of healing needed to occur for Alexis. The complication was that Alexis did not have a strong or positive emotional connection with her parents, so some of the spirituality work had to be based on a positive and trusting relationship with her psychologist.

The core spiritual issue of negative images of God and feeling of abandonment from God had over the years evolved into self-hatred and feelings of unworthiness. These beliefs strongly impeded her ability to have loving relationships with other people. Alexis's religious point of view that truth can be found in many places became a theme during her treatment that allowed her a renewed look at the role of religion and the importance of spiritual connections in her daily life. With some patients, one of the bridges to a new view of God's ability to forgive is constructed as the patient forgives herself, and especially as she forgives that little-girl self who had suffered so much because of the false beliefs and decisions. After forgiveness, other kinds of tender and loving feelings emerge toward herself, past and present, challenging the notion that she is the exception to love or that she is too damaged or undeserving to receive love.

Throughout treatment, Alexis was given opportunities to open up the process of love by giving and receiving love with the staff and other patients. In these loving exchanges no strings were attached, making it safer for her to approach God in private—safer to say, "I want to forgive God for what I believed and how I felt when I was little. I want to ask God to forgive me for how I have felt about him since, and I want to have a fresh start." It was remarkable that over the course of treatment, Alexis's tendency to be consumed emotionally and mentally by the past trauma dramatically decreased and was replaced with a quiet, peaceful kind of self-acceptance along with a faith that she could be healed; she could have peace in her life, and she could have a positive future.

Imagery can be a useful and nonintrusive spiritual intervention in helping people view, understand, and gain new insights or perceptions about themselves, about their relationships with other people, and also in their feelings about God. In the imagery described in Alexis's treatment, she felt and saw things that brought her comfort, peace, and encouragement, along with a new awareness of what might be available in her spiritual relationships. This imagery helped to Alexis to see herself with new eyes and to gain heartfelt convictions about her important place in the journey of life. She discovered an ability to give new and better meanings to old and painful events and experiences. She felt the influence of God and of loving people around her in developing new strategies for dealing with her losses and addictions. To use imagery within a context of clarifying, deepening, and broadening the spiritual aspects of recovery, the therapist provides direction and structure within the imagery, but the patient fills in all of the experiences and images. The therapist can help the patient translate those images and feelings into something meaningful that they can continue to build on as they move forward in the treatment and recovery.

The religious community became a safe place again for Alexis during her gradual reinvolvement with it. As an adult, she could receive support and connection from her religious community, even though it was not the primary source of spiritual renewal for her. Most of the spiritual shifts were internally based for Alexis, but knowing she had a sense of belonging within her religious community was a valuable contribution in her recovery.

12

PATIENT PERCEPTIONS OF THE ROLE OF SPIRITUALITY IN TREATMENT AND RECOVERY

In this chapter, we summarize the findings of a recent qualitative survey we conducted of former patients at our eating disorder treatment center that inquired about their perceptions concerning the role of faith and spirituality in their treatment and recovery. A number of researchers have found that when recovered patients are asked what helped them recover from their eating disorder, many of them report that their faith and spirituality were important (e.g., Hall & Cohn, 1992; Hsu, Crisp, & Callender, 1992; Mitchell, Erlander, Pyle, & Fletcher, 1990; Rorty, Yager, & Rossotto, 1993). Yet these studies have provided little insight into why or in what ways such women found that their spirituality was helpful. Our goal was to extend the findings of the studies cited by inquiring more deeply into the reasons some women regard their spirituality as important in the recovery process.

We sought to gain insight into a number of general research questions, including the following: (a) In what ways did the women perceive that their eating disorder affected their faith and spirituality? (b) How did the women perceive that their faith and spirituality helped them during treatment? (c) What spiritual interventions did the women perceive as most helpful to them during treatment? and (d) How did the women perceive that their faith and spirituality helped them following discharge from inpatient treatment? It was not our purpose to generalize our findings to all women who have eating disorders. Our goal was to gain in-depth descriptive insight into the reasons a sample of women whose faith and spirituality was important to them in recovery perceived that it was helpful.

PROCEDURES

We purposively selected 50 former inpatients whom the treatment staff perceived as having successfully completed treatment and whose faith and spirituality played a significant role in their treatment. Thirty-six of the former patients responded to the survey. Patients' responses to each survey question were analyzed by four researchers who had training in the use of qualitative data analysis procedures, including two undergraduate research assistants, a doctoral student in counseling psychology, and a licensed psychologist. Emergent themes in the patients' responses within each survey question and across the survey questions were identified and categorized. Consensus was sought and achieved on all of the major themes that were identified, including themes described subsequently.

DESCRIPTION OF THE SURVEY

The survey is shown in Exhibit 12.1. It contained 14 questions about the role of faith and spirituality in treatment and recovery, including open-ended questions about how patients' eating disorders hurt their faith and spirituality, how patients' faith and spirituality may have helped them in their treatment and recovery, and what spiritual interventions were perceived as most helpful to them. Patients were also asked to share their story of recovery and to offer suggestions about spirituality that they believed may be helpful to other women who struggle with eating disorders.

SURVEY FINDINGS

In this section we briefly summarize the main themes identified in the patient responses to Survey Questions 1, 2, 7, 8, 9, 12, and 13. We also present quantitative data from survey question 10, which asked patients to rate the five spiritual practices they found most helpful in their healing and recovery. We also comment on several overall themes that we identified across the various survey questions. The manuscript that reports the findings of this study in its entirety is available from the authors on request (Richards, Hardman, Jensen, Berrett, & Jensen, 2006).

EXHIBIT 12.1
Spirituality and Eating Disorders Survey

Directions: Please complete this survey by providing as much detail about the personal and spiritual aspects of your eating disorder treatment and recovery as you feel comfortable sharing. Please take time to reflect, ponder, and contemplate your responses to the questions before answering. Your insights and experiences are important to us. We believe that what you share will ultimately help other women who suffer from eating disorders heal and recover. Please use the reverse side of these pages if you need more room on any of the questions.

1. How did your eating disorder hurt your spirituality and/or relationship with God?

2. In what ways did your faith and spirituality help you during your treatment and stay at Center for Change?

3. What did your therapist or other staff members of the treatment staff at Center for Change do to assist you in using the resources of your faith and spirituality during treatment?

4. Please describe three spiritual interventions or assignments that your therapist or other members of the treatment staff recommended or used that helped you.
   1.
   2.
   3.

5. If you participated in Center for Change's spirituality group, please describe how it was helpful to you.

6. If you participated in Center for Change's 12-step group, please describe how it was helpful to you.

7. In what ways has your faith and spirituality helped you since you left Center for Change?

8. What role has your spirituality and faith played in the overall progress you have made in recovering from your eating disorder?

9. In what ways do you feel God or your higher power has helped you personally and directly in the healing and recovery process?

(continued)

EXHIBIT 12.1 *Continued*

10. In the list below, please check the five spiritual practices that you have found most helpful in your healing and recovery.

__ Praying	__ Giving service to others
__ Meditating	__ Keeping a spiritual journal or diary
__ Reading scriptures	__ Talking about spiritual issues with leaders or friends
__ Attending spiritual services	__ Participating in religious rituals, rites, or ordinances
__ Forgiving others	__ Showing kindness and compassion to others
__ Repenting	__ Expressing gratitude to God and/ or others
__ Experiencing nature	__ Fellowshipping and socializing with religious friends
__ Forgiving myself	__ Experiencing solitude and spiritual contemplation
__ Other (please specify)	__ Other (please specify)

11. Please list the three most important people who have positively influenced the spiritual aspects of your eating disorder recovery and briefly comment on how they helped you.
    1.
    2.
    3.
12. If you could speak to other women who struggle with eating disorders, what are three messages you would you most like to share with them about faith and spirituality that would help them in their recovery?
    1.
    2.
    3.
13. Please share with us in your own words your story of recovery from your eating disorder, beginning with when it was at its worst up until where you are today.
14. Is there anything else about the role of faith and spirituality in your treatment and recovery you would like to share with us?

Thank you for your assistance! Your responses will help us assist other women who struggle with eating disorders.

Stories of Recovery

In question 13 of the survey, we asked the former patients to describe briefly their "stories of recovery." One of the themes in the patients' recovery stories is that most of them had reached "rock bottom" or a crisis point before they entered inpatient treatment. During the crisis point, many patients perceived that their lives were literally in danger, most often from starvation or suicidal impulses. Another theme that was apparent in the recovery stories was the patients' perceptions that it was their faith in God, or personal spirituality that helped them endure the most difficult times of their eating disorder and fight their way back on the pathway toward healing and recovery. The following recovery stories illustrate these themes. A former patient wrote,

> At my worst I was sleeping about 18 hours per day. I couldn't go to school or work, and I barely had energy to go up stairs at my house. I was abusing 10 to 50 laxatives per day, along with diuretics, diet pills, and 1 to 3 bottles of epicac. I was also engaging frequently in self-harm. I remember praying to God and asking Him to take me. I didn't want to live anymore. I was so extreme in my pursuit for perfection that I was convinced that only by dying could I be perfect. My weight got so low that my doctor told my parents I would have a heart attack if I didn't get help.
>
> Today I am at a healthy weight, and I no longer abuse laxatives, diet pills, or epicac. Self-harm is still an addictive temptation, but I fight it with all my might. I know that I can never be perfect and I'm okay with that. I live now to please myself and not everyone around me. I'm no longer afraid of the future and look forward to all the opportunities ahead of me. I still have a difficult time with my body image, but never do I want to go back to being a prisoner to anorexia. Life is much more than being thin. My faith and spirituality were vital in my treatment and recovery. I could not have done it without God and His faith in me.

Another former patient wrote,

> It's hard for me to remember what it was like during the worst times of my eating disorder. It feels like a totally different life. I do remember every second being consumed by eating disorder thoughts and behavior. I was so trapped by the lies I told. I no longer knew the truth.
>
> I wanted to recover, yet I was sure if I gave up my eating disorder, no one would care about me anymore. I felt I was nothing if I wasn't starving myself. Because of the things I was doing to my body, I felt sick most of the time. Somehow that was how I was supposed to be. I was afraid to let myself feel good.
>
> I went for treatment and I learned how to recover and heal, but I didn't choose to do so for about a year. That is when I discovered that I had something big to accomplish and I couldn't do what I needed to if I allowed my life to be engulfed by an eating disorder. I felt God's love for me, and I knew that with His help, I could do anything.
>
> From that moment on, my life was changed. Everyone still told me that I would never completely recover and I would deal with an eating

disorder my whole life, but I knew this was not necessarily God's prognosis for my future. I know God is a forgiving God. He would not let me stay stuck forever if I had faith and if I was willing to do my part.

Sometimes it was hard, and sometimes I questioned if it was really worth it to get rid of the eating disorder. At those times, I always had someone enter my life with just the right words, or just the right support. There was always someone there to lift me up.

I no longer think about my eating disorder stuff. I have no desires to starve myself, or hurt myself. I live. I married my sweetheart after dating him for two years. He is wonderful and he has taught me so much about life and how to have fun. We hope to have children, but that hasn't happened yet. We work together always trying to do what the Lord would have us do, lifting others the way others lifted me.

Another former patient wrote,

At the lowest point in my eating disorder I saw no hope. I had resigned myself to a life of despair and darkness, a life filled with obsessions of food and weight—but never satisfying myself. I felt shameful and worthless before others and God. I told myself how undeserving I was of anything good in my life. I knew my life was not pleasing to God and that only intensified my feelings of shame and guilt. I felt I didn't deserve to get help, but a little something inside of me didn't want to "live" like I had been. I actually didn't know how much longer I could live like that.

Slowly, through the course of treatment, I realized how my life could be without an eating disorder. And even more pivotal, when I realized and decided that was what I wanted—life without an eating disorder—I started to let people in. I let God in. I took steps forward and backward, and started to learn how to forgive myself for the step backwards. My recovery has been all-encompassing and so complex, it is impossible to sum up in a short paragraph. However, I can say that my relationship with God has been the foundation. I came to know my divine and eternal worth as a daughter of God. Now I know that I am of worth and that I have a life worth living.

Another former patient wrote,

At my worst I was purging up to 30 times a day. I isolated myself from everything and everyone. I had no respect for myself. I was failing school because I stayed home to do my eating disorder stuff. I couldn't stop thinking about it. I felt like I was constantly bingeing and purging and fighting with my family. I totally believed in God and how much He loved me, but I didn't feel like He should love me. I've always had a strong relationship with Him, but there were a lot of things I didn't understand. I started going to outpatient therapy, but it did no good. I went for inpatient treatment after a while and I have no words to express how thankful I am to have been able to go there. It has changed my life forever.

During inpatient treatment, I gradually started to open up and I grew to be a stronger person. I learned to eat right and I got healthy, but the most important part was learning to love myself exactly the way I am. Now I know that I am important and that I matter. I really do love myself for who I am, and I have a strong belief that without God, I would be right back to how I was before I went into treatment. I know with all my heart and soul that God is guiding me through this. Spirituality for me is one of the biggest "must haves" to recover and I am so thankful treatment helped me understand that. I've come a long way, and I plan to go even further. Now I'm able to be open with people and say what I'm feeling and thinking. I stick up for myself and what I believe in.

How Eating Disorders Hurt Spirituality

The former patients almost universally said that their eating disorders undermined their spirituality and made them feel unworthy and alienated from God. Many of the patients also mentioned that their eating disorders cut them off from all that was good in their lives, including love and relationships with other people. A former patient wrote,

> I put up a wall between me and God because I wanted to be "good" and "perfect." I continued praying because I knew I "should," but I felt unworthy and ashamed. I did not let God in. I was dulled spiritually.

Another former patient wrote,

> Because of the tremendous guilt over eating disorder-related behavior, I was scared to pray or to allow myself to have any relationship with God. I was afraid He would be just one more person that I would "let down." I was also afraid of feeling "good" things, and I knew praying, reading scriptures, etc., would feel good.

Another wrote,

> I knew that I was hurting my body by continuing in my eating disorder. Every night I would pray that I would be able to stop throwing up. Then one evening as I was praying for help I came to the realization that I didn't want to give it up. I was knowingly and deliberately killing myself. I couldn't continue my prayer that night or any night. I didn't feel worthy to talk with God because I was harming my body—one of His creations. When I was in my eating disorder, I hated everything about myself. I soon believed that I was not good enough to have a relationship with God or with my family and friends. At times I felt as

though no one knew what I was going through and that they never would.

Another former patient wrote,

> Because I was starving myself physically, the rest of me was starving as well: emotionally and spiritually. I didn't have the brainpower to think, let alone to think about my relationship with God. In my quest to be thin, I isolated myself from everyone, including God.

How Faith and Spirituality Help During Treatment

Most of the former patients perceived that their faith in God and personal spirituality helped them face the challenges of treatment and the challenges of the healing process. Many patients expressed that when things got really tough during treatment that it was their faith in God and in His unconditional love that helped them endure. Many patients also mentioned that personal spiritual practices such as prayer and Scripture reading gave them strength and understanding. A former patient wrote,

> My faith gave me the courage to stay in treatment and work the program. Without faith that I could get over my eating disorder, I would never have been able to accomplish what I did. Recovery is incredibly difficult and I can't do it alone.

Another former patient wrote,

> Praying helped me survive. I learned something from my first roommate in the treatment center—that was her persistent prayer. I set a goal to pray at least twice a day, but prayer helped me get though the hardest times.

Another wrote,

> During treatment, all I really had left to hold onto was my faith and spirituality—and it was horrifying at first. It was a real test of my faith. I grew more sincere about spiritual things. It did take time, but slowly I grew to trust my faith and the "higher power" watching over me. Because of the hateful feelings I had within, it was difficult. I thought I would feel so alone at the treatment center, but I never did. There was always this feeling inside of me that was constantly buoying me up. I was so grateful we were able to explore faith, spirituality, and our "higher powers" during treatment.

Another wrote,

> I remember from the very first day of treatment just being so overwhelmed. I felt so alone and the smallest task of eating 100% of dinner was more than I could handle. I just realized I really couldn't do this

alone, so I prayed. I also had some church leaders come and give me blessings of comfort. Not to say I didn't struggle with God issues from then on, because I did. I still felt inadequate and unworthy of His help and I still had perceptions of a stern, judgmental, harsh God. I had to kind of go off of the faith of my therapist that God wasn't like that. I prayed a lot. I prayed for Him to soften and open my heart, to help me get through difficult things . . . so many things. And my faith was strengthened throughout my stay in inpatient treatment. I literally saw miracles occur. And I realized how much I needed God in my life.

How Faith and Spirituality Help in Recovery and Maintenance

Most of the patients stated that their faith and spirituality not only provided strength during treatment but that it continued to provide an anchor during their entire recovery process, including the challenges they faced after being discharged from inpatient treatment. In fact, many of the patients said that their faith and spirituality became even more important to them after treatment when they did not enjoy such a strong and readily available support system. A former patient wrote,

> My faith and spirituality have been the foundation for my recovery process. My sense of self and of worth, my relationships with other people, my letting go of "perfection" have all hinged on my understanding of my relationship with God.

Another former patient wrote,

> Since leaving treatment, I have grown closer to God. It took a couple of years to find out what I believe and then change my behavior to match my beliefs. A seed of faith was planted during my treatment and it has bloomed into a much happier life. Faith is what keeps me going when life has its trials, and negative emotions cloud my judgment. Having this new relationship with God has changed my outlook on life. God wants me to be happy. I know that He loves me unconditionally. I have found out who I am and that I am of great worth.

Another wrote,

> My spirituality and faith have been a key piece to my recovery. While in treatment, I learned many tools I could use to aid in my recovery. They have helped tremendously in the everyday battles I have fought with my eating disorder. But I feel the healing and self-worth that allowed the other tools to be as successful as they were came from God.

Another wrote,

> Life out here (since discharge from inpatient treatment) is much, MUCH harder than it ever was there. In the treatment center, there was always someone to talk to, somewhere to go for help. Out here,

> that's very rare. I have to rely more on God, because I know He will always be there. Also, sometimes spirituality can fill the void that I used to use my eating disorder and other behaviors to fill. Not to say that I've been perfect, or that I haven't messed up, but I notice things are generally better when I choose to be closer to God.

Another wrote,

> My spirituality has helped me become more connected with others. It has also helped me keep my focus on other things and ways to serve others, instead of just focusing on everything that was a stressor in my life. I have found that service to others always makes me feel better. My spirituality has given me a stronger connection with others as well as a deeper sense of who I am.

Another wrote,

> There's no way I would be where I am today without help from God. I honestly was so sick and confused and lost, there's just no way I could've picked myself up. I believe spirituality has given me added strength and insight that I otherwise would not have had. It has also helped me to be more aware of the needs of others. Serving others has really furthered my recovery. Relating to others has also helped me to better realize the progress I have made. Also, having faith that there's more to life than self-destructive hell has helped.

How Has God or a Higher Power Helped You Personally?

Most of the patients reported that they believe God is personally aware of them. Many of the patients mentioned specific ways they have perceived God's providential care in their lives. Most of the patients perceive that they have a meaningful and personal relationship with God. This relationship is an important source of strength and support in their recovery. A former patient wrote,

> My Higher Power placed wonderful people in my life to help me and answered my cries for help and love. Sometimes when I am struggling, I'll hear a song or read something that seems to be God speaking directly to me, addressing specifically whatever I'm worried about. Also, my Higher Power has given me innumerable blessings and opportunities.

Another former patient wrote,

> As I look at my recovery, I feel that just having the chance to get the help that I needed was a personal blessing from God. After I completed treatment, I was having a very hard time facing life and dealing with it. Once again, I felt that suicide was the way to go. As I was reading my scriptures for a religion class, the spirit spoke to me in a way that

> it never had before. This has been one of the most amazing experiences in my life. From having this and other experiences like it, I know that I have a mission here on earth and that I need to finish it. God someday wants to have me be with Him again but I need to finish this life first.

Another wrote,

> This is going to sound incredibly insane, but at times when I have struggled the most during recovery, and I have felt worthless and all alone because "no one understands," I will get a warm feeling inside. Sometimes I have even had dreams where I am surrounded by light, or I have had dreams where I am in heaven and am with my ancestors—relatives I have never met because they have passed on—and in my dream I know who they are—and we are together and happy and everything around me is beautiful.

Another former patient wrote,

> God has helped me directly by introducing very special people into my life at just the moment I needed them. These people helped me with their love, support, friendships, and examples. It was divinely orchestrated. He has introduced thoughts and ideas to me, letting me know He is there and cares.

Another wrote,

> There are many ways God has helped me. For example, on one occasion, I was feeling especially desperate, like I would do anything to end the pain I was feeling at that moment. I prayed for help, and was able to relax and sleep that night. This was an answer to my prayer. The next day, I happened to be in the office of a seminary teacher discussing graduation. He knew nothing about me except I had missed a lot of school the year before. He told me that God loves me, He knows my struggles, and He will help me overcome them. That was just what I needed to hear. Those words gave me strength to keep going. Once I decided I wanted God's help to recover, He has never left me alone. I have always had His support and guidance.

Another wrote,

> God has always been there for me—I just shut and locked the door during my eating disorder. As I started treatment, when I still wouldn't let Him in, God sent other people to help me heal. He provided me with my family and the staff at the treatment center. As I started to let them in—their love and support—I was able to see glimpses of God's love for me. When I was ready and let Him in, He welcomed me. He pulled me from my own hell. I have no doubt now that He is very personally aware of and active in my life.

EXHIBIT 12.2
Spiritual Practices That Former Patients Perceived as Most Helpful

Spiritual intervention	Frequency nominated as most helpful
Praying	30
Expressing gratitude to God and/or others	20
Forgiving myself	20
Giving service to others	14
Keeping a spiritual journal or diary	11
Reading scriptures	11
Showing kindness and compassion to others	11
Talking about spiritual issues with leaders or friends	10
Attending spiritual services	9
Forgiving others	7
Experiencing nature	7
Repenting	6
Participating in religious rituals, rites, or ordinances	3
Meditating	3
Experiencing solitude and spiritual contemplation	3
Fellowshipping and socializing with religious friends	2
Worship through music and hymns	1

What Spiritual Practices and Interventions Were Most Helpful?

Survey Question 10 asked respondents to indicate which 5 spiritual practices (from a list of 16) they had found most helpful in their healing and recovery. The frequency with which the various spiritual interventions were nominated as most helpful by the former patients is shown in Exhibit 12.2. Respondents most often perceived prayer, forgiving self, expressing gratitude to God and others, and giving service to others as being helpful. Patients also noted several other spiritual practices as being most helpful, including keeping a spiritual journal, reading scriptures, showing kindness and compassion to others, and talking about spiritual issues with leaders or friends.

Survey Question 4 asked respondents to describe which spiritual interventions their therapists or other members of the treatment staff used or recommended that were helpful. Following are brief patient descriptions of the wide variety of spiritual interventions they found helpful.

- Our 12-step leader encouraged me to identify the miracles in my life.
- Hearing the miracles of others during 12-step group was helpful.
- I was encouraged to create images of my vision of God through artwork.

- My therapist encouraged me to pray to know if God wants me to get better and if He will help me.
- My therapist asked me to make a list of my dreams or goals (things I want to do, be, or have).
- My therapist taught me that I wasn't hated by God—he reminded me I was a creation and daughter of God.
- My therapist had me read and write a book report on a book about spiritual issues (e.g., forgiveness, grace).
- My dance/movement therapist had me dance my "dreams." She also encouraged me to dance as if God loved me. This seems to free me to be myself.
- In 12-step group we wrote all of our issues and imperfections on a helium balloon and then we went outside and let the balloons go. This helped me believe that I could let them go.
- My therapist asked me to write a letter to God in which I told Him all about everything I was feeling, including my hurt, pain, questions, fears, gratitude, and so forth.
- My therapist asked me to write about the desires of my heart—this helped me see that the intentions of my heart are good.
- My therapist asked me to write a list of everything that I had done that is bad. He read it aloud to me, expressed his love and acceptance to me, and burned my list. I knew he was aware of my deep, dark secrets and he still cared about me.
- My therapist asked me to spend some of my solo time praying, meditating, and contemplating about spiritual things.
- My therapist asked me to write my autobiography and then to read it to other patients in our group.
- My therapist was doing imagery with me and I saw myself as a little girl—as she asked me if I would starve that little girl I realized that I did not want to do that to her.
- My therapist encouraged me to write about my spiritual experiences in my journal.
- My therapist taught me about the importance of finding a calm environment and listening to my heart—this has helped me feel God's love.
- Reading the *Spiritual Renewal* workbook and doing the self-help assignments were very helpful.
- We took some yoga classes, which allowed us to become more in tune with ourselves and our bodies.
- My therapist encouraged me to pray for the specifics (e.g., asking for help to feel the Lord's love, to be able to love myself, to be able to see my body more like He sees it).

- In music therapy we were given a topic and encouraged to share a song that expressed our feelings about the topic—while spirituality may not have been the goal of music therapy it was often the result for me.
- My therapist asked me to write about how my spiritual beliefs could help me in my recovery.
- My therapist asked me to write a letter to myself from God, emphasizing how precious and loved I am to Him.
- I was encouraged to listen to spiritual music which allowed my heart to feel and accept God's love.

Messages From Recovered Patients to Women With Eating Disorders

Survey Question 12 asked the respondents to share messages about faith and spirituality that they believed would be helpful to other women who struggle with eating disorders. The former patients shared a wide variety of messages and suggestions, many of which emphasized the importance of trusting in God, forgiving self and others, and the value of spiritual practices such as prayer, serving others, keeping a journal, and so on. Exhibit 12.3

EXHIBIT 12.3
Messages of Hope From Women Who Have Recovered From Eating Disorders About How Faith and Spirituality Can Assist in Recovery

- Serving others makes you feel better about yourself.
- Praying to God gives you meaning and helps you to realize that you're not alone.
- Forgiving yourself and being free of shame is an essential part of moving on and having a full recovery.
- Be humble. This is so hard because it takes admitting that we have a problem. Next, it takes facing the problem and asking for help. But until we are humble enough to ask for help and face the problem, it will always take over one's life.
- Know that you are precious, beautiful, and loved. God is perfect and all-knowing; therefore, he "doesn't make any junk!"
- Know that there is One who understands with a perfect knowledge . . . how you feel. We are never alone, even when we appear to be.
- Spiritual growth is more empowering, long-lasting, and comforting than the eating disorder ever was or ever will be.
- God heals.
- Find some sort of Higher Power to pray to. Take time to pray for yourself—you are worth praying for!
- Thank your Higher Power for the gift of life and for your body—especially if you have a bad body image—at least you have a body!
- Keep a miracles journal—find at least three miracles each day—these little miracles help you keep a perspective that is positive.
- You are a creation, a daughter of God. Don't ever forget the divine nature that is in you.

(continued)

EXHIBIT 12.3 *Continued*

- God will never stop loving you! Don't be afraid to ask for His help.
- Never lose hope no matter how difficult things seem. Always hold on to the hope that there is a God who loves you, who knows your pain, and who will never leave you.
- Remember that all your challenges can be turned into experiences for your own good. Instead of letting your eating disorder destroy you, focus on recovering so you can be an inspiration and blessing in others' lives.
- Sometimes you can't do it on your own. That's when you must turn your pain and struggles over to your Higher Power and let Him carry your burdens for you.
- Learning to listen to your heart and trust is a key and most helpful.
- Faith is a key to recovery—feel the fear and do it anyway!
- Don't be afraid to speak honestly to God—tell Him your pains, fears, rage at Him. Tell Him about your thankfulness, love, and trust in Him.
- There is so much good in you. Listen to God because He will always love and comfort you.
- Risk losing the disorder. Believe you can get fully better!
- Know that God loves you no matter what you have done or what the eating disorder tries to tell you differently.
- Do the little things—keeping a journal, praying out loud, and focusing on your own spirituality and trying to better yourself for God and no one else.
- When we lose being able to be in tune with our hearts, it is as if we have lost our compass. Things become dark and we soon begin to wander in the darkness. Learn to listen to your heart and never lose sight of that "compass" again.
- If there seems to be nothing left to believe in, believe that there is a God and that He loves you. Try to let that love in.
- Don't stop praying, and if you never have, start. Be consistent and don't give up even when there seem to be no answers or help coming to you. It will help—I believe that.
- Knowing that God loves you is so much more fulfilling than worrying about other people liking you.
- Remember that you are never alone with your suffering; God is always there to help.
- Be brave! Gaining your faith back and accepting God's love is immensely hard, but it is worth it in the end.
- Fight the temptation! Remember who you are and what you're about. Don't give into the eating disorder, which will bring you unhappiness.
- God is not controlling, vengeful, or warlike. God is like a gentle mother who sang the world into creation and holds each one of us as a precious baby.
- Dare to dream! God gives us dreams to help push us forward. God will help us find a way to accomplish every good thing.
- Count your blessings. Look for the good things, and be grateful for each and every thing in your life. When we express gratitude, we will receive more. If God leads you to it, He will lead you through it.
- Forgive; forgive the people that hurt you. This is not easy but it must be done. This does not mean that you have to let them back into your life. You need to go through all of the stages of forgiveness; feel the anger and hurt.
- Forgive yourself; as you do this you will see that you are not bad.
- Trust God, not your eating disorder. God loves you so much and He wants to help you so much. You need to do your part and ask, but I promise you, if you take that leap of faith and call on God for some help, He will help you get through this.

Note. From *Patient Perceptions of the Role of Faith and Spirituality in Recovery From Eating Disorders,* by P. S. Richards, R. K. Hardman, B. Jensen, M. E. Berrett, and F. Jensen, 2006. Unpublished manuscript.

lists some of these messages. Practitioners may find it helpful to share these with their patients in treatment for eating disorders as "messages of hope" from women who have recovered from an eating disorder about how they perceive that faith and spirituality may help other women who struggle.

CONCLUSION

Our survey provided further qualitative evidence that many women who struggle with an eating disorder perceive that faith in God and spirituality are essential in their treatment and recovery. The survey also provided considerable insight into why and how spirituality is perceived as helpful by women recovering from eating disorders. It provides a perspective into the types of spiritual practices and interventions that may be helpful in treatment and recovery. We hope this information proves useful for practitioners and researchers who wish to further explore the role of faith and spirituality in eating disorder treatment and recovery.

REFERENCES

Alcoholics Anonymous World Services. (1990). *Alcoholics Anonymous 1989 membership survey*. New York: Author.

Alcoholics Anonymous World Services. (2001). *Alcoholics Anonymous Big Book*. New York: Author.

Allport, G. W. (1966). The religious context of prejudice. *Journal for the Scientific Study of Religion, 5*, 447–457.

Allport, G. W., & Ross, J. M. (1967). Personal religious orientation and prejudice. *Journal of Personality and Social Psychology, 5*, 432–443.

American Counseling Association. (1995). *Code of ethics and standards of practice*. Alexandria, VA: Author.

American Heritage dictionary of the English language (3rd ed.). (1992). Boston: Houghton Mifflin.

American Psychiatric Association. (1994). *Diagnostic and statistical manual of mental disorders* (4th ed.). Washington, DC: Author.

American Psychiatric Association. (2000a). *Diagnostic and statistical manual of mental disorders* (4th ed., text revision). Washington, DC: Author.

American Psychiatric Association. (2000b). *Practice guideline for the treatment of patients with eating disorders* (2nd ed.). Arlington, VA: Author.

American Psychological Association. (2002). Ethical principles of psychologists and code of conduct. *American Psychologist, 57*, 1060–1073.

Apple, R. E., & Agras, W. S. (1997). *Overcoming eating disorders: A cognitive–behavioral treatment for bulimia nervosa and binge-eating disorder, client workbook*. San Antonio, TX: The Psychological Corporation.

Azhar, M. Z., & Varma, S. L. (1995a). Religious psychotherapy as management of bereavement. *Acta Psychiatrica Scandinavia, 91*, 223–235.

Azhar, M. Z., & Varma, S. L. (1995b). Religious psychotherapy in depressive patients. *Psychotherapy and Psychosomatics, 63*, 165–173.

Azhar, M. Z., Varma, S. L., & Dharap, A. S. (1994). Religious psychotherapy in anxiety disorder patients. *Acta Psychiatrica Scandinavia, 90*, 1–3.

Banks, C. G. (1992). "Culture" in culture-bound syndromes: The case of anorexia nervosa. *Social Science Medicine, 34*, 867–884.

Banks, C. G. (1997). The imaginative use of religious symbols in subjective experiences of anorexia nervosa. *Psychoanalytic Review, 84*, 227–236.

Barrett, D. B., & Johnson, T. M. (2002). Religion. In *Britannica Book of the Year* (p. 303). Chicago: Encyclopedia Britannica.

Bell, R. M. (1985). *Holy anorexia*. Chicago: University of Chicago Press.

Benson, H. (1996). *Timeless healing: The power and biology of belief*. New York: Scribner.

Bergin, A. E. (1980). Psychotherapy and religious values. *Journal of Consulting and Clinical Psychology, 48,* 75–105.

Bergin, A. E. (1985). Proposed values for guiding and evaluating counseling and psychotherapy. *Counseling and Values, 29,* 99–116.

Bergin, A. E. (1991). Values and religious issues in psychotherapy and mental health. *American Psychologist, 46,* 394–403.

Bergin, A. E. (2002). *Eternal values and personal growth: A guide on your journey to spiritual, emotional, and social wellness.* Provo, UT: BYU Studies.

Birmingham, C. L., & Beumont, P. J. V. (2004). *Medical management of eating disorders: A practical handbook for health care professionals.* Cambridge, England: Cambridge University Press.

Bridges, R. A., & Spilka, B. (1992). Religion and the mental health of women. In J. F. Schumaker (Ed.), *Religion and mental health* (pp. 43–53). New York: Oxford University Press.

Brown, P. (1988). *The body and society: Men, women and sexual renunciation in early Christianity.* New York: Columbia University Press.

Brownell, K. D., & Fairburn, C. G. (Eds.). (1995). *Eating disorders and obesity: A comprehensive handbook.* New York: Guilford Press.

Bruch, H. (1978). *The golden cage.* Cambridge, MA: Harvard University Press.

Bryk, A. S., & Raudenbush, S. W. (1992). *Hierarchical linear models: Applications and data analysis methods.* Newbury Park, CA: Sage.

Butcher, J. N., Dahlstrom, W. G., Graham, J. R., Tellegen, A. M., & Kaemmer, B. (1989). *MMPI–2: Manual for administration and scoring.* Minneapolis: University of Minnesota Press.

Bynum, C. (1987). *Holy feast and holy fast. The religious significance of food to medieval women.* Berkeley: University of California Press.

Castaneda, R., & Galanter, M. (1987). A review of treatment modalities for alcoholism and their outcome. *American Journal of Social Psychiatry, 7,* 237–244.

Chirban, J. T. (2001). Assessing religious and spiritual concerns in psychotherapy. In T. G. Plante & A. C. Sherman (Eds.), *Faith and health: Psychological perspectives* (pp. 265–290). New York: Guilford Press.

Cole, B. S. (2000). The integration of spirituality and psychotherapy for people confronting cancer: An outcome study (Doctoral dissertation, Bowling Green State University, 2000). *Dissertation Abstracts International Section B: The Sciences and Engineering, 61*(2-B), 1075.

Collins, P. L. (2000). Eating disorders: A multiple-case investigation of the Internet e-mail correspondence of women's lived experience (Doctoral dissertation, Texas Tech University, 2000). *Dissertation Abstracts International Section A: Humanities and Social Sciences,* 60(11-A), 3916.

Cooper, P. J., Taylor, M., Cooper, Z., & Fairburn, C. G. (1987). The development and validation of the Body Shape Questionnaire. *International Journal of Eating Disorders, 6,* 485–494.

Dancyger, I., Fornari, V., Fisher, M., Schneider, M., Frank, S., Wisotsky, W., et al. (2002). Cultural factors in orthodox Jewish adolescents treated in a day program for eating disorders. *International Journal of Adolescent Medicine and Health, 14,* 317–328.

Dare, C., & Eisler, I. (1995). Family therapy and eating disorders. In K. D. Brownell & C. G. Fairburn (Eds.), *Eating disorders and obesity: A comprehensive handbook* (pp. 318–323). New York: Guilford Press.

Dare, C., & Eisler, I. (1997). Family therapy for anorexia nervosa. In D. M. Garner & P. E. Garfinkel (Eds.), *Handbook of treatment for eating disorders* (2nd ed., pp. 307–326). New York: Guilford Press.

Davis, W. B. (1985). Epilogue. In R. M. Bell (Ed.), *Holy anorexia* (pp. 181–183). Chicago: University of Chicago Press.

Denzin, N. K., & Lincoln, Y. S. (Eds.). (1994). *Handbook of qualitative research.* Thousand Oaks, CA: Sage.

Dossey, L. (1993). *Healing words: The power of prayer and the practice of medicine.* San Francisco: HarperCollins.

Dupont, R. L., & McGovern, J. P. (1994). *A bridge to recovery: An introduction to 12-step programs.* Washington, DC: American Psychiatric Press.

Eisler, I., le Grange, D., & Asen, E. (2003). Family interventions. In J. Treasure, U. Schmidt, & E. van Furth (Eds.), *Handbook of eating disorders* (2nd ed., pp. 233–251). West Sussex, England: Wiley.

Elkins, D. N. (1995). Psychotherapy and spirituality: Toward a theory of the soul. *Journal of Humanistic Psychology, 35,* 78–98.

Ellison, C. W. (1983). Spiritual well-being: Conceptualization and measurement. *Journal of Psychology and Theology, 11,* 330–340.

Ellison, C. W., & Smith, J. (1991). Toward an integrative measure of health and well-being. *Journal of Psychology and Theology, 19,* 35–48.

Ellsworth, S. G. (1995). *How I got this way and what to do about it.* Draper, UT: Author.

Emery, E. E. (2003). Living history-spiritually . . . or not? A comparison of conventional and spiritually integrated reminiscence groups (Doctoral dissertation, Bowling Green State University, 2003). *Dissertation Abstracts International Section B: The Sciences and Engineering,* 63(10-B), 4898.

Emmons, R. A. (1999). *The psychology of ultimate concerns: Motivation and spirituality in personality.* New York: Guilford Press.

Epstein, M. (1995). *Thoughts without a thinker: Psychotherapy from a Buddhist perspective.* New York: Basic Books.

Epstein, S., & O'Brien, E. J. (1983). *The Multidimensional Self-Esteem Inventory.* Odessa, FL: Psychological Assessment Resources.

Fairburn, C. G., & Cooper, Z. (1993). The Eating Disorder Examination (12th ed.). In C. G. Fairburn & G. T. Wilson (Eds.), *Binge eating: Nature, assessment, and treatment* (pp. 317–360). New York: Guilford Press.

Faiver, C., Ingersoll, R. E., O'Brien, E. M., & McNally, C. (2001). *Explorations in counseling and spirituality: Philosophical, practical, and personal reflections*. Belmont, CA: Thomson Learning–Brooks/Cole.

First, M. B., Spitzer, R. L., Gibbon, R. L., Gibbon, M., & Williams, J. B. W. (1994). *Structured clinical interview for Axis I* DSM–IV *disorders, patient edition* (Version 2.0). New York: Biometrics Research Department, New York State Psychiatric Institute.

Fowler, J. W. (1981). *Stages of faith: The psychology of human development and the quest for meaning*. New York: Harper & Row.

Frankl, V. E. (1959). *Man's search for meaning*. New York: Washington Square Press.

Friends in Recovery. (1994). *The twelve steps for Christians: Based on biblical teachings* (rev. ed.). San Diego, CA: RPI Publishing.

Friends in Recovery. (1995). *The twelve steps: A way out: A spiritual process for healing* (rev. ed.). San Diego, CA: RPI Publishing.

Ganje-Fling, M. A., & McCarthy, P. R. (1991). A comparative analysis of spiritual direction and psychotherapy. *Journal of Psychology and Theology*, *19*, 103–117.

Garfinkel, P. E., & Garner, D. M. (1982). *Anorexia nervosa: A multidimensional perspective*. New York: Brunner/Mazel.

Garner, D. M. (1991). *The Eating Disorder Inventory—2*. Odessa, TX: Psychological Assessment Resources.

Garner, D. M., & Garfinkel, P. E. (1979). The Eating Attitudes Test: An index of the symptoms of anorexia nervosa. *Psychological Medicine*, *9*, 273–279.

Garrett, C. (1996). Recovery from anorexia nervosa: A Durkheimian interpretation. *Social Science Medicine*, *43*, 1489–1506.

Garrett, C. (1998). *Beyond anorexia: Narrative, spirituality, and recovery*. New York: Cambridge University Press.

Gilbert, S. C., Keery, H., & Thompson, J. K. (2005). The media's role in body image and eating disorders. In E. Cole & J. H. Daniel (Eds.), *Featuring females: Feminist analysis of media* (pp. 41–57). Washington, DC: American Psychological Association.

Gorsuch, R. L., & McPherson, S. E. (1989). Intrinsic/extrinsic measurement: I/E-revised and single-item scales. *Journal for the Scientific Study of Religion*, *28*, 348–354.

Gorsuch, R. L., & Miller, W. R. (1999). Assessing spirituality. In W. R. Miller (Ed.), *Integrating spirituality into treatment: Resources for practitioners* (pp. 47–64). Washington, DC: American Psychological Association.

Greenberger, D., & Padesky, C. A. (1995). *Mind over mood: Change how you feel by changing the way you think*. New York: Guilford Press.

Griffin, D. R. (2000). *Religion and scientific naturalism: Overcoming the conflicts*. Albany: State University of New York Press.

Griffith, J. L., & Griffith, M. E. (2002). *Encountering the sacred in psychotherapy: How to talk with people about their spiritual lives*. New York: Guilford Press.

Hall, L., & Cohn, L. (1992). *Bulimia: A guide to recovery*. Carlsbad, CA: Gurze Books.

Hardman, R. K., Berrett, M. E., & Richards, P. S. (2003). Spirituality and ten false pursuits of eating disorders: Implications for counselors. *Counseling and Values, 48,* 67–78.

Hawkins, R. S., Tan, S. Y., & Turk, A. A. (1999). Secular versus Christian inpatient cognitive–behavioral therapy programs: Impact on depression and spiritual well-being. *Journal of Psychology and Theology, 27,* 309–318.

Hedayat-Diba, Z. (2000). Psychotherapy with Muslims. In P. S. Richards & A. E. Bergin (Eds.), *Handbook of psychotherapy and religious diversity* (pp. 289–314). Washington, DC: American Psychological Association.

Helminiak, D. A. (1996). *The human core of spirituality: Mind as psyche and spirit.* Albany: State University of New York.

Herzog, D. B. (1995). Psychodynamic psychotherapy for anorexia nervosa. In K. D. Brownell & C. G. Fairburn (Eds.), *Eating disorders and obesity: A comprehensive handbook* (pp. 330–335). New York: Guilford Press.

Hill, C. (1967). *Reformation to industrial revolution.* London: Weidenfeld & Nicholson.

Hill, C. H., & Hood, R. W. (1999). *Measures of religiosity.* Birmingham, AL: Religious Education Press.

Hill, P. C., & Pargament, K. I. (2003). Advances in the conceptualization and measurement of religion and spirituality. *American Psychologist, 58,* 64–74.

Hoek, H. W., & van Hoeken, D. (2003). Review of the prevalence and incidence of eating disorders. *International Journal of Eating Disorders, 34,* 383–396.

Hopson, R. (1996). The 12-step program. In E. P. Shafranske (Ed.), *Religion and the clinical practice of psychology* (pp. 533–558). Washington, DC: American Psychological Association.

Hsu, L. K., Crisp, A. H., & Callender, J. S. (1992). Recovery in anorexia nervosa—the patient's perspective. *International Journal of Eating Disorders, 11,* 341–350.

Huline-Dickens, S. (2000). Anorexia nervosa: Some connections with the religious attitude. *British Journal of Medical Psychology, 73,* 67–76.

Jacoby, G. E. (1993). Eating disorder and religion. *Psychotherapy, Psychosomatic Medicine and Psychology, 43,* 70–73.

James, W. (1936). *The varieties of religious experience.* New York: Modern Library. (Original work published 1902)

Jersild, A. (2001). Field mice and mustard seeds: Approaching spirituality as a therapeutic tool. *Eating Disorders: Journal of Treatment and Prevention, 9,* 267–273.

Jewison, N. (Producer/Director). (1971). *Fiddler on the roof* [Motion picture].United States: The Mirisch Production Company.

Johnson, C. (1985). Initial consultation for patients with bulimia and anorexia nervosa. In D. M. Garner & P. E. Garfinkel (Eds.), *Handbook of psychotherapy for anorexia nervosa and bulimia* (pp. 19–51). New York: Guilford Press.

Johnson, C. (1995). Psychodynamic treatment of bulimia nervosa. In K. D. Brownell & C. G. Fairburn (Eds.), *Eating disorders and obesity: A comprehensive handbook* (pp. 349–353). New York: Guilford Press.

Johnson, C. L., & Sansone, R. A. (1993). Integrating the 12-step approach with traditional psychotherapy for the treatment of eating disorders. *International Journal of Eating Disorders, 14,* 121–134.

Johnson, W. B. (1993). Outcome research and religious psychotherapies: Where are we and where are we going? *Journal of Psychology and Theology, 21,* 297–308.

Johnson, W. B., DeVries, R., Ridley, C. R., Pettorini, D., & Peterson, D. R. (1994). The comparative efficacy of Christian and secular rational–emotive therapy with Christian clients. *Journal of Psychology and Theology, 22,* 130–140.

Johnson, W. B., & Ridley, C. R. (1992). Brief Christian and non-Christian rational–emotive therapy with depressed Christian clients: An exploratory study. *Counseling and Values, 36,* 220–229.

Jones, S. L. (1994). A constructive relationship for religion with the science and profession of psychology: Perhaps the boldest model yet. *American Psychologist, 49,* 184–199.

Joughin, N., Crisp, A. H., Halek, C., & Humphrey, H. (1992). Religious belief and anorexia nervosa. *International Journal of Eating Disorders, 12,* 397–406.

Kaplan, A. S., & Garfinkel, P. E. (Eds.). (1993). *Medical issues and the eating disorders: The interface.* New York: Brunner/Mazel.

Kashubeck-West, S., & Saunders, K. (2001). Inventories used to assess eating disorder symptomatology in clinical and non-clinical settings. In J. J. Robert-McComb (Ed.), *Eating disorders in women and children: Prevention, stress management, and treatment* (pp. 59–85). New York: CRC Press.

Kass, J. D., Friedman, R., Lesserman, J., Zuttermeister, P., & Benson, H. (1991). Health outcomes and a new index of spiritual experience. *Journal for the Scientific Study of Religion, 30,* 203–211.

Kaye, W. H. (2002). Central nervous system neurotransmitter activity in anorexia nervosa and bulimia nervosa. In C. G. Fairburn & K. D. Brownell (Eds.), *Eating disorders and obesity: A comprehensive handbook* (2nd ed., pp. 222–277). New York: Guilford Press.

Kaye, W. H., Devlin, B., Barbarich, N., Bulik, C. M., Thornton, L., Bacanu, S. A., et al. (2004). Genetic analysis of bulimia nervosa: Methods and sample description. *International Journal of Eating Disorders, 35,* 556–570.

Kazdin, A. E. (1994). Methodology, design, and evaluation in psychotherapy research. In A. E. Bergin & S. L. Garfield (Eds.), *Handbook of psychotherapy and behavior change* (4th ed., pp. 19–71). New York: Wiley.

Keel, P. A. (2005). *Eating disorders.* Upper Saddle River, NJ: Pearson/Prentice Hall.

Kelly, E. W. (1995). *Religion and spirituality in counseling and psychotherapy.* Alexandria, VA: American Counseling Association.

Koenig, H. G., McCullough, M. E., & Larson, D. B. (2001). *Handbook of religion and health.* New York: Oxford University Press.

Lacey, J. H. (1982). Anorexia nervosa and a bearded female saint. *British Medical Journal, 285*, 1816–1817.

Lambert, M. J., & Burlingame, G. M. (1996). *The Outcome Questionnaire*. Stevenson, MD: American Professional Credentialing Services.

Lambert, M. J., & Hill, C. E. (1994). Assessing psychotherapy outcomes and processes. In A. E. Bergin & S. L. Garfield (Eds.), *Handbook of psychotherapy and behavior change* (4th ed., pp. 72–113). New York: Wiley.

Lelwica, M. M. (1999). *Starving for salvation: The spiritual dimensions of eating problems among American girls and women*. New York: Oxford University Press.

Levine, P. (1996). Eating disorders and their impact on family systems. In F. W. Kaslow (Ed.), *Handbook of relational diagnosis and dysfunctional family patterns* (pp. 463–476). New York: Wiley.

Lewis, L. (2001). Spirituality. In R. McComb & J. Jacalyn (Eds.), *Eating disorders in women and children: Prevention, stress management, and treatment* (pp. 317–324). Boca Raton, FL: CRC Press.

Lovinger, R. J. (1984). *Working with religious issues in therapy*. Northvale, NJ: Jason Aronson.

Luks, A. (1993). *The healing power of doing good*. New York: Ballantine Books.

Malony, H. N. (1985). Assessing religious maturity. In E. M. Stern (Ed.), *Psychotherapy and the religiously committed patient* (pp. 25–33). New York: Haworth Press.

Manley, R. S., & Leichner, P. (2003). Anguish and despair in adolescents with eating disorders: Helping to manage suicidal ideation and impulses. *Crisis, 24*, 31–36.

Martin, J. E., & Carlson, C. R. (1988). Spiritual dimensions of health psychology. In W. R. Miller & J. E. Martin (Eds.), *Behavior therapy and religion* (pp. 57–110). Newbury Park, CA: Sage.

McCabe, M. P., & Ricciardelli, L. A. (2004). Weight and shape concerns of boys and men. In J. K. Thompson (Ed.), *Handbook of eating disorders and obesity* (pp. 606–634). Hoboken, NJ: Wiley.

McCourt, J., & Waller, G. (1996). The influence of sociocultural factors on the eating psychopathology of Asian women in British society. *European Eating Disorders Review, 4*, 73–83.

McCrady, B. S., & Delaney, S. I. (1995). Self-help groups. In R. K. Hester & W. R. Miller (Eds.), *Handbook of alcoholism treatment approaches* (2nd ed., pp. 160–175). Boston: Allyn & Bacon.

McCullough, M. E. (1999). Research on religion-accommodative counseling: Review and meta-analysis. *Journal of Counseling Psychology, 46*, 92–98.

McGee, R. S., & Mountcastle, W. D. (1990). *Rapha's 12-step program for overcoming eating disorders. A new biblically integrated approach to recovery from the ABC's of eating disorders*. Houston, TX: Rapha/Word.

McMinn, M. R. (1996). *Psychology, theology, and spirituality in Christian counseling*. Wheaton, IL: Tyndale House Publishers.

Mehler, P. S., & Andersen, A. E. (Eds.). (1999). *Eating disorders: A guide to medical care and complications.* Baltimore: John Hopkins University Press.

Miller, L., & Lovinger, R. (2000). Psychotherpay with conservative and reform Jews. In P. S. Richards & A. E. Bergin (Eds.), *Handbook of psychotherapy and religious diversity* (pp. 259–286). Washington, DC: American Psychological Association.

Miller, W. R. (1999). *Integrating spirituality into treatment: Resources for practitioners.* Washington, DC: American Psychological Association.

Minuchin, S., Rasman, B., & Baker, L. (1978). *Psychosomatic families: Anorexia nervosa in context.* Cambridge, MA: Harvard University Press.

Mitchell, J. E., Erlander, M., Pyle, R. L., & Fletcher, L. A. (1990). Eating disorders, religious practices and pastoral counseling. *International Journal of Eating Disorders, 9,* 589–593.

Mitchell, J. E., & Peterson, C. B. (Eds.). (2005). *Assessment of eating disorders.* New York: Guilford Press.

Mogul, S. L. (1980). Asceticism in adolescence and anorexia nervosa. *Psychoanalytic Study of the Child, 35,* 155–175.

Morgan, J. F., Marsden, P., & Lacey, J. H. (2000). "Spiritual starvation?": A case series concerning Christianity and eating disorders. *International Journal of Eating Disorders, 28,* 476–480.

Murray-Swank, N. A., & Pargament, K. I. (2004, March). *Solace for the soul: A journey towards wholeness.* Paper presented at the APA Division 36 Mid-Winter Conference on Religion and Spirituality, Columbia, MD.

Myers, T. C., & Mitchell, J. E. (2005). Counseling patients with bulimia nervosa. In D. J. Goldstein (Ed.), *The management of eating disorders and obesity* (pp. 13–21). Totowa, NJ: Humana Press.

Newmark, G. R. (2001, September–October). Spirituality in eating disorder treatment. *Healthy Weight Journal,* 76–77.

Nohr, R. W. (2001). Outcome effects of receiving a spiritually informed vs. a standard cognitive–behavioral stress management workshop (Doctoral dissertation, Marquette University, 2001). *Dissertation Abstracts International Section B: The Sciences and Engineering, 61*(7-B), 3855.

O'Brien, E. J., & Epstein, S. (1998). *The Multidimensional Self-Esteem Inventory manual.* Odessa, FL: Psychological Assessment Resources.

Oman, D., & Thoresen, C. E. (2001, August). *Using intervention studies to unravel how religion affects health.* Paper presented at the annual convention of the American Psychological Association, San Francisco, CA.

Paloutzian, R. F., & Ellison, C. W. (1991). *Manual for the Spiritual Well-Being Scale.* Nyack, NY: Life Advances.

Pargament, K. I. (1999). The psychology of religion and spirituality? Yes and no. *International Journal for the Psychology of Religion, 9,* 3–16.

Pargament, K. I., Kennell, J., Hathaway, W., Grenvengoed, N., Newman, J., & Jones, W. (1988). Religion and the problem-solving process: Three styles of coping. *Journal for the Scientific Study of Religion, 27,* 90–104.

Pecheur, D. R., & Edwards, K. J. (1984). A comparison of secular and religious versions of cognitive therapy with depressed Christian college students. *Journal of Psychology and Theology, 12,* 45–54.

Piedmont, R. L. (1999). Does spirituality represent the sixth factor of personality? Spiritual transcendence and the five-factor model. *Journal of Personality, 67,* 985–1013.

Pike, K. M., Devlin, J. J., & Loeb, K. L. (2004). Cognitive–behavioral therapy in the treatment of anorexia nervosa, bulimia nervosa, and binge eating disorder. In J. K. Thompson (Ed.), *Handbook of eating disorders and obesity* (pp. 130–162). Hoboken, NJ: Wiley.

Piran, N., Jasper, K., & Pinhas, L. (2004). Feminist therapy of eating disorders. In J. K. Thompson (Ed.), *Handbook of eating disorders and obesity* (pp. 263–278). Hoboken, NJ: Wiley.

Propst, R. L. (1980). The comparative efficacy of religious and nonreligious imagery for the treatment of mild depression in religious individuals. *Cognitive Therapy and Research, 4,* 167–178.

Propst, R. L., Ostrom, R., Watkins, P., Dean, T., & Mashburn, D. (1992). Comparative efficacy of religious and nonreligious cognitive–behavioral therapy for the treatment of clinical depression in religious individuals. *Journal of Consulting and Clinical Psychology, 60,* 94–103.

Puchalski, C. M., & Larson, D. B. (1998). Developing curricula in spirituality and medicine. *Academic Medicine, 73,* 970–974.

Puchalski, C. M., Larson, D. B., & Lu, F. G. (2000). Spirituality courses in psychiatry residency programs. *Psychiatric Annals, 30,* 543–548.

Rabinowitz, A. (1999). *Judaism and psychology: Meeting points.* Northvale, NJ: Jason Aronson.

Rabinowitz, A. (2000). Psychotherapy with orthodox Jews. In P. S. Richards & A. E. Bergin (Eds.), *Handbook of psychotherapy and religious diversity* (pp. 237–258). Washington, DC: American Psychological Association.

Richards, P. S. (1996). *The Eating Disorder Self-Monitoring Scale* (Technical report). Orem, UT: Center for Change.

Richards, P. S. (1999, August). *Spiritual influences in healing and psychotherapy.* William C. Bier Award Invited Address, Division 36 (Psychology of Religion), presented at the annual meeting of the American Psychological Association, Boston, MA.

Richards, P. S., Baldwin, B., Frost, H., Hardman, R., Berrett, M., & Clark-Sly, J. (2000). What works for treating eating disorders: A synthesis of 28 outcome reviews. *Eating Disorders: Journal of Treatment and Prevention, 8,* 189–206.

Richards, P. S., & Bartz, J. (2006). *Systematic review of religion and spirituality in eating disorder research, theory, and practice.* Manuscript submitted for publication.

Richards, P. S., & Bergin, A. E. (1997). *A spiritual strategy for counseling and psychotherapy*. Washington, DC: American Psychological Association.

Richards, P. S., & Bergin, A. E. (Eds.). (2000). *Handbook of psychotherapy and religious diversity*. Washington, DC: American Psychological Association.

Richards, P. S., & Bergin, A. E. (2004). *Casebook for a spiritual strategy in counseling and psychotherapy*. Washington, DC: American Psychological Association.

Richards, P. S., & Bergin, A. E. (2005). *A spiritual strategy for counseling and psychotherapy* (2nd ed.). Washington, DC: American Psychological Association.

Richards, P. S., Berrett, M. E., Hardman, R. K., & Eggett, D. L. (in press). Comparative efficacy of spirituality, cognitive, and emotional support groups for treating eating disorder inpatients. *Eating Disorders: Journal of Treatment and Prevention.*

Richards, P. S., Hardman, R. K., & Berrett, M. E. (2000). *Spiritual renewal: A journey of faith and healing.* Orem, UT: Center for Change.

Richards, P. S., Hardman, R. K., Frost, H. A., Berrett, M. E., Clark-Sly, J. B., & Anderson, D. K. (1997). Spiritual issues and interventions in the treatment of patients with eating disorders. *Eating Disorders: Journal of Treatment and Prevention, 5,* 261–279.

Richards, P. S., Hardman, R. K., Jensen, B., Berrett, M. E., & Jensen, F. (2006). *Patient perceptions of the role of faith and spirituality in recovery from eating disorders.* Unpublished manuscript.

Richards, P. S., & Potts, R. W. (1995). Using spiritual interventions in psychotherapy: Practices, successes, failures, and ethical concerns of Mormon psychotherapists. *Professional Psychology: Research and Practice, 26,* 163–170.

Richards, P. S., Rector, J. R., & Tjeltveit, A. C. (1999). Values, spirituality, and psychotherapy. In W. R. Miller (Ed.), *Integrating spirituality in treatment: Resources for practitioners* (pp. 133–160). Washington, DC: American Psychological Association.

Richards, P. S., & Smith, T. B. (2000, June). *Development and validation of the Spiritual Outcome Scale.* Paper presented at the annual convention of the Society for Psychotherapy Research, Chicago, IL.

Richards, P. S., Smith, T. B., Schowalter, M., Richard, M., Berrett, M. E., & Hardman, R. K. (2005). Development and validation of the Theistic Spiritual Outcome Survey. *Psychotherapy Research, 15,* 457–469.

Ringwald, C. D. (2002). *The soul of recovery: Uncovering the spiritual dimensions in the treatment of addictions.* New York: Oxford University Press.

Romano, S. J. (2005a). Bulimia nervosa. In D. J. Goldstein (Ed.), *The management of eating disorders and obesity* (2nd ed., pp. 3–11). Totowa, NJ: Humana Press.

Romano, S. J. (2005b). Anorexia nervosa. In D. J. Goldstein (Ed.), *The management of eating disorders and obesity* (2nd ed., pp. 61–70). Totowa, NJ: Humana Press.

Rorty, M., Yager, J., & Rossotto, E. (1993). Why and how do women recover from bulimia nervosa? The subjective appraisals of forty women recovered for a year or more. *International Journal of Eating Disorders, 14,* 249–260.

Rowland, C. V. (1970). Anorexia nervosa—A survey of the literature and review of 30 cases. *International Psychiatric Clinics, 7,* 37–137.

Rubin, J. B. (1996). *Psychotherapy and Buddhism: Toward an integration.* New York: Plenum Press.

Rye, M. S., & Pargament, K. I. (2002). Forgiveness and romantic relationships in college: Can it heal the wounded heart? *Journal of Clinical Psychology, 58,* 419–441.

Sargent, J., Liebman, R., & Silver, M. (1985). Family therapy for anorexia nervosa. In D. M. Garner & P. E. Garfinkel (Eds.), *Handbook of psychotherapy for anorexia nervosa and bulimia* (pp. 257–279). New York: Guilford Press.

Schwartz, R. C., Barrett, M. J., & Saba, G. (1985). Family therapy for bulimia. In D. M. Garner & P. E. Garfinkel (Eds.), *Handbook of psychotherapy for anorexia nervosa and bulimia* (pp. 280–307). New York: Guilford Press.

Shafranske, E. P. (Ed.). (1996). *Religion and the clinical practice of psychology.* Washington, DC: American Psychological Association.

Shafter, R. (1989). Women and madness: A social historical perspective. *Issues in Ego Psychology, 12,* 77–82.

Shea, J. D. (1992). Religion and sexual adjustment. In J. F. Schumaker (Ed.), *Religion and mental health* (pp. 70–84). New York: Oxford University Press.

Slife, B. D. (2004). Theoretical challenges to therapy practice and research: The constraint of naturalism. In M. J. Lambert (Ed.), *Bergin and Garfield's handbook of psychotherapy and behavior change* (5th ed., pp. 44–83). New York: Wiley.

Smart, N. (1983). *Worldviews: Cross-cultural explorations of human beliefs.* New York: Scribner.

Smart, N. (1994). *Religions of the West.* Englewood Cliffs, NJ: Prentice Hall.

Smith, F. T., Richards, P. S., Fischer, L., & Hardman, R. K. (2003). Intrinsic religiosity and spiritual well-being as predictors of treatment outcome among women with eating disorders. *Eating Disorders: Journal of Treatment and Prevention, 11,* 15–26.

Smith, J. C. (1975). Meditation as psychotherapy: A review of the literature. *Psychological Bulletin, 82,* 558–564.

Smith, M. H., Richards, P. S., & Maglio, C. J. (2004). Examining the relationship between religious orientation and eating disturbances. *Eating Behaviors, 5,* 171–180.

Smolak, L., & Murnen, S. K. (2004). A feminist approach to eating disorders. In J. K. Thompson (Ed.), *Handbook of eating disorders and obesity* (pp. 590–605). Hoboken, NJ: Wiley.

Spearing, M. (2001). *Eating disorders: Facts about eating disorders and the search for solutions.* Bethesda, MD: National Institutes of Health.

Sperry, L., & Shafranske, E. P. (Eds.). (2005). *Spiritually oriented psychotherapy.* Washington, DC: American Psychological Association.

Stice, E. (2001). Risk factor for eating pathology: Recent advances and future directions. In R. H. Stiegel-Moore (Ed.), *Eating disorders: Innovative directions in research and practice* (pp. 51–73). Washington, DC: American Psychological Assocation.

Striegel-Moore, R. H., & Smolak, L. (2001). *Eating disorders: Innovative directions in research and practice*. Washington, DC: American Psychological Association.

Sue, D. W., & Sue, D. (1990). *Counseling the culturally different: Theory and practice* (2nd ed.). New York: Wiley.

Sue, S., Zane, N., & Young, K. (1994). Research on psychotherapy with culturally diverse populations. In A. E. Bergin & S. L. Garfield (Eds.), *Handbook of psychotherapy and behavior change* (4th ed., pp. 783–817). New York: Wiley.

Sykes, D. K., Gross, M., & Subishin, S. (1986). Preliminary findings of demographic variables in patients suffering from anorexia nervosa and bulimia. *International Journal of Psychosomatics, 33,* 27–30.

Sykes, D. K., Leuser, B., Melia, M., & Gross, M. (1988). A demographic analysis of 252 patients with anorexia nervosa and bulimia. *International Journal of Psychosomatics, 35,* 5–9.

Tait, G. (1993). "Anorexia nervosa": Asceticism, differentiation, government. *Australian and New Zealand Journal of Sociology, 29,* 194–208.

Tan, S. Y. (1994). Ethical considerations in religious psychotherapy: Potential pitfalls and unique resources. *Journal of Psychology and Theology, 22,* 389–394.

Tan, S. Y. (2003). Integrating spiritual direction into psychotherapy: Ethical issues and guidelines. *Journal of Psychology and Theology, 31,* 14–23.

Tantleff-Dunn, S., Gokee-LaRose, J., & Peterson, R. D. (2004). Interpersonal psychotherapy for the treatment of anorexia nervosa, bulimia nervosa, and binge eating disorders. In J. K. Thompson (Ed.), *Handbook of eating disorders and obesity* (pp. 163–185). Hoboken, NJ: Wiley.

Thelen, M. H., Mintz, L. B., & Vander Wal, J. S. (1996). The Bulimia Test—Revised: Validation with *DSM–IV* criteria for bulimia nervosa. *Psychological Assessment, 8,* 219–221.

Treasure, J., & Szmukler, G. I. (1995). Medical complications of chronic anorexia nervosa. In G. I. Szmukler, C. Dare, & J. Treasure (Eds.), *Handbook of eating disorders: Theory, treatment, and research* (pp. 197–220). Oxford, England: Wiley.

Ulrich, W. L., Richards, P. S., & Bergin, A. E. (2000). Psychotherapy with Latter-Day Saints. In P. S. Richards & A. E. Bergin (Eds.), *Handbook of psychotherapy and religious diversity* (pp. 185–209). Washington, DC: American Psychological Association.

Vandereycken, W., & Van Deth, R. (1994). *From fasting saints to anorexic girls: The history of self-starvation.* London: Athlone Press.

Vizzini, J. (2003). *A comparison study of puppet therapy to regular therapy in a chemical dependency 12-step treatment model.* Unpublished doctoral dissertation, Loyola College, Columbia, MD.

Waller, G., & Kennerley, H. (2003). Cognitive–behavioral treatments. In J. Treasure, U. Schmidt, & E. VanFurth (Eds.), *Handbook of eating disorders* (2nd ed., pp. 233–251). West Sussex, England: Wiley.

Walsh, B. T. (1995). Pharmacotherapy of eating disorders. In K. D. Brownell & C. G. Fairburn (Eds.), *Eating disorders and obesity: A comprehensive handbook* (pp. 313–317). New York: Guilford Press.

Walsh, B. T. (2002). Pharmacological treatment of anorexia nervosa and bulimia nervosa. In C. G. Fairburn & K. D. Brownell (Eds.), *Eating disorders and obesity: A comprehensive handbook* (2nd ed., pp. 325–329). New York: Guilford Press.

Wasson, D. H., & Jackson, M. (2004). An analysis of the role of Overeaters Anonymous in women's recovery from bulimia nervosa. *Eating Disorders: Journal of Treatment and Prevention, 12,* 337–356.

West, W. (2000). *Psychotherapy and spirituality: Crossing the line between therapy and religion.* Thousand Oaks, CA: Sage.

Wilbur, C., & Colligan, R. (1981). Psychological and behavioural correlates of anorexia nervosa. *Journal of Developmental and Behavioural Paediatrics, 2,* 89–92.

Wilfley, D., Stein, R., & Welch, R. (2003). Interpersonal psychotherapy. In J. Treasure, U. Schmidt, & E. VanFurth (Eds.), *Handbook of eating disorders* (2nd ed., pp. 253–270). West Sussex, England: Wiley.

Williamson, D. A. (1990). *Assessment of eating disorders: Obesity, anorexia, and bulimia nervosa.* New York: Pergamon.

Wilson, T. G., & Pike, K. M. (2001). Eating disorders. In D. H. Barlow (Ed.), *Clinical handbook of psychological disorders* (3rd ed., pp. 332–375). New York: Guilford Press.

Wormer, K., & Davis, D. R. (2003). *Addiction treatment: A strengths perspective.* Pacific Grove, CA: Brooks/Cole.

Worthington, E. L., Jr., Kurusu, T. A., McCullough, M. E., & Sanders, S. J. (1996). Empirical research on religion and psychotherapeutic processes and outcomes: A ten-year review and research prospectus. *Psychological Bulletin, 119,* 448–487.

Worthington, E. L., Jr., & Sandage, S. J. (2001). Religion and spirituality. *Psychotherapy, 38,* 473–478.

Worthington, E. L., Jr., Wade, N. G., Hight, T. L., Ripley, J. S., McCullough, M. E., Berry, J. W., et al. (2003). The Religious Commitment Inventory—10: Development, refinement, and validation of a brief scale for research and counseling. *Journal of Counseling Psychology, 50,* 84–96.

Wulff, D. M. (1991). *Psychology of religion: Classic and contemporary views.* New York: Wiley.

Yapko, M. D. (1997). *Breaking the patterns of depression.* New York: Broadway Books.

Yeary, J. (1987). The use of Overeaters Anonymous in the treatment of eating disorders. *Journal of Psychoactive Drugs, 19,* 303–309.

Ziegler, R., & Sours, J. A. (1968). A naturalistic study of patients with anorexia nervosa admitted to a university medical centre. *Comprehensive Psychiatry*, 9, 644–651.

Zinnbauer, B. J., Pargament, K. I., & Scott, A. B. (1999). The emerging meanings of religiousness and spirituality: Problems and prospects. *Journal of Personality*, 67, 889–919.

INDEX

ABOUT THE AUTHORS

P. Scott Richards, PhD, is a professor of counseling psychology at Brigham Young University. He received his doctoral degree in counseling psychology in 1988 from the University of Minnesota. He is the senior coauthor of the book *A Spiritual Strategy for Counseling and Psychotherapy*, which was published in 1997 by the American Psychological Association (APA) and is now available in a second edition. Dr. Richards is also the senior coeditor of another APA book, *Handbook of Psychotherapy and Religious Diversity* (with A. Bergin, 2000). Dr. Richards has published numerous journal articles on the topics of religion and mental health, spiritual issues in psychotherapy, and spirituality and eating disorders. In 1999, he was awarded the William C. Bier Award by Division 36 (Psychology of Religion) of the APA for "outstanding contributions to religious and allied issues." He was named a fellow of APA Division 36 in August 2002 and served as division president from August 2004 through August 2005. Dr. Richards is a licensed psychologist and maintains a private practice at Center for Change, in Orem, Utah, where he also serves as the director of research.

Randy K. Hardman, PhD, received his doctoral degree in counseling psychology with a minor in marriage and family therapy from Brigham Young University in 1984. He is a cofounder and vice president of Center for Change, a mental health clinic that specializes in the inpatient treatment of women with eating disorders. Dr. Hardman has been a private practitioner in Indiana, Colorado, and Utah for more than 18 years, providing outpatient psychological evaluations and psychotherapy for individuals, couples, and families with a wide range of problems. He developed and facilitated intensive treatment programs at the Human Development Institute in Aurora, Colorado, and the Depression Center at the Utah Valley Regional Medical Center in Provo. He has published professional articles about spirituality and eating disorders in *Eating Disorders: The Journal of Treatment & Prevention* and *Counseling and Values*.

Michael E. Berrett, PhD, received his doctoral degree in counseling psychology with a minor in marriage and family therapy from Brigham Young University in 1986. He is a cofounder, corporate president, and coclinical director of Center for Change. Prior to opening Center for Change, Dr. Berrett worked at the Utah Valley Regional Medical Center where he provided inpatient treatment for adults and adolescents. There he was the program coordinator for a specialty eating disorder program and served as the chief of psychology from 1989 to 1991. He remains a member of the medical staff at the Utah Valley Regional Medical Center. He has published professional articles about spirituality and eating disorders in *Eating Disorders: The Journal of Treatment & Prevention* and *Counseling and Values*.